CIAO!

TEACHER'S RESOURCE BOOK

Terzo libro

Michael Buckby	project co-ordinator
Jenny Jackson	principal author
Co-authors:	Kathy Wicksteed
	Teresa Huntley
	Ian Skelton
	Colin Yarwood
	Nia Griffith

Nelson

Thomas Nelson and Sons Ltd
Nelson House   Mayfield Road
Walton-on-Thames   Surrey
KT12 5PL   UK

51 York Place
Edinburgh
EH1 3JD   UK

Thomas Nelson (Hong Kong) Ltd
Toppan Building 10/F
22A Westlands Road
Quarry Bay   Hong Kong

Thomas Nelson Australia
102 Dodds Street
South Melbourne   Victoria 3205
Australia

Nelson Canada
1120 Birchmount Road
Scarborough   Ontario
M1K 5G4   Canada

© Language Teaching Centre, University of York 1992

First published by Thomas Nelson and Sons Ltd 1992

ISBN 0-17-439653-8

NPN 9 8 7 6 5 4 3 2 1

Printed in Hong Kong

Acknowledgements
The authors and publishers would like to thank the following people
for their help and encouragement in the production of this course:

Mr J E Trickey, HMI
Mr Michael V Salter, OBE, BA, FIL, Educational Consultant
Mrs June Farrel
Professor Brian Moloney, Department of Italian, University of Hull
Mr Bob Pullin, University of Sheffield
Dr Bob Powell, University of Bath
Mr Derek Aust, South Devon College of Arts and Technology
Professor A Vaciago
Anna Maria Lelli
Angela Vegliante, Italian Cultural Institute, London
Dr Silvana Quadri, Italian Cultural Institute, London
Lorella Martini

The authors and publishers would like to thank the following
companies and institutions for their financial support:

Banco di Roma
Banco di Santo Spirito
Italian International Bank
Stirling International Civil Engineering Limited (Mr Peter Bruell)
The Hilden Charitable Trust
The Department of Education and Science
The Central Bureau for Educational Visits and Exchanges
The Mary Glasgow Trust
Schools Abroad
The Italian Cultural Institute, London
The Italian Government, Ministry of Foreign Affairs, Cultural Division

CONTENTS

The aims, methodology and layout of **Ciao! 3** are essentially as presented in **Books 1** and **2**.

The course shares the aims of the syllabuses based on the National Criteria:

– to develop the ability to use Italian effectively for the purposes of practical communication

– to form a sound basis of the skills, language and attitudes required for further study, work and leisure

– to offer insights into the culture and civilisation of Italian–speaking communities

– to make foreign language learning an enjoyable, successful and intellectually stimulating experience

– to contribute to the general education of learners

– to encourage positive attitudes to foreign language learning, to speakers of other languages and to other civilisations

– to encourage an awareness of the language learning process and to make the learning of other languages easier at a later stage.

Book 3 consists of 15 units covering different transactional or interactional situations.

As in **Books 1** and **2** each unit contains the following common elements:

– A statement of aims

– *Adesso, tocca a te!* This section contains a number of exercises which aim to show both the student and the teacher that the language and skills of the unit have been mastered.

These exercises are directly linked to the statements on the **Ciao! 3 Profile Statement** (Copymaster 77). It is intended that this should be photocopied and distributed to the students. When a student thinks he/she is able to complete a particular task successfully, he/she ticks the appropriate box on the chart. He/she then asks a classmate to assess whether or not the task can be completed successfully. The classmate only initials the second box if the task is completed satisfactorily. The third box is provided so that you can monitor the students' progress yourself.

We hope that the exercises in *Adesso, tocca a te!* and the statements on the accompanying profile statement will encourage students to become more aware of their own strengths and weaknesses and that they will take increasing responsibility for their own, and each other's, learning.

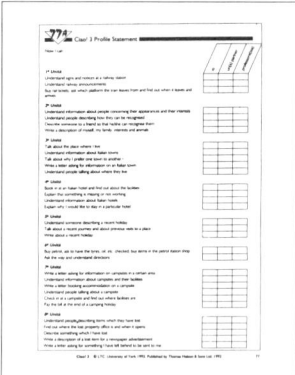 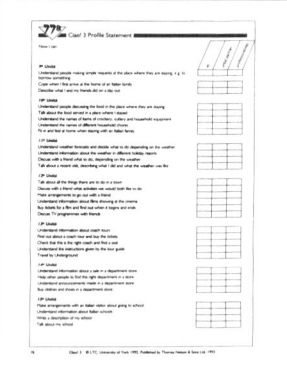

– *Ora sai.* This section summarises in English what has been covered in the unit. The Teacher's Book contains suggestions for using the *Ora sai* grid for reference and revision purposes.

The emphasis throughout is on the communicative use of Italian for real and meaningful purposes.

Learning to communicate

In each unit of **Ciao! 3**, the language necessary to complete the language tasks set out in the Statement of Aims is presented in a variety of ways. There is no set pattern as the intention is to provide the students with a variety of learning activities.

This key language is then used by students in a series of activities allowing them to listen to, and to practise using, key phrases in a controlled situation. Examples of such activities, including games, are found in both the Students' Book and the Teacher's Book.

Students then gradually move away from set phrases to a more independent and creative use of language, using a variety of communicative tasks. Communicative tasks are based on situations which students can relate to and understand. Communicative activities also require authentic use of Italian for communicative purposes. In **Ciao! 3** examples of such tasks generally involve an element of oral work. They often require students to make decisions, and can also include an element of negotiation.

Each unit of **Ciao! 3** contains activities which develop the four skills of listening, reading, speaking and writing. Many of the activities contain an element of oral work, much of which takes place in pairs or groups. Such activities not only increase motivation and enjoyment, but also encourage the development of self–confidence and a greater willingness to communicate.

The notes in the Teacher's Book provide a variety of suggestions for preparation and exploitation of all the material and activities in the Students' Book.

Effective use of language

Everyday communication is rarely predictable, and in order to use language effectively for practical communication students must be able to deal effectively with the unexpected in almost any situation.

In **Ciao! 3** students are encouraged to develop strategies for dealing with unexpected problems or situations. Many of these are straightforward. For example, asking someone to repeat what they said, asking questions, apologising and so on. The Teacher's Book also contains suggestions for developing such strategies.

Appropriateness of language

It is also important for students to be aware of register and to be able to use an appropriate style of language to suit the occasion. Having been introduced to the polite form very early in the course, students are provided with many opportunities in **Ciao! 3** to practise and use correctly the different forms of address.

A feature of **Book 3** is the emphasis on using language for doing things – influencing people, persuading them to do something and so on. In role play situations, in particular, students are encouraged to play different roles in different ways and then to decide which is the most socially acceptable and which is likely to be the most effective.

The use of Italian in the classroom

The research shows that Italian should be used by teachers and learners as much as possible. **Ciao!** sets out to encourage this from **Book 1**, and by **Book 3**, all rubrics and instructions in the main body of the book are in Italian. In addition, throughout the book, whenever new vocabulary is presented, students are encouraged to ask for further information in Italian.

For example:
Se vuoi sapere dire qualcos'altro in italiano, chiedilo al tuo professore/alla tua professoressa così:

Tu: Professore, come si dice 'I wear contact lenses' in italiano?

Professore: Si dice 'porto le lenti a contatto'. (Unit 2)

Students are also encouraged to manage pairwork activities in Italian wherever possible.

The notes in the Teacher's Book also contain suggestions for presenting preparation and extension activities in Italian. It is hoped that the increasing use of Italian in the book will be mirrored in the classroom, with both students and teachers using Italian for an increasing proportion of lesson time. The successful use of Italian for virtually all classroom management constitutes genuine communication for practical purposes in the target language.

Scoprite qualcosa di più

As with **Books 1** and **2**, after Unit 15 there follows a grammar section entitled *Scoprite qualcosa di più*. This does not mean that grammar should be seen as a separate part of language learning. Each grammar point is practised extensively in the unit in which it arises. It is also presented in context in the *Scoprite qualcosa di più* section. Students are encouraged to deduce the principles underlying the key structures for themselves. A formal explanation is then given, followed by exercises designed to practise these points.

Establishing links with Italy

Book 3 is based in Tuscany, with particular reference to Arezzo, and deals with the kinds of situation which students are likely to encounter on a school–to–school exchange or on a holiday with their parents or other adults.

The important benefits that can accrue from links with Italians are stressed throughout **Book 3**. The Italian assistant obviously has an important role to play.

However, the positive results from contacts with other young Italians can also have a great effect on motivation. Unit 2 actively encourages students to set up links with young Italians who have similar interests to their own, either through a link school, or by finding a penfriend.

The notes in the Teacher's Book also contain suggestions and useful addresses for making contact with schools and other organisations in Italy.

It is hoped that by following **Ciao!** over a period of three to five years, students will grow in self–confidence and independence. Similarly, working along the lines suggested here and throughout the Teacher's Book should ensure that students continue to enjoy learning Italian, and look forward to continuing to do so in the future.

Games and activities

Most teachers and classes will already have their favourite games and activities for learning new language. Some suggestions for a variety of activities are given here, and more are suggested throughout the Teacher's Book.

1 Verbal tennis

This can be played either in pairs or teams. One team serves by asking a question, and the other should return with the answer. The first team then volleys back with another question. A team wins a point when the other hesitates or replies incorrectly.

2 Il gioco di Kim (Kim's game)

Kim's game involves showing students between 10 and 15 objects/words for a short time, then taking them away/covering them and asking students to say or write down a list of the objects/words.

This game can be played at different levels, by gradually removing objects/words, and by asking for greater or lesser precision in the answers.

3 Tombola

This is another game that has a number of variations. The most common game uses numbers. Students write down six or eight numbers between a fixed limit, and the teacher (or a student) calls out numbers within that limit, in any order. The first to cover or cross out all the numbers is the winner. It is important to keep a record of the numbers called, as a check.

4 Ripetete se è vero

A very simple game which gives some purpose to repetition exercises. Students listen to the teacher making certain statements. When he or she says something true, the students repeat it. When he or she says something false, they remain silent. This can be developed into a competition between teacher and students, by allocating points for a correct response (or lack of response).

5 Chinese whispers

This game involves passing a message along a row of students, trying to do so without changing the message. Only a quiet whisper is allowed. This can be a team game, with the message being an instruction. The student at the end of the row is required to carry out the instruction. The first team to do so is the winner.

6 Noughts and crosses

Draw on the board/OHP nine squares, in a three x three grid. Each square will contain a picture/symbol/flashcard/ number/word. This can be played either in pairs or in two teams, one the 'noughts' and the other the 'crosses'. Each team must try to complete a row of three symbols. This can be adapted to use a larger grid, colours or symbols instead of noughts and crosses and so on. To indicate where they would like their symbol to go, the team must say what is in that equivalent square of flashcards or drawings.

7 Categorie

Students draw three columns in their rough book, and then categorise a given list of words/objects in the correct column.

8 Jigsaw words or phrases

Present on the board/OHP words that have been written in two parts. Students have to label photos or drawings by matching up the two parts of the word.

9 Domande

Write on the board/OHP a list of questions. On the other side of the board/OHP write a list of possible answers, in the wrong order. Students match up the questions and answers. This can be developed so that all the questions and answers are taken from one topic area and can be put together to form a simple dialogue. This activity can also be presented on cards, which students work on in pairs. One has the questions, the other has the answers.

Teachers will no doubt devise their own activities for learning key language. The following books may be of some use:

Games for language learning, Andrew Wright, Michael Buckby, David Betteridge, Cambridge University Press, 1984

Take 5, Michael Carrier, Nelson Harrap, 1980

Grammar games, Mario Rinvolucri, Cambridge University Press, 1985

INDEX OF MAIN TEACHING POINTS

Main aims	Grammar points	Productive vocabulary		Revision points
1ª Unità				
– to be able to travel by train	More about verbs: The present tense Regular and irregular verbs Regular present tense verb endings The 'we' form of some irregular verbs	un'andata un'andata e ritorno il binario da partire prima classe prossimo seconda classe solo stamattina il treno		Using the telephone (Book 2, Unit 2) Devi, deve, dovete + infinitive (Book 2, Unit 2) Free time and leisure activities (Book 2, Unit 10) Present tense: 'io' and 'tu' forms (Book 2, Unit 10)
2ª Unità				
– to be able to get a penfriend/ exchange partner – to be able to understand and fill in exchange forms – to be able to say that you collect something – to be able to describe personality and appearance – to be able to begin and end a letter to a partner appropriately	Comparative adjectives	allegro alto bello biondo calmo i capelli corto fare collezione di grasso un hobby lungo magro maturo meno...di gli occhiali la pallavolo	un(a) partner i passatempi più ... di portare una ragazza un ragazzo rispondimi presto scuro sensibile serio socievole sono nato(a) sportivo studioso tanti cari saluti timido	Family, pets, interests (Book 2, Unit 1) Avere: present tense (Book 2, Unit 1) Possessive adjectives, 1st-3rd person singular (Book 2, Unit 1) School (Book 2, Unit 8) Fare: present tense (Book 2, Unit 8) Travelling by train (Book 3, Unit 1) Present tense (Book 3, Unit 1)
3ª Unità				
– to write for information about Italian towns – to talk about the town/ village in which you live – to understand information about Italian towns – to ask other people about their home towns	Superlative adjectives	un abitante antico brutto centrale un chilometro una città com'è commerciale la contea da quanto tempo l'est una località noioso il nord	l'ovest un paese la regione storico il sud si può tranquillo turistico vedere visitare vivo	Meals and buying food (Book 2, Unit 3) Di + definite article (Book 2, Unit 3) Daily routine (Book 2, Unit 9) Reflexive verbs: present tense (Book 2, Unit 9) Talking about interests and personality (Book 3, Unit 2) Comparative adjectives (Book 3, Unit 2)

Main aims	Grammar points	Productive vocabulary	Revision points
4ª Unità – to be able to get by in an Italian hotel – to be able to understand hotel guides and brochures	Direct object pronouns after 'ecco'	aria condizionata un asciugamano la carta igienica la chiave con da la doccia doppia funzionare il gabinetto un letto libero la luce mancare matrimoniale la notte il passaporto prenotare il riscaldamento (centrale) il sapone una settimana servire i servizi singolo (con) vista sul mare	Introductions and greetings (Book 1, Unit 1) Buying ice creams, snacks and pizza (Book 2, Unit 4) Talking about free-time activities (Book 2, Unit 10) Present tense: 'io' and 'tu' forms (Book 2, Unit 10) Talking about a town (Book 3, Unit 3) Superlative adjectives (Book 3, Unit 3)
5ª Unità – to understand and give an account of a recent holiday – to understand and give opinions regarding journeys, accommodation, etc	Perfect tense with 'essere'	un aereo il disastro la discoteca divertente fa interessante il mare la montagna il monumento noioso perfetto rimanere salire sciare scorso la settimana la spiaggia la vacanza il viaggio visitare	Using Italian in the classroom (Book 1, Unit 2) Talking about homes and their location (Book 2, Unit 5) Present tense of -are verbs, 1st-3rd person singular (Book 2, Unit 5) Travelling by train (Book 3, Unit 1) Present tense of regular -are, -ere, -ire verbs (Book 3, Unit 1) Direct object pronoun after 'ecco' (Book 3, Unit 4) Booking hotel accommodation (Book 3, Unit 4)

Main aims	Grammar points	Productive vocabulary	Revision points
6ª Unità – to be able to buy petrol – to be able to ask for essential services – to be able to check your route – to be able to buy drinks, snacks and maps, etc	Indirect object pronouns	la benzina una bibita le caramelle una cartina della regione chiedere la strada controllare un distributore fare benzina i fazzoletti di carta il gasolio la gomma una lattina normale l'olio il parabrezza il pieno la pressione della gomme senza piombo una stazione di servizio super	Obtaining information about places in town and opening times (Book 1, Unit 3) Definite articles: il, l' la (Book 1, Unit 3) Buying presents and souvenirs (Book 2, Unit 6) Agreement of adjectives (Book 2, Unit 6) Interests and personality (Book 3, Unit 2) Comparative adjectives (Book 3, Unit 2) Talking about a recent holiday (Book 3, Unit 5)
7ª Unità – to understand information about campsites – to book in at a campsite – to find your way around the site – to understand signs and notices – to settle the bill – to book accommodation at a campsite in advance	Potere: present tense	un adulto una piazzuola all'ombra un posto un bambino potere un campeggio prenotare un camper una settimana il campo da tennis i servizi il campo giochi sistemarsi fermarsi lo spaccio il locale ritrovo una tenda lontano da una macchina	Understanding and giving directions (Book 1, Unit 4) Al, alla, all' (Book 1, Unit 4) Irregular plurals of nouns (Book 2, Unit 7) Town and region (Book 3, Unit 3) Indirect object pronouns (Book 3, Unit 6)
8ª Unità – to be able to understand lost and found advertisements, and relevant signs and notices – to be able to understand procedures involved in a lost property office and a police station – to be able to report and describe articles lost, stolen or found	Perfect tense with 'avere'	a che ora apre? perdere (perso) a che ora chiude? plastica argento trovare contiene ufficio oggetti una gattina smarriti lasciare una valigia una macchina vecchio fotografica i vestiti mi hanno rubato nuovo oro un orologio pelle	Travelling by bus (Book 1, Unit 5) School (Book 2, Unit 8) Fare: present tense (Book 2, Unit 8) Hotels (Book 3, Unit 4) Direct object pronouns after 'ecco' (Book 3, Unit 4) Camping (Book 3, Unit 7) Potere + infinitive (Book 3, Unit 7)

Main aims	Grammar points	Productive vocabulary		Revision points
9ª Unità — to fit in and feel at home when staying with an Italian family	Pronouns following prepositions: me, te, lui, lei, etc	l'aeroporto avere caldo avere fame avere freddo avere sete avere sonno il dentifricio un fon una giacca un incidente Lei lei lui loro la macchina me nel, nella, nell' il pigiama	prestare un ritardo una scarpa uno sciopero lo shampoo sopra sotto lo spazzolino da denti stanco su, sul, sulla la valigia i vestiti il viaggio	Buying postcards and stamps (Book 1, Unit 6) Plural of nouns (Book 1, Unit 6) Daily routine (Book 2, Unit 9) Reflexive verbs: present tense (Book 2, Unit 9) Talking about a recent holiday (Book 3, Unit 5) Perfect tense with 'essere' (Book 3 Unit 5) Lost property (Book 3, Unit 8) Perfect tense with 'avere' (Book 3, Unit 8)
10ª Unità — to ask and tell people about arrangements for meals — to react to offers of food and pay compliments — to ask for things at table — to offer to help	Impersonal 'si'	altrettanto apparecchiare asciugare una bistecca buon appetito cin-cin un coltello un cucchiaino un cucchiaio delizioso i fagioli fare male una forchetta un frigorifero frutti di mare il pepe un piatto i piselli un pollo un po' di provare il sale salute una scodella sparecchiare vegetariano(a) volentieri		Buying drinks in a bar or café (Book 1, Unit 7) Indefinite article: un' (Book 1, Unit 7) Free time, leisure activities (Book 2, Unit 10) Present tense: 'io' and 'tu' forms (Book 2, Unit 10) Indirect object pronouns (Book 3, Unit 6) Staying with an Italian family (Book 3, Unit 9) 'Noi' and 'voi': present and perfect tenses (Book 3, Units 1, 5, 9) Pronouns following prepositions (Book 3, Unit 9)

Main aims	Grammar points	Productive vocabulary		Revision points
11ª Unità – to understand and talk about the weather	Prepositions and the definite article: a, di, da, in, su	l'autunno bello brutto caldo il cielo coperto domani l'estate forte freddo l'inverno la nebbia la neve oggi la pioggia piove	la primavera sereno il sole la stagione il tempo il temporale il vento	Arranging activities (Book 1, Unit 8) Agreement of adjectives (Book 1, Unit 8) Essere: present tense (Book 1, Unit 8) Present tense of regular verbs (Book 3, Unit 1) Staying at a campsite (Book 3, Unit 7) Potere: present tense (Book 3, Unit 7) Impersonal 'si' (Book 3, Unit 10)
12ª Unità – to make arrangements for things to do during your free time – to see a film at the cinema	Using infinitives	andare a trovare una camminata un concerto divertente domani dare (un film) era una festa un giro in bicicletta il luna park ottimo	una partita una passeggiata il pomeriggio potremmo preferirei sarebbe possibile la sera sono rimasto un po' deluso lo spettacolo ti è piaciuto vorresti	Changing money (Book 1, Unit 9) Collections, personality, appearance (Book 3, Unit 2) Comparative adjectives (Book 3, Unit 2) Lost property (Book 3, Unit 8) Weather (Book 3, Unit 11) Prepositions (Book 3, Unit 11)
13ª Unità – to be able to understand announcements, information and notices on guided coach tours – to be able to understand the working of the 'metropolitana' – to book tickets on guided coach tours and to use the 'metropolitana'	Perfect tense: 'avere' and 'essere' verbs, regular and irregular past participles	bisogna un giro una gita la guida le informazioni libero la linea la metropolitana occupato il pullman quanto ci mette una sosta turistico(a) una visita		Getting a penfriend (Book 2, Unit 1) Avere (Book 2, Unit 1) Talking about your town (Book 3, Unit 3) Comparative and superlative adjectives (Book 3, Unit 3) Staying with an Italian family (Book 3, Unit 9) 'Noi' and 'voi': present and perfect tenses (Book 3, Units 1, 5, 9) Going to the cinema (Book 3, Unit 12) Potere (Book 3, Unit 7) Perfect tense

Main aims	Grammar points	Productive vocabulary	Revision points
14ª Unità – to be able to buy clothes and shoes – to ask for the correct size – to ask to try a different size or colour	Demonstrative adjectives: questo, quello	le calze una camicetta una camicia cercare che numero ha? che taglia porta? elegante una felpa una giacca una gonna lo/la/li/le posso provare? una maglietta i pantaloni pratico quello questo il reparto le scarpe sportivo gli stivali	Phoning home (Book 2, Unit 2) Possessive adjectives (Book 2, Unit 1) Avere: present tense (Book 2, Unit 1) Mealtimes and offering to help (Book 3, Unit 10) Impersonal 'si' (Book 3, Unit 10) Guided tours (Book 3, Unit 13) Bisogna + infinitive (Book 3, Unit 13)
15ª Unità – to talk about your school, how you get there and its facilities	Uscire: present tense Di, da: further uses	un alunno un'aula una biblioteca circa la corriera il cortile entrare l'istituto un laboratorio di lingue un laboratorio di scienze il liceo una palestra a piedi il preside la sala dei professori la segretaria uscire venire	Introductions, saying hello (Book 1, Unit 1) At a petrol station (Book 3, Unit 6) Indirect object pronouns (Book 3, Unit 6) Main verb + infinitive (Book 3, Unit 12)

  # 1ª Unità
ALLA STAZIONE

Main aim

~ To be able to travel by train

Materials

~ Tape
Alla biglietteria (Teacher's Book page 15)
A che ora parte? Da che binario parte? (Teacher's Book page 16)
Matilde informatissima! (Teacher's Book page 16)
C'è un treno per Firenze stamattina? (Teacher's Book page 17)
È in orario? (Teacher's Book page 18)
Dove vanno? (Teacher's Book page 18)
Adesso, tocca a te! (Teacher's Book page 20)
~ Copymasters 1–6
~ Tourist brochures for Florence, Milan, Bologna
~ Italian railway timetables

Grammar in *Scoprite qualcosa di più*

~ More about verbs: The present tense
                     Regular and irregular verbs
                     Regular present tense verb endings
                     The 'we' form of some irregular verbs

Revision

~ Using the telephone (Book 2, Unit 2)
~ Devi, deve, dovete + infinitive (Book 2, Unit 2)
~ Free time and leisure activities (Book 2, Unit 10)
~ Present tense: 'io' and 'tu' forms (Book 2, Unit 10)

Vocabulary

A: Productive

un'andata	prossimo
un'andata e ritorno	seconda classe
il binario	solo
da	stamattina
partire	il treno
prima classe	

B: Receptive

acqua (non) potabile	donne
aspettare	è pericoloso sporgersi
la biglietteria	un espresso
il buffet	(non) fumatori
carrozzelle (per persone handicappate)	gabinetti
il deposito bagagli	

un gruppo	un rapido
un Intercity	una riduzione
in arrivo	la sala d'attesa
in orario	sottopassaggio
in partenza	lo sportello
in ritardo	un supplemento
un locale	l'ufficio prenotazioni
l'orario	uomini
un posto	l'uscita
prenotato	vietato attraversare i binari
prezzo ridotto	

Alla stazione (page 5)

Main aim: **To present the main objectives of this unit**

Present, and discuss, the aims of this unit with the students. Make sure that they understand the aims and try to arouse their enthusiasm. You could try to involve them by asking, for example, if anyone has travelled by train in Italy and, if so, to talk about it. You could also ask if anyone has travelled by train in any other country. The students could be asked to suggest when they would find it useful to travel by train in Italy and to suggest what sorts of things they would need to know and say to do this successfully.

Le ferrovie italiane (page 5)

Main aims: **To introduce some of the language needed for travelling by rail**

                  To present some information about travelling by rail in Italy

A Tell the students that one of their teachers, who does not understand Italian, is thinking of going to Italy soon and would like the following information about rail travel there. They should try to find this information and to write it down for the teacher.

1   Are there Intercity trains in Italy?
2   If so, do they cost the same as other trains?
3   Where can you buy train tickets?
4   Is it possible to reserve seats?
5   Is there a railway station at Arezzo?

Present these questions on the board/OHP and give the class eight minutes only to find and write the answers. Then discuss their answers and correct as necessary.

B Write the following words on the board:

the railways
an express train
a supplement
a station
a train
travel agent's
reservation office
first class

Ask the students to look in the text to find the Italian equivalent of each one. When a student reads the correct equivalent for 'the railways', get the students to write the English and Italian words in their books while you say, many times, the Italian words. Then ask a few students to say the Italian. Repeat this procedure with the other words.

C Say that you would like the class to learn all these words. Ask the students to suggest how they could do this. This allows you to find out something about the sorts of learning activities which your students enjoy and find useful. It also helps them to become more effective learners by learning ideas from each other. You could, if necessary, suggest some possible activities, e.g.

1 List the words in the order in which you are most likely to need to use them when speaking in Italy.
2 Write two lists: one in which the Italian words look like their English equivalent and the other in which they do not.

Vero o falso? (page 5)

Main aim: **To check that students have understood the information on travelling by train in Italy**

A Give the class just two minutes to read the information on page 5 again and to find the answers to the quiz. You could ask a student to read the first sentence and to choose who should say if it is true or false, e.g.

Student A: I treni locali si fermano solo nelle grandi città. Andrew, è vero o falso?

The student who gives the correct reply can read the next sentence and decide who should respond.

B Ask the students to tell you, in English, everything they have now learnt about Italian railways. Allow each student to say one thing only and see how many correct things the class can tell you in three minutes. This should prove to be very encouraging.

La stazione ferroviaria (page 6)

Main aim: **To present some of the key language needed for travelling by train**

A Use techniques for presenting this language which have proved popular and successful in the past. You could:

1 Encourage the students to ask you to say each expression, e.g.

– Scusi, il numero uno che cos'è?
– Scusi, il numero nove che cos'è?

You could then reverse this and ask students what the various parts of the station are called, first with the names visible and then with them covered up.

2 Make a statement and ask the students to say where they would be most likely to hear that at a station, e.g.

Teacher: Ah, guarda! Lì ci sono gli autobus.
Student: L'uscita.
Teacher: A che ora parte il treno per Roma?
Student: L'orario.

3 Call out the place names in random order. The students listen and point to the appropriate part of the drawing. Say each place several times and walk round the class as you do so, helping students to point correctly. At first, do this with the captions visible, and then covered up.

B To make quite sure that everyone has understood these terms, say the English equivalents in random order and ask students to find and read out the appropriate Italian, e.g.

Teacher: Come si dice 'the left luggage office'?
Student: Il deposito bagagli.
Teacher: Bravo(a). E come ...

C You could start a 'word tree' on the board. The students suggest words that you could add, e.g.

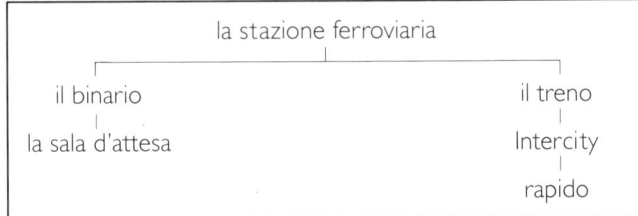

Stop after a short while and ask the students to copy the 'tree' from the board and to add to it as much as they can, looking back over the unit. They could also be encouraged to add to the tree as they work through the unit.

Matilde fa la guida (page 6)

Main aim: To practise asking and answering questions about places at a railway station

A You could begin by reading each question in turn and seeing how many times you can say it before a student gives you the correct answer.

B Give the class two minutes only to try to learn Matilde's answers. They then cover them up and you repeat activity A above.

C Give the class three minutes only. In that time, each person in pairs should ask and answer all the questions. Then see if they can do it in two minutes!

D With the answers covered up again, you could use this for a game of Verbal Tennis. One team serves by asking a question, the other should return with the answer and the first team volleys back with another question. A team wins a point when the other hesitates or replies incorrectly.

Alla biglietteria (page 7)

Main aims: To present the language needed for buying a railway ticket

To develop listening skills

A Read each caption several times to give the students a good chance to hear it. Then ask them what they think it means, in English, e.g.

– 'Un'andata', cosa vuol dire in inglese?

B Say several times a simple sentence using these words, e.g.
– Vorrei un'andata per Milano.
– Uno per Arezzo, andata e ritorno.
– Due per Roma, seconda classe, per favore.
– Vorrei tre biglietti di prima classe.

Ask the students to explain in English what you have said.

C Give the class two minutes to try to learn all the captions. In pairs, one student covers up the captions and the other tests him/her, e.g.
– Cosa vuol dire questo?
– Vuol dire un'andata.
– Bravo(a).

Write this exchange on the board and leave it there as a model.

D Give each student four minutes only to write as many variations as possible on the speech bubble in the drawing.

They could read these aloud, and you could award points, two for each correct caption and ten if it is correct and no other student has written the same thing.

E Play the recorded dialogues. Present each one twice and ask students to say which ticket, and how many, were bought.

Answers:
1 F × 1
2 B × 3
3 E × 1

Alla biglietteria

Esempio
Man: Uno per Arezzo, per favore.
Clerk: Come?
Man: Uno per Arezzo.
Clerk: Andata e ritorno?
Man: No, solo andata.
Clerk: Undicimiladuecento.
Man: Dodicimiladuecento?
Clerk: No, undicimiladuecento.
Man: Grazie.
Clerk: Prego.

Dialogo 1
Woman: Uno per Venezia.
Clerk: Andata e ritorno?
Woman: Sì. Andata e ritorno.
Clerk: Prima o seconda classe?
Woman: Seconda classe. Quant'è?
Clerk: Quarantunomilaquattrocento.
Woman: Quanto?
Clerk: Quarantunomilaquattrocento lire ... Grazie.
Woman: Grazie a Lei.

Dialogo 2
Man: Tre per Ciampino, per favore.
Clerk: Ciampino?
Man: Sì. Quanto costa?
Clerk: Vuole andata e ritorno?
Man: No, solo andata.
Clerk: Duemilaquattrocento lire, signore ... Grazie.

Dialogo 3
Woman: Un biglietto per Ventimiglia, per favore.
Clerk: Solo andata?
Woman: No, andata e ritorno.
Clerk: Prima o seconda?
Woman: Seconda.
Clerk: Ventunomilaseicento lire.

Woman: Prego? Vuol ripetere?
Clerk: Ventunomilaseicento lire.
Woman: Grazie.

F Explain that you would now like the students to expand the speech bubble with the drawing into a dialogue. To help them, they should listen once more to the recorded dialogues. They could then each write a dialogue, based on the drawing: this could be done as homework.

G In pairs, the students play-read the dialogue at the bottom of the page. They then adapt this for tickets A and D by changing the words underlined. You could give a model for this by playing the part of a traveller and asking a few students, in turn, to play the other part.

H Make copies of Copymaster 1A and 1B so that one partner in each pair has A and the other has B. Students work in pairs along the lines suggested on the copymasters.

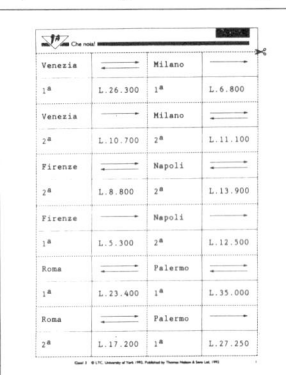 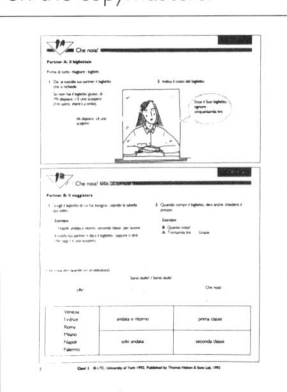

A che ora parte? Da che binario parte? (page 8)

Main aims: **To practise asking for, and giving, information about when and where trains leave**

To practise understanding announcements about trains

The students read the model dialogue silently to themselves and ask about anything they do not understand. They then listen to the recording before play-reading it in pairs, reading each part in turn.

A che ora parte? Da che binario parte?

Passenger: Scusi, a che ora parte il prossimo treno per Roma?
Employee: Alle sedici e cinquantotto.
Passenger: Da che binario parte?
Employee: Binario numero uno.

Matilde informatissima! (page 8)

Main aim: **To develop listening skills and the language needed to ask for, and give, information about departure times and platform**

A Work on the model in the Students' Book. You and a student could read it aloud, and several students say the answer. Base some questions on the *Treni in partenza* information to ensure that everyone can understand it, e.g.

– A che ora parte il treno per Milano?
– E da che binario parte, per favore?

B Play the recording. Ask the students to write V or F after hearing each item once only, and then to listen again to check their answers. Then ask them to say if it is 'vero' or 'falso' and agree on the answer before going on.

Answers: 1 – V, 2 – F, 3 – F, 4 – F, 5 – V, 6 – F.

Matilde informatissima!

Esempio
Man: Scusi, a che ora parte il prossimo treno per Orvieto?
Matilde: Alle dodici e due.
Man: Da che binario?
Matilde: Binario numero due.

Dialogo 1
Woman: Scusi, a che ora parte il prossimo treno per Perugia?
Matilde: Perugia? ... Alle quattordici e trentasei, signora.
Woman: Alle quattordici e trentasei?
Matilde: Sì.
Woman: Da che binario?
Matilde: Binario numero tre.
Woman: Grazie.

Dialogo 2

Man: Scusi, signora, da che binario parte il treno per Milano?
Matilde: Il treno per Milano ... binario numero uno.
Man: Numero uno. A che ora parte?
Matilde: Alle quattordici e venticinque.
Man: Alle quattordici e venticinque? Grazie.

Dialogo 3

Woman: Mi dica, il prossimo treno per Ravenna, da che binario parte?
Matilde: Ravenna ... numero due.
Woman: Due. A che ora parte?
Matilde: Alle nove e cinquantadue.
Woman: Va bene, grazie.

Dialogo 4

Man: Buongiorno. Il prossimo treno per Torino, a che ora parte?
Matilde: Il prossimo treno per Torino parte alle quindici e venticinque, signore.
Man: Ha detto, alle quindici e venticinque?
Matilde: Esatto.
Man: Da che binario?
Matilde: Dal binario due.
Man: Grazie.

Dialogo 5

Woman: Senta, da che binario parte il prossimo treno per Bologna?
Matilde: Per Bologna, dal quarto binario.
Woman: Prego?
Matilde: Per Bologna? Quarto binario.
Woman: A che ora parte?
Matilde: Alle dodici e quarantanove.
Woman: Grazie.

Dialogo 6

Man: Buongiorno, mi può dire a che ora parte il prossimo treno per Napoli, per favore?
Matilde: Per Napoli deve aspettare un bel po', signore. Parte alle 19.20.
Man: Alle diciannove e venti?
Matilde: Sì.
Man: Da che binario?
Matilde: Dal binario numero quattro.
Man: Grazie ... che noia ...

C Some pairs could make up similar dialogues for the class to listen to and respond 'vero/falso'.

C'è un treno per Firenze stamattina? (page 8)

Main aim: To practise asking for, and giving, information about departure and arrival times of trains

A The students read the dialogue silently to themselves and ask about anything they do not understand. Ask a few questions to ensure that everyone has understood, e.g.

- Dove vuole andare?
- Quando parte il treno?
- A che ora arriva a Firenze?
- Quanti minuti ci vogliono per andare da Arezzo a Firenze?

B The students listen to the recording and follow the dialogue in the Students' Book. Do this once without pauses. Then do it again, pausing occasionally without warning and pointing to someone who should carry on from exactly the right place.

▆ C'è un treno per Firenze stamattina?

Passenger: Scusi, c'è un treno per Firenze stamattina?
Clerk: Sì.
Passenger: A che ora parte il prossimo treno?
Clerk: Alle dieci e sei.
Passenger: A che ora arriva a Firenze?
Clerk: Vediamo ... alle undici e quattro.
Passenger: Grazie.
Clerk: Prego.

C The students play-read the dialogue in pairs, playing each role in turn. Then give them one minute only in which to read it twice, with each student reading each role in turn.

D Ask some questions based on the timetable to ensure that everyone knows how to use the timetable. Clear up any problems and then ask more questions, e.g.

- Sono a Roma. Sono le otto di mattina. A che ora parte il prossimo treno per Arezzo?

E Try to get tourist brochures about Florence, Bologna, Milan and any of the other places mentioned in the timetable. The Italian State Tourist Office, 1 Princes Street, London W1R 8AY, tel: 071-408 1254 is a good source for such things. Give these to different students, or groups, and they read them and then tell each other about the town they have been reading about. Each pair decides, on the basis of what they have read and heard, which town to visit. They then make up a dialogue to get there by train, adapting the model in the Students' Book.

F This would be a good time to start work on *Scoprite qualcosa di più* (page 146).

È in orario? (page 9)

Main aim: To develop the ability to understand station announcements

A Make sure that everyone understands the notice board, e.g.

— Il treno in arrivo da Venezia deve arrivare a che ora?
— Da dove viene il treno che arriva alle dieci e cinquanta?

B Make sure that everyone understands what to do. You could give a few examples for the students to respond to, holding your nose to make your voice sound like a railway announcement, e.g.

— Il treno proveniente da Venezia arriverà alle 10.20.

The students respond accordingly, e.g.

— È in ritardo.

Then play each announcement twice, stopping after each for the students to respond. Clear up any problems before playing the next announcement.

C Play each announcement once only and ask the students to tell you at what time the train is due in and at which platform. Set the class the challenge of doing this with all the announcements in four minutes.

D Return to these announcements in another lesson and use them to revise 'dovere' + infinitive. Introduce each one, e.g.

Teacher: Lei aspetta il treno rapido da Venezia, alle 10.10. Ascolta l'annuncio. Che cosa deve fare?
Student: Devo aspettare cinque minuti. Devo andare al binario numero quattro.

🔊 È in orario?

Esempio

— Il treno rapido da Venezia arriverà alle 10.15 al binario 4.
— Il rapido da Milano è in arrivo alle 10.30 al binario 8.

1 Il rapido proveniente da Ancona arriverà al binario 2 alle 10.40.
2 L'Intercity da Napoli, atteso in stazione al binario 7, arriverà alle undici.
3 L'espresso proveniente da Bologna viaggia con dieci minuti di ritardo. È in arrivo alle undici e dieci.
4 Il rapido da Roma, atteso in stazione al binario numero 9, arriverà alle undici e quindici.
5 Il treno proveniente da Trieste arriverà alle undici e trentacinque al binario 3.
6 Il locale proveniente da Lecce arriverà alle undici e cinquantacinque al binario 14.

7 Siamo spiacenti di annunciare che il diretto da Reggio Calabria viaggia con venti minuti di ritardo. Arriverà alle 12.45.
8 L'Intercity da Torino è in arrivo al binario 1 alle 13.40.

E This would be a good time to work on another part of *Scoprite qualcosa di più* (page 146).

Dove vanno? (page 9)

Main aim: To develop listening skills on the topic of train travel

A Give the students three minutes to revise the phrases and dialogue on page 7 from *Alla biglietteria*.

B The students look at the illustrations on page 9 of the Students' Book and write three words or phrases which they think go with each one. They compare these in pairs.

C Make sure that everyone knows what to do. Then play the recorded dialogues and, after each one, ask the students to say where the travellers are going. An example is provided in the Students' Book.

🔊 Dove vanno?

Esempio

Man:	Due per Venezia, per piacere, seconda classe.
Clerk:	Due per Venezia?
Man:	Sì.
Clerk:	Andata e ritorno?
Man:	Sì.
Clerk:	Trentaseimilaseicento ... grazie ... Buon viaggio.

Dialogo 1

Woman:	Buongiorno, mi può dire, per favore, se c'è una riduzione per gruppi?
Clerk:	Per quante persone?
Woman:	Venti giovani e due adulti.
Clerk:	Hanno la Carta Verde?
Woman:	No.
Clerk:	Hanno più di 12 anni?
Woman:	Sì, hanno 14 e 15 anni.
Clerk:	Allora c'è una riduzione del 20%.
Woman:	Anche per i professori?
Clerk:	Sì, per tutti. Dove volete andare?
Woman:	A Bologna, per favore.
Clerk:	Andata e ritorno?
Woman:	Sì.
Clerk:	Ecco ... 10, 20, 22 biglietti per Bologna.
Woman:	Grazie.

Dialogo 2

Woman:	Buongiorno. Un biglietto per Torino, per favore.
Clerk:	Prima o seconda?
Woman:	Prima classe. Devo comprare un biglietto anche per Fifi?
Clerk:	Per chi?
Woman:	Per il mio cane. Fifi, vieni qui.
Clerk:	Il cane viaggia a metà tariffa.
Woman:	Quant'è in tutto?
Clerk:	Per Torino?
Woman:	Sì.
Clerk:	Cinquantaduemilaottocento lire ... Grazie.

Dialogo 3

Man:	Rimini, due adulti e quattro bambini. Scusi, la piccola, ha bisogno di un biglietto? Ha tre anni.
Clerk:	No, non si paga sotto i quattro anni.
Man:	Allora, due adulti, tre bambini.
Clerk:	Ha la Carta Famiglia?
Man:	No.
Clerk:	Per Rimini?
Man:	Rimini, andata e ritorno, seconda classe. Quanto viene?
Clerk:	Quarantatremilaquattrocento ... Grazie.

Dialogo 4

Student:	Uno per Napoli, per favore, solo andata.
Clerk:	Uno?
Student:	Sì.
Clerk:	Prima o seconda?
Student:	Seconda. Ho la Carta Verde. Tenga.
Clerk:	Grazie. Allora c'è una riduzione del 30% ... 15.600 lire, per favore ... Grazie.
Student:	Il prossimo treno per Napoli, a che ora parte?
Clerk:	Alle quattordici e ventidue.
Student:	Grazie.

D Play the 'detective' game. Listen to each dialogue again and see how many different pieces of information the class can give you. Encourage them to go beyond the obvious, e.g.

– È ricca la signora? Come fai a saperlo?
– Quanto deve pagare in tutto?
– Quanto deve pagare per il suo cane?

E This would be a good time to do some more work on *Scoprite qualcosa di più* (pages 146-147).

È pericoloso sporgersi! (page 9)

Main aim: To introduce some common signs and notices

A Make sure that the students understand all these signs and notices. Then ask a few questions, e.g.

– Che cosa non si deve fare qui?
– Perché non dovete bere quest'acqua?

B The students draw a symbol for each sign, drawing them on the left of a page and writing the appropriate sign next to the symbol, on the right. This could be done at home.

C The students cover the captions and show their drawings to each other to see if they can recognise them all.

D You could make an attractive wall display with these drawings.

E Give each student a copy of Copymaster 2. They could write the four advantages and compare what they have written, in pairs.

Ask them to find the English words used in this text. Do words exist in Italian for: breakfast, snack, drinks?
Why do the students think that English is used here?
The students read the text again to find, in two minutes, two important pieces of advice to give to someone thinking of using this service.

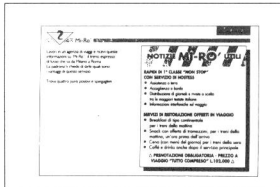

Adesso, tocca a te! (page 10)

Main aim: To demonstrate that the language of this unit has been mastered

Exercise 1
Language area: Finding places at the station
Skill area: Reading

The students write their answers. They then check each other's work and help their partners to get everything right.

Exercise 2
Language area: Train announcements
Skill area: Listening

The students write an explanation, in English, of this announcement, after listening to it twice.

🔊 Adesso, tocca a te!

— Siamo spiacenti di annunciare che il rapido per Bologna al binario 5 partirà con dieci minuti di ritardo.

Exercise 3

Language area: Travel by train
Skill area: Listening and speaking

Make a copy of Copymaster 3 onto an OHP transparency. This provides a model for the activity which students will do in pairs. Explain that students will act out two conversations in which they will take turns to play the part of the passenger and the part of the clerk. The passenger must base what he/she says on symbols similar to those in the model dialogue. Work through the model dialogue with the class until everyone understands what to do. Now give a copy of Copymasters 4A and 4B to each pair. The student playing the part of the 'viaggiatore' asks questions based on the symbols and writes down the information supplied by the 'bigliettaio'. The student playing the part of the 'bigliettaio' only needs to write down details of the ticket asked for. They then change roles in the second situation.

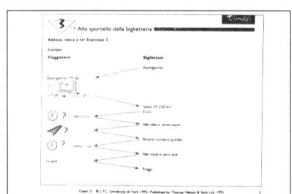

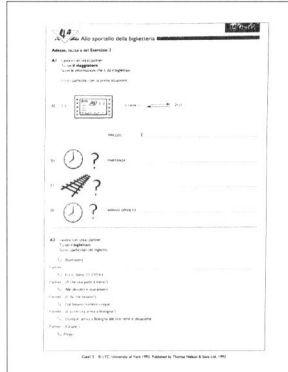
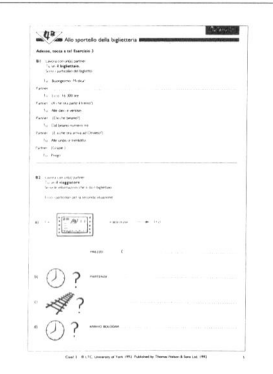

Ora sai ... (page 10)

Main aim: **To act as a summary and reference point for the main language of this unit**

Base a few activities on this page.

● Ask students to repeat and adapt some of the sentences, e.g.

— Due per Venezia, per favore, solo andata.

● They say how you would ask for one (three, etc.) single (return) ticket(s) to Rome (Milan, etc.).

● The students make up dialogues which use one sentence from each box.

● The students test each other in pairs. One has his/her book open and asks the other (whose book is closed) for Italian expressions which illustrate the English descriptions in the left-hand boxes.

Revision

1   Using the telephone (Book 2, Unit 2)

A   Write the following two lists of words on the board/OHP.

1 Introdurre ...	il ricevitore
2 Sollevare ...	il tasto
3 Comporre ...	delle monete
4 Introdurre ...	il ricevitore
5 Riagganciare ...	altre monete
6 Premere ...	il numero

Students select the words that complete the instructions correctly. They write down the instructions in the correct order and then use these to explain to a partner, in Italian, how to use a public telephone.

B   Make two copies of Copymaster 5 for each group of players. Cut up each sheet into 16 'cards' so that you have a pack of 32 cards.

Rules

1   Suitable for between two and four players.
2   Deal five cards to each player face down.
3   Place the remaining cards face down in the centre of the table.
4   Take the top card from the centre pile and place it face up next to the pile to form the 'discard' pile.
5   The object of the game is to play cards face upwards on the table in such a way that they form a realistic telephone conversation.
6   Each card played must be added to the end of the conversation that has so far been put down on the table. Cards may not be inserted into the beginning or middle of the conversation.
7   Only one conversation may be built up at a time.
8   The dialogue must make sense. If a majority of players cannot accept a card as a valid continuation of the dialogue, the player must take it back and start his/her turn again.
9   The player to the left of the dealer starts.

10 The first card played must be either 'Pronto, Hotel Bellavista' or 'Pronto?'.

11 Players in turn place a card face up on the table to continue the dialogue. Only one card may be played at each turn.

12 If none of their cards can be added to the dialogue, players must pick up one card from either the face down pile or the discard pile, and discard one card face up onto the discard pile (as in Rummy). They may play the card they pick up immediately, if it is suitable.

13 The words on a new card placed on the table do not have to be the words of a new speaker in the dialogue. They could be the words which the same speaker goes on to say e.g.

Player A: Vorrei parlare con la Signora Wilson, per favore.
Player B: Un momento ...
Player C: Mi dispiace, in questo momento non c'è.

14 Conversations must end with 'Grazie' or 'Prego'.

15 When a conversation has ended, the next player starts a new one.

16 If there is no possible card that can be played to continue a dialogue, the cards so far played are returned to the centre pile and a new conversation is started.

17 The first person to get rid of all their cards wins.

18 Or, when no-one can play any more cards, the player with the lowest number of cards wins.

Simpler version

Distribute the cards in single sets of 16 cards, shuffled. Students, working in pairs, must sort out the cards so that they make a sensible conversation. They then practise reading it aloud.
The longer game could follow on from this activity.

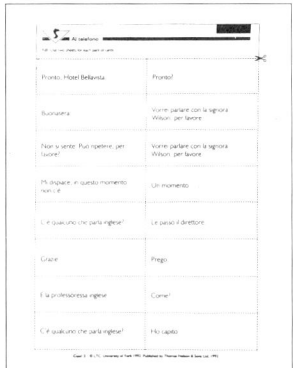

2 Devi, deve, dovete + infinitive (Book 2, Unit 2)

A Organise a brief period of verb circle practice (see Teacher's Book 2, page 67), e.g.

– Devo telefonare alla stazione.

B The students copy these words and grid from the board:

Devi				
Deve				
Dovete				

They listen and write next to each of these words the numbers of the sentences in which they occur. The first to fill all twelve boxes correctly wins, e.g.

Numero uno: Dovete finire quest'esercizio a casa.
Numero due: Per i francobolli devi andare dal tabaccaio.

C Show the students some appropriate signs and notices from your country. They say how they would explain to an Italian visitor what these mean, e.g.

– Qui, non devi fumare.

– Qui, dovete andare sempre dritto.

3 Free time and leisure activities (Book 2, Unit 10)

A Give each student a copy of Copymaster 6. They could work on this at home, deciding what to give to each friend. In class, ask several students what they are giving to each friend and why.

B Ask some students to adapt what the Italians say to talk about their free time. The others suggest appropriate presents. They could then all do this in pairs.

4 Present tense: 'io' and 'tu' forms (Book 2, Unit 10)

These verb forms can be revised by using a mime game, first with the whole class and then in small groups. Students in turn volunteer to mime an activity. The others guess what it is, using the 'tu' form, e.g. "Giochi a scacchi?"
The mimer replies in the 'io' form, e.g. "No, non gioco a scacchi."
To get the game off to a good start, you could ask the class to name as many activities as they can think of, and write them all on the board in the infinitive. They can of course include things such as 'comprare della frutta', 'prendere/bere una birra' and 'andare alla farmacia' as well as the key vocabulary from Book 1, Unit 8 and Book 2, Units 9 and 10.

2ª Unità
FACCIAMO UNO SCAMBIO!

Main aims

~ To be able to get a penfriend/exchange partner
~ To be able to understand and fill in exchange forms
~ To be able to say that you collect something
~ To be able to describe personality and appearance
~ To be able to begin and end a letter to a partner appropriately

Materials

~ Tape
Intervista (Teacher's Book page 23)
Ascolta questi ragazzi (Teacher's Book page 25)
L'alunno modello (Teacher's Book page 27)
Adesso, tocca a te! (Teacher's Book page 31)
In treno (Teacher's Book page 34)

~ Copymasters 7–13

Grammar in *Scoprite qualcosa di più*

~ Comparative adjectives

Revision

~ Family, pets, interests (Book 2, Unit 1)
~ Avere: present tense (Book 2, Unit 1)
~ Possessive adjectives 1st-3rd person singular (Book 2, Unit 1)
~ School (Book 2, Unit 8)
~ Fare: present tense (Book 2, Unit 8)
~ Travelling by train (Book 3, Unit 1)
~ Present tense (Book 3, Unit 1)

Vocabulary

A: Productive

allegro	un(a) partner
alto	i passatempi
bello	più ... di
biondo	portare
calmo	una ragazza
i capelli	un ragazzo
corto	rispondimi presto
fare collezione di	scuro
grasso	sensibile
un hobby	serio
lungo	socievole
magro	sono nato(a)
maturo	sportivo
meno ... di	studioso
gli occhiali	tanti cari saluti
la pallavolo	timido

B: Receptive

un adesivo	un'inserzione
un'amica	liscio
un amico	del materiale
una casalinga	i passatempi
una cassetta	il prefisso
castano	la professione
una collezione	riccio
il/la corrispondente	riconoscere
data di nascita	uno scambio
divorziato	simpatico
gentile	un testo di canzone
giovane	uscire

Facciamo uno scambio! (page 11)

Main aim: **To present the main objectives of this unit**

A Ask the class to read the text and to respond to it, e.g.

- What do you think of this?
- Has anyone got an Italian penfriend?
- Do you think it is a good idea to have one?
- What other advantages can you think of apart from those mentioned?

B Encourage any students without an Italian penfriend to get one. They could write to:
International Youth Service,
PB 125 SF-20101 Turku 10,
Finland.

Class exchanges of letters, magazines, recordings, realia, etc. can be arranged through:
Central Bureau for Educational Visits and Exchanges,
Seymour Mews House,
Seymour Mews,
London W1H 9PE

Tel. 071-486 5101

C Encourage the students to talk about the photo on this page, e.g.

- Che cos'ha ricevuto la ragazza?
- Chi gliel'ha mandato? Suo zio? Un amico?

D Using the words on this page, and any other words they know, the students write lists of things they would like to receive from an Italian penfriend. They compare these in pairs.

Un modulo da riempire (page 11)

Main aim: To practise understanding, and giving, information required by an exchange school

A The students read this form and each decide if they would like to have this person as an exchange partner. Ask them to explain their decisions. Ask them also who (else) he would suit as a partner and why. Ask several students to say what they have in common with him: they should all try to find at least one thing.

B Make sure that everyone understands the headings on the exchange form. Then read aloud some of the headings and ask students for the relevant information. When this starts to be easy, ask them for two pieces of information, e.g.

– Cognome e nome.
– Nazionalità e luogo di nascita.

The students can continue to do this in pairs.

C Make enough copies of Copymaster 7 for each student to have one. Cut them into 'cards' and put each set of cards into a separate envelope for each student. The students match the heading cards with the appropriate information cards. They compare their results with a partner.
You could point out that you use the feminine form of the adjective for nationality, whoever you are describing. The adjective agrees with the word 'nazionalità' and not with the person concerned.

D Play the recording. The students listen and check that their cards are correctly paired. They could put the cards into correct sequence too.

▬ Intervista

Teacher:	A chi tocca? Ah, a te Valentina? Benissimo. Dunque, per lo scambio devo riempire questo modulo con te, allora ... vediamo ... cognome ... Righetti.
Valentina:	Sì.
Teacher:	Nome, Valentina ... femmina ... Dove sei nata?
Valentina:	A Costalpino.
Teacher:	Costalpino. Data di nascita?
Valentina:	Il sei giugno, settantotto.
Teacher:	Nazionalità, italiana.
Valentina:	Sì.
Teacher:	Età. Quanti anni hai?
Valentina:	Quattordici.
Teacher:	Indirizzo?
Valentina:	Via Cellini, 19, ad Arezzo.
Teacher:	Via Cellini, 19, Arezzo, 52100. Numero di telefono?
Valentina:	920025.
Teacher:	920025 ... e poi il prefisso ... 0575. Hai fratelli?
Valentina:	Sì, una sorella e un fratello.
Teacher:	E come si chiamano?
Valentina:	Dunque ... mia sorella si chiama Romina e mio fratello si chiama Marco.
Teacher:	E quanti anni hanno?
Valentina:	Romina è più grande di me, ha sedici anni e Marco è più piccolo; ne ha dieci, lui.
Teacher:	Adesso ... professione del padre. Che lavoro fa tuo papà?
Valentina:	Lavora all'ufficio postale. È impiegato.
Teacher:	Professione della madre. Tua mamma va al lavoro?
Valentina:	Sì, è maestra.
Teacher:	Ah, sì ... è vero. Avete degli animali a casa?
Valentina:	Sì, abbiamo un cane e due gatti.
Teacher:	Benissimo. Adesso, passatempi, hobby, tempo libero? Cosa fai la sera, per esempio?
Valentina:	Mi piace giocare a ping-pong ... andare al cinema ... leggere dei fumetti e poi il weekend mi piace andare a sciare.
Teacher:	Perfetto. Adesso ... classe ... prima C. Materie preferite?
Valentina:	Mm.. Mi piace italiano, scienze ... e poi mi piace l'inglese!
Teacher:	Grazie.

E Give each student a copy of Copymaster 8. They complete the form for themselves, as if they are taking part in the exchange.
Alternatively, the students could work in pairs.
Student A plays the part of a teacher organising the exchange.

Student B is a student taking part in the exchange. Put these questions on the OHP board for students to refer to.

- Nome?
- Cognome?
- Qual è la tua data di nascita?
- Dove sei nato(a)?
- Nazionalità?
- Qual è il tuo indirizzo?
- Qual è il tuo numero di telefono?
- Qual è il prefisso?
- Hai fratelli?
- Come si chiamano?
- Quanti anni hanno?
- Che lavoro fa tuo padre?
- Che lavoro fa tua madre?
- Avete degli animali a casa?
- Hai qualche hobby?
- Che classe fai?
- Quali sono le tue materie preferite?

Student A asks questions and completes a form for B. They then change roles.

F Pass round the completed forms so that everyone has a chance to read what the others have written. They could decide who they would like as a partner and each write their own name, and their preferred partner's name, on a piece of paper. They give these to you. You could read out the names of those who would like to be partners. You could arrange for some of these to work together the next time the class works in pairs.

Le collezioni (page 12)

Main aim: To present some of the key language associated with talking about things you collect

A The students read this and you ask a few questions, e.g.

- Chi fa collezione di francobolli (cartoline, dischi)?

Encourage the students to talk a little about their collections, e.g.

- Quanti dischi hai nella tua collezione?
- Di dove sono i tuoi francobolli? Di quali paesi?
- Dove le metti/tieni le tue cartoline?
- Sei membro di un club?
- C'è una rivista che leggi sulle monete estere?

Also encourage the other students to ask about these collections.

B The students copy a grid from the board to help with the class survey, e.g.

Cognome	Nome	Collezioni

They each try to find three people in the class with a collection and write down the details. You could ask about the results and summarise them on the board or OHP, e.g.

- Francobolli: Jane, John, Anthony ...
- Dischi: Clare, Catherine, Michael ...

C Each student draws something to illustrate what they collect, or would like to collect. They make sure that they know how to say that they collect, or would like to collect, this, and write it with their picture. They try to learn this and then go round, asking each other, e.g.

- Fai qualche collezione?
- Ti piacerebbe fare collezione di (francobolli)?

Il mercatino (page 12)

Main aim: To develop reading and writing skills on the topic of collections

A Ask the students to scan this to find out what the magazine extracts are. They then read the adverts and try to find:
- someone they would like to write to;
- someone another student in the class would like to write to.

B Bearing in mind what they found out in their class survey, the students could comment on similarities and differences between them and these Italians.

C The students read the postcard and then adapt it orally to suit other adverts. You could write on the board key words which they need. Use these to play Kim's Game. The students have two minutes to study, and to try to learn, the words. They then close their eyes and you rub off one of the words. The students try to say what you have rubbed off and a volunteer can come to the board and write in the missing word, using a different colour chalk.

Leave these words on the board while the students all write a card in response to one of the adverts.

D As students finish writing their cards, ask them to write an advert, based on those in the Students' Book. You could use these for a class display.

If possible, use the display as a means of arranging real exchanges involving students in other classes. You could also organise a class auction for charity, with students bringing in objects and auctioning them.

E You could base some scanning practice on these adverts, e.g.

– Chi fa collezione di poster (testi di canzoni, dischi, ecc.)?
– Chi abita a Napoli (Verona, Milano, ecc.)?

You could also ask questions which require the students to make connections between different adverts, e.g.

– Trovate i nomi di tre persone che fanno collezione di francobolli.
– Trovate i nomi di due persone che vorrebbero vendere dei dischi.

Scriviamoci! (page 13)

Main aim: To develop the ability to read letters from, and write letters to, an exchange partner

A The students read the letter and the form: they try to find any things they have in common with Aster and report what these are.

B Using the form which they filled in giving their own personal details on Copymaster 8, the students now write a letter to go with the form, using the letter on this page as a model.

Ascolta questi ragazzi (page 13)

Main aim: To develop listening skills in the context of talking about yourself, family and interests

A Present a technique which can often be used to prepare for listening. Each student looks at the four photos and tries to guess six words or phrases which the people in each photo will say. They write these down. In pairs, they compare their lists and agree on ten words or phrases for each photo. Ask some students to read their lists aloud and encourage the others to comment.

B Play the recordings. The students listen first to see which of the words and phrases on their lists are used. This should encourage them and help them to realise that this is an effective technique to help them to understand: to anticipate what people are likely to say. Discuss this with the class. They should now be able to tell you the name of each person in each photo.
Answers: A = Stefania, B = Luca, C = Paola, D = Carlo.

🔊 Ascolta questi ragazzi

Numero uno

– Ciao. Sono Carlo. Carlo Bucchini. Allora, invece di mandare una lettera, ho deciso di spedire una cassetta. Allora, come ho già detto mi chiamo Carlo Bucchini. Sono nato l'undici gennaio 1975. Ho sedici anni. Sono nato ad Arezzo e sono italiano. Abito in via Umbria, 22, sempre ad Arezzo. Ho un fratello, Andrea. È più grande di me; ha diciotto anni. Mio padre è impiegato alla Lebole e mia madre è disegnatrice. Come passatempo ... mi piace soprattutto uscire in motorino con i miei amici. E come hobby mi piace la filatelia, cioè la collezione dei francobolli. Frequento il liceo classico. Le mie materie preferite sono, a parte la ginnastica e l'intervallo, la matematica e la storia, ma per me la ginnastica è più interessante di tutte le altre materie.

Numero due

– Ciao. Sono Luca, un ragazzo italiano di quindici anni. Vivo a Pieve al Toppo, vicino ad Arezzo. Sono nato il venti gennaio. Non ho fratelli; sono figlio unico. I miei genitori lavorano; mio padre è notaio e mia mamma lavora in una farmacia. Come animali abbiamo un gatto e un cane. Il nostro gatto si chiama Egor e il cane si chiama Boris. Preferisco il cane - è più affettuoso del gatto! Pratico molti sport; tennis, pallavolo e Kung Fu. Il mio hobby è la collezione di testi di canzoni. Le mie materie preferite sono la matematica e le scienze. Secondo me le scienze sono più utili delle lingue. La mia scuola si chiama Francesco Redi e sono nella Iª A.

Numero tre

— Ciao! Sono Stefania Fauci e anch'io vorrei partecipare allo scambio. Ho quindici anni e sono nata il 23 agosto. Sono italiana. Abito a San Leo, un piccolo paese vicino ad Arezzo. Ho due sorelle; una più grande di me, di diciassette anni, Cristina, e l'altra (più piccola) di dodici anni che si chiama Daniela. Mio padre fa il carabiniere e mia madre è impiegata alla questura. Ho un animale, un canarino, di nome Biffi. Come passatempo mi piace giocare con il computer, ascoltare la musica e guardare le partite di calcio. Non sono molto sportiva ma mi piace il nuoto. Frequento il primo anno di Liceo Scientifico, 1ª B e le mie materie preferite sono inglese e biologia.

Numero quattro

— Ciao. Io sono Paola e ho deciso di mandare una cassetta invece di scrivere una lettera. Allora, mi chiamo Paola Luciani e voglio fare una piccola descrizione ... Ho quindici anni e il mio compleanno è il 3 luglio. Sono italiana e vivo ad Arezzo. Il mio appartamento è situato in centro, non lontano dal centro sportivo. Il mio indirizzo è Via Anardi, 14. Ho una sorella più piccola di me, di nome Laura, ha otto anni, ma non abbiamo animali. Vivo con la mamma perché i miei genitori sono divorziati. Mia madre si chiama Maria Elena ed è redattrice. Mio padre lavora nel settore pubblicitario. Per quanto riguarda il tempo libero pratico molti sport come il tennis, la pallavolo, il nuoto e lo sci. Faccio collezione di cartoline di tutto il mondo. Le mie materie preferite sono informatica e inglese.

C The students listen again to decide which of these people they would prefer to have an exchange with, and why. They could suggest a suitable penfriend for their partners and see if they agree. They could each write a letter to the person they choose, using the one on page 13 as a model.

D Give students four copies each of the form on Copymaster 8. They listen again to the recordings and fill in a form for each person.

They could then discuss what sorts of information are called for on official forms which people do not usually talk about when introducing themselves. They could also say what sorts of things people talk about but which are not asked for on the forms.

You could point out that it is useful to have a M/F section on such forms because there are a number of Italian boys' names which look feminine, e.g. Andrea, Luca, Nicola.

Mandami una cassetta! (page 13)

Main aim: To practise talking about yourself, family and interests

A The students could use the suggestions here, and the information on Copymaster 8, to write some brief notes to help them to make a recording. Stress that they should work from notes to get the best results and not write out what they want to say. They could practise in pairs, working from their notes to talk about themselves. They may wish, on the basis of this, to improve their notes.

B Invite some students to practise what they wish to say as you and the class listen. You could write the key words on the board as you listen and then compare your notes with those of the student.

C Everyone should make a recording, either at home or at school. You could play some of the best ones to the class and encourage them to say why you think they are good. If you judge them by the criteria used in exams, this will help the students to understand these criteria better. Those with penfriends in Italy should be encouraged to send their recordings to them. You could suggest that they also record a paragraph in English and a favourite song or piece of music.

La personalità (page 14)

Main aim: To present and practise some useful adjectives for describing people's personality

A The students read this to themselves and ask about anything with which they need help. They try to learn the adjectives in the box and then, each in turn, try to teach them to their partners in a memorable way.

B They say how they think their parents would answer the question on the form. Give each a copy of Copymaster 9. The students take these home and ask their parents to fill them in, with the students explaining what the adjectives mean.
In class, the students compare what they thought their parents would say with what they actually said. You could write some helpful models on the board, e.g.

— A casa i miei genitori dicono che sono timido, ma sul modulo dicono che sono socievole.
— A casa i miei genitori dicono che sono allegra, ma sul modulo non dicono che lo sono.

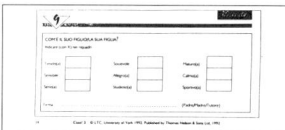

C Each student uses the adjectives on the form to write a brief description of an ideal exchange partner for themselves and for their class partner based on the model given. You could write one or two further models on the board and leave them there for the students to refer to as they write, e.g.

– Alla mia partner piacerebbe fare uno scambio con una ragazza matura, una ragazza molto allegra ma anche calma.

In pairs, the students compare what they have written about each other.

D Discuss the form with the class. Do they think that the most useful adjectives are included? Which would they add? Write on the board adjectives which they ask for or suggest, e.g.

simpatico, ordinato, comprensivo, dolce, apprensivo, intelligente, disponibile, independente, forte, religioso, tollerante, gentile, generoso, severo, energico.

Leave these on the board while the students produce a better form, one which includes the features they think are important.

E Using the grid below, written on the board or OHP, the students write as many correct and sensible sentences as they can in ten minutes, completing their sentences with appropriate adjectives:

un buon professore una buona madre un buon amico una buona amica il marito ideale la moglie ideale un poliziotto uno studente	è ... dev' essere ...

Take in and correct these sentences. The students then compare their sentences in pairs and/or groups.

F For homework, each student could write a list of the adjectives which describe the character of:

un professore
uno studente
un poliziotto
un'infermiera

When reporting back, they could say, e.g.

– Questa persona dev'essere calma, socievole, matura, sensibile, allegra e simpatica. Chi è?

The others guess who is being described.

G The students speculate about which characteristics they have inherited from their parents. To help them, they could first copy the following from the board and complete them:

– Mio padre è ...
– Mia madre è ...
– Io sono ...

È una questione di punti di vista (page 14)

Main aim: To practise describing one's own character and compare it with that of others

A The students read this to themselves. Check that they understand it: you could ask someone, for example, to summarise in English how each person is described.

B Each student writes a description of a favourite famous person. They read these aloud to their friends who try to guess who the famous people are.

C Give out Copymaster 10. Make sure that everyone understands the sheet and knows what to do. Then play the recording, stopping and repeating as necessary. Discuss with the students their answers and the conclusions they reach on the teachers. *Answers:*

Qualità	Numero 1	Numero 2	Numero 3	Numero 4
maturo		1		
calmo				
socievole				5
serio			1	
tollerante				
curioso	4			2
studioso	2		2	
organizzato	1	3	6	
disciplinato			3	
timido				
gentile		4		3
onesto			4	
allegro	3			1
paziente	5			
spiritoso				4
coscienzioso		2	5	

L'alunno modello

Numero uno

Interviewer: Buongiorno.
Teacher: Buongiorno.
Interviewer: Senta, stiamo facendo un'inchiesta sull'alunno modello. Vorremmo sapere se tutti gli insegnanti vedono l'alunno modello sotto la stessa luce o se per certi insegnanti alcune qualità sono più importanti di altre. Dunque ... Lei mi potrebbe descrivere l'alunno modello?

Teacher: Mm ... è difficile ... non so ... l'alunno modello deve essere organizzato. Deve essere studioso ma non troppo, allegro, curioso – cioè deve interessarsi a tante cose diverse ... e poi deve essere paziente.

Interviewer: Grazie.

Teacher: Prego.

Numero due

Interviewer: Buongiorno.

Teacher: Buongiorno.

Interviewer: Senta, professoressa, mi potrebbe descrivere l'alunno modello? Per Lei, l'alunno modello, com'è?

Teacher: Vediamo ... per me l'alunno modello deve essere maturo, una persona coscienziosa, organizzata, gentile, quest'è importante. Sì, per me deve essere organizzato e gentile.

Interviewer: Grazie.

Teacher: Prego.

Numero tre

Interviewer: Scusi, per favore ... Lei ha qualche minuto per parlarci dell'alunno modello?

Teacher: L'alunno modello?

Interviewer: Sì, secondo Lei, l'alunno modello com'è?

Teacher: Dunque ... l'alunno modello è serio, studioso ... cioè s'interessa agli studi ... è disciplinato, cioè non ci sono problemi di disciplina. È onesto: quando non capisce una cosa lo dice. Poi è coscienzioso; fa bene tutto il lavoro ed è molto ben organizzato. Ecco.

Interviewer: Ho capito. La ringrazio.

Teacher: Di niente.

Numero quattro

Interviewer: Scusi ...

Teacher: Sì?

Interviewer: Mi potrebbe fare una breve descrizione dell'alunno modello? Cioè, secondo Lei quali sono le caratteristiche più importanti dell'alunno modello?

Teacher: Mm ... dirlo così è difficile ... vediamo ... Sì, prima di tutto deve essere allegro, vivo. Poi deve essere curioso; deve avere voglia di imparare, di capire le cose. Deve essere gentile; gentile con l'insegnante, ben inteso, ed anche gentile con gli altri ragazzi. Poi mi piacciono i ragazzi spiritosi, che hanno un buon senso dell'umorismo ... i ragazzi socievoli, che lavorano bene con tutti quanti.

Interviewer: Allora, allegro, curioso, gentile, spiritoso, socievole.

Teacher: Esatto.

Interviewer: Grazie.

Teacher: Prego.

D This would be a good time to start work on *Scoprite qualcosa di più* (page 148).

Messaggi personali (page 15)

Main aim: To develop reading skills on the topic of describing people and their personalities

A Ask the students to read this page for one minute only to find out what the texts are. Then ask them to suggest, in English, the sorts of words and phrases they expect to find in such texts. Write these on the board. The students then try to find the Italian equivalents of these.

B Draw attention to some of the conventions used in these adverts, e.g.
– How age is given ('32 enne,' etc).
– How to tell if the person is male or female (form of adjectives, 'ragazzo(a)', 'mamma', etc).

The students could, after some discussion, look for and write down the key link phrases in these adverts, e.g.

disposto(a) ...		
cerca vorrebbe conoscere desidera conoscere conoscerebbe		compagno max 40 enne ragazzi(e) persona ... amici/amiche ragazza donna signorina un uomo
per	affettuosa amicizia amicizia eventuale unione divertirsi nel tempo libero sentirsi amata e protetta trascorrere tempo libero eventuale matrimonio formare compagnia eventuale legame costruire una vita a due (scopo unione) passare il tempo libero (scopo matrimonio)	

C The students read the adverts and try to find who could contact whom. They could do this individually or in pairs.

D Students could write adverts of their own, e.g.
– for themselves
– for their partners
– for you.
These could be displayed, compared and discussed.

E Each student lists the adjectives used in these advertisements in two columns, headed + (for positive characteristics) and - (for negative ones). What conclusions do they reach by comparing the content and length of the two lists?

F Give out copies of Copymaster 11A. When the students have each drawn a tree, give out Copymaster 11B. They could study these interpretations at home and discuss them in the next lesson.

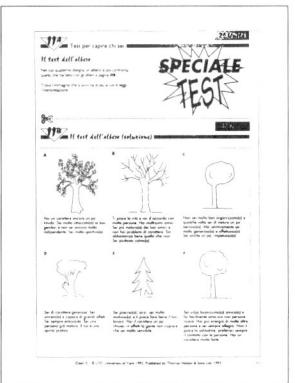

Mi riconosci? (page 15)

Main aim: To introduce the key language associated with describing appearance

A The teacher describes someone in the class using phrases from the list e.g.
- Who would say 'sono molto bello, ho i capelli neri, gli occhi castani e porto gli occhiali'?
- Questa persona è molto alta, non porta gli occhiali ... ecc. Chi è?

Play the game suggested in the Students' Book.

B Divide the class into two teams, A and B. Each member of team A writes a description of someone in team B and vice-versa. Can the people described recognise themselves in the descriptions?

C Drawing dictation
Explain to the students that you are going to pretend to be an alien from outer space and that you are going to describe yourself. Without looking at each other's work, the students must draw a picture of what they imagine you to look like. They can then compare their pictures.

- Ciao, ragazzi! Mi presento. Mi chiamo Ernesto Extraterrestre. Sono molto alto e ho la testa molto grande. Ho gli occhi neri e porto gli occhiali. Sono occhiali speciali. Ho i capelli neri,

corti e ricci. Sono un po' grasso. Purtroppo non sono molto bello. Ho le braccia lunghissime e ho delle grosse mani. Sono molto socievole e mi piace stare insieme a persone simpatiche e aperte.

You could then display two pictures and invite the students to compare them, e.g.

- Questo extraterrestre è più alto di quello.
- Questo extraterrestre ha i capelli più corti di quello.

This could be played as a team game. Teams score points for every correct statement they can make comparing the two aliens.

The description revises the names of parts of the body (Book 2, Unit 7).

D The students make a photo collage with the eyes of one person, the hair of another, the nose of another, etc. by cutting up magazines and newspapers. They write a simple physical description of their photo collage. Display the collages around the room. Distribute the descriptions to the students, in random order. The students read these and identify the picture which goes with each one.

E This is an alternative to **D**. Cut out pictures of famous people in magazines, colour supplements, etc. Each student takes a picture and writes a short description of the person in the picture using the phrases in the list in the Students' Book. Display all the pictures around the classroom. One student reads a description, and the others identify the picture. This could be done in groups of five.

F Witness game
Divide the class into six groups of five, say, (Groups 1-6). Each student in each group has a letter A-E. Give each group a picture to study and then display all the pictures. Students form new groups with all the As going together and all Bs going together, etc. Student A1 describes his/her picture. Student A2 describes his/her picture, and so on. The others in the group identify the pictures described.

G Identity parade / Confronto all'americana
One student (A) goes out of the room. Eight students line up in an identity parade. Another student (B) from the rest of the class goes out and describes one of the eight in the parade to the person already outside (A). Student A comes back in and has to identify the 'criminal'.

H Chi sono. Come ti vorrei
Make copies of Copymaster 12. The students fill in both forms by answering questions, supplying details and ticking appropriate boxes.

Form A is *Chi sono*. Students give details concerning themselves.

Form B is *Come ti vorrei*. Students give details of their ideal partner.

Separate form A from form B. Display *Chi sono* (A) forms around the room (with no names on them!). The students read the forms and see if any self-description matches their *Come ti vorrei* (B) requirements. They then find out who in the class would be their ideal partner.

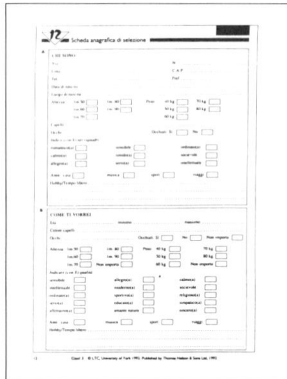

I This would be a good time to do some more work on *Scoprite qualcosa di più* (pages 148-149).

Indovinello (page 16)

Main aim: To present and practise some comparative adjectives

A Complete work on *Scoprite qualcosa di più* (pages 148-149) before working on this item.

B The students could work on this at home in order to name the three girls and to prepare an explanation for their choice. In class, you could ask, e.g.

– Chi ha i capelli più lunghi / corti di quelli di A?
– Che è più alto(a) di C, ma meno alto(a) di B?

Then ask students to identify and describe each girl. Write the descriptions on the board, e.g

– Patrizia porta gli occhiali. È meno alta di Stefania e di Raffaella. Ha i capelli ...

Answers: **A** Raffaella **B** Patrizia **C** Stefania

When all three descriptions are on the board, you could play 'Kim's game' (see Teacher's Book page 6): give the students four minutes to study the descriptions and then, while they shut their eyes, remove a word, ask various students to say the word and one to write it back on the board. You could concentrate on comparative adjectives.

C Draw three matchstick boys on the board, describing them as you do so and encouraging the students to add details for you to include, e.g.

– Paolo è meno alto di Enrico.

When you have finished the drawings, the students describe the boys orally and then write a description of them, similar to the one on page 16 for the girls.

D As students finish work on the above activity, they could copy and complete these sentences which you can present on the board/OHP:

I Il treno rapido è meno _____ dell'Inter City.
2 Una bicicletta è meno _____ di una macchina.
3 Una macchina è più _____ di un autobus.
4 Il taxi è più _____ di un autobus.
5 L'autobus è meno _____ del taxi.
6 I treni moderni sono più _____ di quelli di un tempo.

E Present the following on the board or OHP. The students should compare one item in each pair with the other:

il treno e l'autobus; la matematica e la storia; le ragazze e i ragazzi; gennaio e giugno; una lettera e una cartolina ...

Encourage the students to find as many ways as possible of comparing the two words in each pair.

F This is a game to be played by the whole class or by groups of six to eight students. The players sit in a circle which includes one empty chair. Whoever has the empty chair on their right has to invite someone to sit on it by making a true comparison, e.g.

– Sue, vieni qua perché sei più grande di me.
– Andrew, vieni qua perché hai i capelli meno corti di me.

Write two or three such examples on the board and leave them there as a model for students to refer to if necessary.

Davanti allo specchio (Copymaster 13)

Main aim: To practise describing people, personality and appearance

A Give each student a copy of Copymaster 13. Introduce this quiz to ensure that everyone understands it. Work on the first few questions orally, encouraging several students to answer each one and stimulating discussion.

When it is clear that everyone is ready, the students write their answers to each question.

They then compare their replies, in pairs.

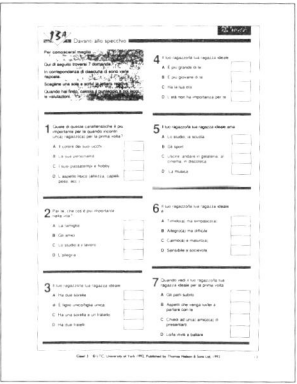 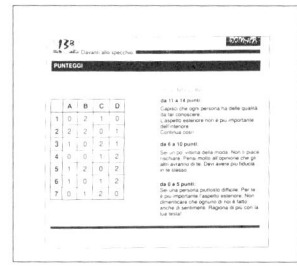

B The students add up their points and read their evaluation. Encourage them to react to this and to express agreement or disagreement.

Ci vediamo alla stazione! (page 16)

Main aim: To practise reading and writing personal descriptions

A Spend a few minutes working on page 15 (*Mi riconosci?*). The students could choose from the list and read aloud as many phrases as possible to describe, for example, the headteacher, another teacher, a famous singer or TV star; this could be done in a time limit of one minute, trying with each person to say more things in a minute.
As an alternative, you could use a large photo of someone, cut from a magazine. Show it for just three seconds and then see how many things the students can say to describe the person. Write what they say on the board. Then show the photo again, for five seconds, and give the class the chance to change and add to the description on the board. Finally, put the photo next to the description, get students to read the description aloud and to correct it if necessary.

B Ask the students to read to themselves the introduction to this item and the letter. Ask them to say, e.g.
– what the introduction says
– what the letter is about.
The students then read the letter again and try to find Francesca in the picture. When a student claims to have found her, ask the student to describe her.

Using the letter, each student writes down what they would say to explain to a parent what Francesca looks like.

C The students look at the letter again and choose what they think are the eight key words in it, the words which convey the most important information. They write these and then compare them in pairs.

Ask some students to read out their key words, and invite others to comment, e.g.

– Secondo me, 'T shirt' è più importante di 'paio'.

D Each student writes eight to ten key words for describing themselves. As they do so, you write on the board eight to ten key words for describing yourself. When everyone has finished, get them to help you to expand your key words into a full description of you: write this on the board. All the students then write a self-description based on their key words.

When you give back the corrected version of these, read a few aloud and see how well they work: can everyone identify the writer?

E For homework everyone can adapt this description to write a letter like the one on page 16.

Adesso, tocca a te! (page 17)

Main aim: To demonstrate that the language of this unit has been mastered

Exercise 1
Language area: Describing someone
Skill area: Reading

The students read this and write down what they find in it which would interest a friend.

Exercise 2
Language area: Describing someone
Skill area: Listening

The students listen twice to the recording and write a description of the young man so that a parent would recognise him.

Adesso, tocca a te!

– Ciao! Io sono il tuo partner e ti voglio fare una piccola descrizione per ... così almeno, il 20 agosto, quando mi verrai a prendere all'aeroporto, potrai riconoscermi. Sono abbastanza alto, un metro e ottanta, magro ... direi magro. Non porto gli occhiali. E ho i capelli castani, tendenti al rosso, un po' ricci. Ho gli occhi castani. Mm ... e penso che quel giorno, se il tempo lo consente, indosserò un paio di jeans ... mm ... una T-shirt nera e una maglia verde. Avrò con me una grossa valigia nera. Molto probabilmente un walkman. E ti aspetterò davanti all'uscita.

Exercise 3

Language area: Describing someone
Skill area: Speaking

As one student describes his/her parents, the other writes notes in English: they check these before changing roles.

Exercise 4

Language area: Describing yourself
Skill area: Writing

Each student writes an introductory letter about themselves, in reply to this advert.

Exercise 5

Language area: Making comparisons
Skill areas: Writing, reading and speaking

Students work individually to list all the ways in which they are different from other people in the class. You may wish to discuss with the class the positive side of being different from other people. You could point out that very often the most interesting and most memorable people are those who are different in certain ways from others. Once the students have written their own lists, they could read each other's and discuss/challenge any statements with which they do not agree.

Ora sai (page 18)

Main aim: To act as a summary and reference point for the main language of this unit

Help the students to develop techniques for using this to learn and revise the key language.

Give them five minutes to study it and then get them to cover up the Italian. Then ask them for as many Italian words as they can think of to illustrate the English summaries.

Present the following on the board and give the class five minutes to copy them and to find and copy the opposite of each one:

padre	corti
socievole	grassa
ragazza	ricci
biondi	un po'

Present the following on the board and ask the students to say what each is an example of:

Francesco	40 31 12
Verdi	Giornalista
Inglese	Francobolli
Roma	Lo sci
5	24 . 05 . 80

See how quickly the students can find three examples to illustrate each of the following categories:

una collezione	una professione
un hobby	una città italiana
un nome	una via
una nazionalità	un passatempo
un cognome	una canzone

Repeat this once or twice, trying each time to improve on the time taken.

Revision

1   Family, pets, interests (Book 2, Unit 1)

A Call out, in random order, words which go into one of these categories: 'la famiglia', 'gli animali,' 'i passatempi,' e.g.

madre, nonno, pesce rosso, zio, calcio, cane, lo sci, suonare il pianoforte, fratello

Write on the board the three words: 'Famiglia', 'Animale', 'Passatempo'.

As you say the words, the students call out the appropriate category. As soon as someone says the correct category, you say another word. See how many words the class can categorise in one minute. Then see if they can improve on this score.

B Each student writes ten key words which they would use to talk about their family, pets and interests. They give these to a partner who uses them to say as much as they can about the writer's family, pets and interests. The writer confirms and corrects.

2   Avere: present tense (Book 2, Unit 1)

A Organise a few minutes of verb circle practice based on, e.g.

– Ho due fratelli.
– Ha una sorella.
– Non ho un gatto.

B Each student writes five true sentences beginning with 'Ho' and five true sentences beginning with 'Non ho'. They do not show these to their partners.

In pairs, each student has two minutes to guess what the other has written. Student A says a number of sentences beginning with 'Hai' and 'Non hai'. Each time that Student A says something which Student B has written, Student B ticks it. They then change roles. Finally, they compare results and sentences.

To prepare the class for this, you could play this with an assistant or student. You present your ten sentences on the board or OHP. The other person stands with his/her back to this and guesses what you have and do not have.

3 Possessive adjectives (Book 2, Unit 1)

A Present on the board or OHP a table like this:

		maglia
	il mio	t-shirt
È	la mia	zaino
		borsa
Sono	i miei	penne
	le mie	matite
		ombrello

Encourage the students briefly to make up sentences based on the table.
You now describe an item owned by someone in the class, e.g.

– È azzurro. È più grande di una borsa ...

The student who owns the item tries to recognise it first and say, e.g.

– È il mio zaino.

The others also try to recognise it first and to point and say, e.g.

– È il suo zaino.

B Cut pictures from magazines. Show them one at a time and encourage each student to write a sentence expressing their opinions, e.g.

– Mi piace il suo cane.
– Non mi piace la sua maglia.

Then ask students to read aloud their opinions and see how many different ones there are about each picture.
You could ask students to give opinions in a particular mood, e.g. sarcastic, flattering, kind, cruel, critical, aggressive.

C If possible, begin this activity with an assistant or student on teaching practice. Ask him/her for a number of things, e.g.

– Mi puoi dare la tua penna (matita, gomma, chiave)?

Put these on a desk where everyone can see them, along with similar things which belong to you. Point at these things, one after another, and ask who each thing belongs to, e.g.

– È questa la tua matita (chiave, etc.)?
– È questo il mio righello (libro, etc.)?

Your partner replies 'Sì' or 'No' to each question. Encourage the others to join in.

The students could soon play this in pairs, trying to catch their partners out as often as possible.

4 School (Book 2, Unit 8)

A You could play a game of Categories (see Activity 1 above), with these categories: 'materie', 'treni', 'passatempi'. Call out appropriate words, e.g.

rapido, tennis, matematica, storia, biglietto, il windsurf, un'andata e ritorno, inglese, italiano, geografia, binario

B Write on the board a number of incomplete sentences, e.g.
1 A _____ non piace la storia.
2 A _____ piace la matematica.
3 A _____ non piace l'inglese.
4 A _____ piace la musica.
5 _____ è molto bravo in scienze.

You and other students can ask various students about which subjects they like, dislike, are good at, etc. Everyone listens for the information needed to complete one of the sentences and then writes the sentence. The first to complete them all reads them aloud and is declared the winner if they are all correct.

5 Fare: present tense (Book 2, Unit 8)

A Organise a few minutes of verb circle practice based on, e.g.

– Il lunedì faccio matematica e storia.
– Non facciamo musica in questa scuola.
– Che cosa fate alle 10?

B Play a game of 'Il gioco degli spazi' (see Teacher's Book 1, page 110), e.g.
1 _____ fa collezione di francobolli.
2 ____ e _____ fanno una collezione di cartoline.
3 Che cosa _____ domani mattina alle 9.30?
4 La sera dopo scuola ho molti _____ da fare.
5 Cosa _____ stasera? Andiamo al cinema?
6 Ti piacerebbe _____ del windsurf?
7 Mi _____ male i piedi.
8 E tu, Marisa, che classe _____ ?
9 A scuola _____ fa chimica e fisica.
10 Che lavoro _____ tuo padre?

6 Travelling by train (Book 3, Unit 1)

A The students imagine that they have a job in a travel agency. They listen to these Italian tourists and:

– after one hearing, say where each wants to go
– after a second hearing, say what sort of ticket each wants
– after a third hearing, say what else they have understood

🔊 In treno

Dialogo 1

Italian:	Lei parla italiano?
Employee:	Sì.
Italian:	Perfetto. Senta, vorrei un biglietto di andata e ritorno per Leicester, per favore.
Employee:	Dove voleva andare?
Italian:	A Leicester.
Employee:	Ah, Leicester. Ho capito. Prima o seconda classe?
Italian:	Seconda.
Employee:	A che ora voleva partire?
Italian:	Verso le dieci.
Employee:	Va bene. C'è un treno che parte da Londra alle 10.16. Le faccio il biglietto?
Italian:	Sì. Grazie.

Dialogo 2

Italian:	Qualcuno che capisce l'italiano! Che bello!
Employee:	Mi dica!
Italian:	Senta, vorrei fare un biglietto per il treno delle dieci da Londra a Birmingham.
Employee:	Sì. Quando vuole partire?
Italian:	Giovedì.
Employee:	Solo andata, o andata e ritorno?
Italian:	Solo andata.
Employee:	In prima o in seconda classe?
Italian:	Seconda.
Employee:	Dunque, un'andata per Birmingham, seconda classe per il treno delle dieci, partendo giovedì, vero?
Italian:	Esatto.
Employee:	Un momento, allora. Le faccio il biglietto.

Dialogo 3

Employee:	Buongiorno.
Italian:	Buongiorno. Senta, mi può prenotare un posto sul treno da Manchester a Edimburgo, per favore?
Employee:	Sì. Quando vuole partire?
Italian:	C'è un treno che parte da Manchester verso le due del pomeriggio?
Employee:	Un momento ... ce n'è uno che parte alle due e quarantaquattro, che arriva a Edimburgo alle sei e cinquantasette.
Italian:	Va bene. Allora mi può fare un biglietto di andata e ritorno, seconda classe, per il treno delle due e quarantaquattro, per mercoledì?
Employee:	Certo.
Italian:	E vorrei anche prenotare il posto, se è possibile.
Employee:	Certo. Glielo faccio subito.

Dialogo 4

Italian:	Buonasera.
Employee:	Buonasera.
Italian:	Lei parla italiano, vero?
Employee:	Un po', sì.
Italian:	Benissimo. Mi sa dire se c'è un treno che va da Londra a Carlisle, per favore?
Employee:	Da Londra a ...?
Italian:	A Carlisle.
Employee:	Ah... vuol dire Carlisle. Si dice Carlisle, in inglese.
Italian:	Ah, Carlisle. C'è un treno?
Employee:	Sì, sì. A che ora vuole partire?
Italian:	La mattina ... verso le undici.
Employee:	Allora, c'è un treno che parte da Euston proprio alle undici. Vuole che Le faccia il biglietto?
Italian:	Sì, grazie. Mi può fare un biglietto di solo andata, prima classe, per il treno delle undici, per favore.
Employee:	Subito.
Italian:	Senta, mi sa dire se c'è servizio ristorante su quel treno?
Employee:	Sì, c'è servizio ristorante e anche un self-service.
Italian:	Grazie.
Employee:	Prego.

Dialogo 5

Employee:	Hello, can I help you?
Italian:	Mi hanno detto che Lei parla molto bene l'italiano.
Employee:	Lo parlo un po', sì.
Italian:	Benissimo. Dunque, vorrei quattro biglietti di andata e ritorno, seconda classe, per il treno delle dodici e ventidue da Londra a Southampton.
Employee:	Per che giorno?
Italian:	Per domani, martedì.
Employee:	Quattro biglietti ha detto?
Italian:	Sì.
Employee:	È vuol anche la prenotazione?
Italian:	Sì, grazie.
Employee:	Un momento, glieli faccio subito.
Italian:	Grazie.
Employee:	Prego.

Dialogo 6

Italian:	Buongiorno.
Employee:	Buongiorno.
Italian:	Senta, c'è un treno che va da Londra a Canterbury, per favore?
Employee:	C'è un treno, sì. A che ora vuole partire?
Italian:	Beh ... vorrei visitare la cattedrale, allora se c'è un treno che parte presto la mattina... e un altro che torna a Londra verso le sei di sera ...
Employee:	C'è un treno che parte alle 8.30 che arriva a Canterbury alle 9.55. Va bene quello?
Italian:	Sì. E per il ritorno?
Employee:	Per il ritorno, c'è un treno che parte da Canterbury alle 16.22 che arriva a Londra alle 17.47.
Italian:	Perfetto. Mi può fare un biglietto di andata e ritorno, seconda classe, per favore?
Employee:	È per domani?
Italian:	No, per venerdì.
Employee:	Allora, un'andata e ritorno, seconda classe per venerdì 25.
Italian:	Giusto.

You could present a few more place names from your country and the students could have fun asking for a ticket there, pronouncing the place names as they think an Italian might. This activity raises the importance of good pronunciation if communication is to be effective. Get the students to practise asking for train tickets to, e.g.
Arezzo, Firenze, Perugia, Pisa, Venezia, Milano, Torino, Napoli.

They could also practise asking, e.g.
– Is there an express to Naples?
– When does the train leave for Rome?
– When does the train get to Florence?
– From which platform does the train for Milan leave?
– I'd like a return ticket to Venice, second class.
– I'd like two single tickets to Turin, first class.

B Each student decides which are the six most useful sentences for someone travelling by train in Italy. They write these down and ask you to check them. They then try to teach their six sentences to someone in the class.

7 Present tense (Book 3, Unit 1)

A Organise a few minutes of verb circle practice, based on, e.g.
– La mattina mangio un panino o dei biscotti.
– Marco prende l'autobus per andare a scuola.
– Partiamo da casa alle otto meno dieci.

B Divide the class into two teams and organise a game of Noughts and crosses.
The first team to complete correctly one of the sentences on the board (examples below) can begin. Teams then take turns: they can put a nought or a cross in the square corresponding to the sentence they complete.

1 Marco _____ alle otto di mattina.
2 Noi _____ carne e verdura.
3 A scuola io _____ francese e italiano.
4 Tu _____ troppe caramelle.
5 Io _____ la televisione ogni sera.
6 Ragazzi! _____ a pagina 18.
7 Il treno da Milano _____ alle 11.52.
8 Toni e Simone _____ a tennis sulla spiaggia.
9 Stefania _____ la musica la sera.

1	2	3
4	5	6
7	8	9

3ª Unità

COM'È LA TUA CITTÀ?

Main aims

~ To write for information about Italian towns
~ To talk about the town/village in which you live
~ To understand information about Italian towns
~ To ask other people about their home towns

Materials

~ Tape

E tu, dove abiti? (Teacher's Book page 39)
Conversazioni (Teacher's Book page 39)
All'ufficio turistico (Teacher's Book page 40)
Ti piace abitare a Subbiano? (Teacher's Book page 42)
Adesso, tocca a te! (Teacher's Book page 45)

~ Copymasters 14–20
~ A supply of leaflets, maps and brochures relating to Italian towns and cities

Grammar in *Scoprite qualcosa di più*

~ Superlative adjectives

Revision

~ Meals and buying food (Book 2, Unit 3)
~ Di + definite article (Book 2, Unit 3)
~ Daily routine (Book 2, Unit 9)
~ Reflexive verbs: present tense (Book 2, Unit 9)
~ Talking about interests and personality (Book 3, Unit 2)
~ Comparative adjectives (Book 3, Unit 2)

Vocabulary

A: Productive

un abitante	il nord
antico	l'ovest
brutto	un paese
centrale	la regione
un chilometro	storico
una città	il sud
com'è	si può
commerciale	tranquillo
la contea	turistico
da quanto tempo	vedere
l'est	visitare
una località	vivo
noioso	

B: Receptive

avere intenzione di	lungo
una biblioteca	maggiore
la cattedrale	il panorama
una chiesa	un porto
circa	praticare
(in) collina	la provincia
l'Ente Provinciale per il Turismo	la questura
esattamente	situato
famoso	lo stadio
il fiume	il teatro
una guida	una visita
industriale	vi ringrazio in anticipo
un'isola	vi sarei grato(a) se mi
un lago	poteste inviare

Com'è la tua città? (page 19)

Main aim: To introduce the objectives of this unit

A The students read this introduction and then list, in English, the points in it which interest them most; they could list these points under two headings: 'Italian I can learn' and 'What I can learn to do'.

They could compare their lists and change them as a result if they wish.

B The class could discuss with you any other things that they would like to learn in order to talk about their town, or an Italian town. After this discussion, each student could add to their two lists their own additional objectives. Using the Students' Book, you, the assistant or other resources, they should aim to achieve all the objectives on their lists by the end of the unit.

Informazioni... informazioni... (page 19)

Main aims: To provide information on how to find out about Italian towns

To provide a model letter for students to adapt and send

A After reading through this page with the class, you could give each student a card with the address of a different EPT on each card.

Students adapt the model letter for the place on their cards. You can send off the letters.

'Italia – Travellers' Handbook' is available from the Italian State Tourist Office:
1 Princes Street, London W1R 8AY (tel. 071-408 1254) or 47 Merrion Square, Dublin 2 (tel. 766-397, 766-025).

This lists addresses of regional, provincial and local tourist information offices.
You will need to look up postal codes for the towns in guides such as the 'Michelin Red Guide' or the 'Touring Club Italiano Campsite Guide'.

For the purposes of Book 3, which is set in Arezzo, the addresses of agencies providing tourist information are:
Automobile Club d'Italia, Viale Signorelli 24/a, 52100 Arezzo;
Ente Provinciale per il Turismo, Piazza Risorgimento, 116, 52100 Arezzo.

Another useful address is:
CIT, 50-51 Conduit Street, London W1.

B   Mature students could take more of the responsibility than suggested in **A** above. They could find for themselves an appropriate guide book (e.g. in the school, college or local library), choose a place for themselves and write a letter. The replies could be used for some 'jigsaw' reading: students read what they receive and report on it, answering any questions from the other students. They could also make wall displays.

La mia città (page 20)

Main aim: **To present some of the main language of this unit**

A   The students could first work on this as homework. To help them to learn these key phrases, you could advise them to find and try to learn any sentences which, without change, describe where they live. Alternatively, you could suggest that they find sentences which, by changing only one word, can be used to describe where they live, and that they then make this change. A variation on this could be finding sentences where they need to change two words.

The main point to make is that the students should respond actively and thoughtfully to such lists.

B   Read out the Italian sentences in random order, reading each one two or three times while the students race to find it on the list and to tell you the English equivalent.
When this seems too easy, change slightly some of the sentences, e.g.

– È la più importante città commerciale della regione.
– È la cittadina più noiosa della zona.

The students race to find the sentence you have changed and give the English for the sentence you said.

C   Encourage the students to adapt the sentences in the list to describe their own town, region or a nearby town or region. Write on the board additional words which are needed for this and use these to play 'Kim's game' (Teacher's Book page 6).

D   Each student writes a brief description of where they live, using the model and the other sentences in the list. In pairs, they help each other to make these descriptions correct and interesting.

E   When you hand back the corrected descriptions, ask the students to read their own descriptions carefully to themselves several times and to choose eight to ten key words in it. They then write these key words on a piece of paper, writing them in the same positions as in the complete descriptions. You could demonstrate this on the board or OHP, e.g.

– Abito a York. York si trova nel nord est dell'Inghilterra. È a due ore da Londra in treno. È il capoluogo della contea di North Yorkshire. È una città turistica.

	York		nord est	
due ore	Londra		capoluogo	contea
		città turistica		

The students now practise describing where they live using only their key words, doing this first on their own (referring back to their full texts when necessary) and then in pairs. If possible, get some to record their descriptions, using only their key words. Others could do this for the whole class, using 'abitiamo'.

This technique can be used to help learn other key texts. In any conversations, including oral examinations, it is a great help to have some 'islands of security' - things which the students can talk about with confidence.

La città di Arezzo (pages 20-21)

Main aims: **To introduce the names of more places in town**
            To present the town of Arezzo

A   Work on the map along the lines suggested in the Students' Book. After doing this as a class, the students could do it in pairs.

B   Other activities to help the students to familiarise themselves with Arezzo include the following:

● Students could look at the street names and decide what the names tell them about each street, if anything.

- You could revise way-finding with the map. You could ask the students to start from the cathedral, for example, and direct them to various places: they follow your directions and say where they lead to. You could then ask them for directions to various places from the swimming pool. They could continue this in pairs.
- Give the students two minutes to try to learn the map and then base a 'Kim's game' on it. You could ask, for example:

- La piscina è a nord della città?
- La cattedrale è vicina alla biblioteca?
- C'è un parco ad Arezzo?
- Il cinema Corso si trova in che via?
- Quale ufficio si trova vicino al teatro?

Give the students two more minutes to study the map again. Then see how many of your questions they can answer in two minutes. Finally, give them a chance to beat this score after studying the map for one more minute.

C Ask the students to suggest facilities, places of interest, shops, etc. in your town which would interest Italian visitors. Write these on the board as they are suggested by the students or yourself, writing them in random order.
The students copy the words from the board, categorising them in three lists, according to purpose. e.g. 'uffici e luoghi pubblici', 'negozi', 'tempo libero'.

D Arezzo is an ideal town for a family holiday. Tell the students this and suggest that they make a list of places, amenities, shops, etc. which would help them and their families to enjoy a holiday there. Encourage them to ask you for any words they need.

Discuss their lists with them and encourage them to continue this in pairs, e.g.

- Dove ti piacerebbe andare?
- Tuo padre, dove gli piacerebbe andare?
- E tua sorella?
- Chi nella tua famiglia vorrebbe andare alla biblioteca?

E Write these questions on the board:
- In che via ti piacerebbe vivere? Perché?

As the students study the map and think about their answers, you could write this model answer on the board:

- Mi piacerebbe vivere in via della Minerva perché la via non è troppo grande, ed è vicina al mercato e al cinema. E poi il parco non è troppo lontano. Mi piace giocare a calcio.

Each student adapts this to write his/her own answers. They read these to each other and respond appropriately. Go round as they do this, listening, helping and joining in.

The students then form new pairs. Each student tries to guess which street the other has chosen. Write some helpful questions on the board, e.g.

- La tua via è nella parte sud della città?
- Abiti vicino ad una chiesa?
- C'è qualche posto importante nella tua via? La biblioteca, per esempio?

Informazioni turistiche (pages 22-23)

Main aims: To develop reading skills

To present more information about Arezzo

A Begin with some practice of scan reading skills. Ask the students to race to find, e.g.

- What is said to be one of the most important places in town?
- Which is the most beautiful romanesque church in Tuscany?
- What is the emblem of Arezzo?
- When was the amphitheatre built?
- What is the name of the biggest square in Arezzo?
- What else is said about this square?
- Why might you go to Arezzo on the first Sunday in September?

B Now practise the more demanding skills involved in finding links within a text, e.g.

- Which buildings were constructed before A.D. 1300?
- Which buildings are not given a date?
- The introduction says that Arezzo has many 'monumenti': what are these?
- How many churches are described? Which seems to be the oldest?
- Which is the oldest building mentioned?

You could draw the students' attention to the ways in which Italians refer to different centuries, e.g.

'Nel cinquecento' = In the 1500s = In the 16th century.
'Nel secolo XIII' = In the 13th century = In the 1200s.
'Nel ventesimo secolo' = In the 20th century = In the 1900s.
'Nel novecento' = In the 1900s = In the 20th century.

C Use this text to practise important comprehension strategies. Ask the students to find, and to work out the meanings of, the following words in the text:

una collina	greco
un campanile	un capolavoro
un vaso	si svolge

As they work on this, move around talking to and helping individuals. At the end, check that everyone understands all the words on the list. Even more importantly, help them to see how they can work out the meanings of such words by strategies such as using visuals, using context and using similarities to English.

D The students could now prepare a visit and a commentary in English for a group of young people visiting Arezzo. They could try these on you and on each other.

E Working in groups of four to six, the students produce a brief presentation in Italian of an important place in their own town or region. Each group should work on a different place. They should use any visual material which is available (e.g. from a local tourist office). The finished products could form an interesting wall display which parents and the local tourist officer could be invited to view on an open day or parents' evening. You could send information on your town to your link school in Italy.

F This would be a good time to start work on *Scoprite qualcosa di più* (page 150).

G You could base a quiz on your town and region, possibly at the open day or parents' evening, using the format of a popular TV quiz such as Blockbusters.
Questions could include, e.g.

- Qual è la strada più lunga a Leighton Buzzard?
- Qual è il supermercato più grande/brutto/bello/caro di Leighton Buzzard?

E tu, dove abiti? (page 24)

Main aims: To practise talking about your own town

To increase the students' awareness of topics of conversation which serve to oil the social wheels

To practise asking other people about the place where they live

A Discuss with the students topics of conversation frequently used to get to know someone, e.g. when you meet for the first time.
Discuss the purpose and nature of such conversation.

B The students listen to the recording and then practise this dialogue in pairs.

E tu, dove abiti?

A: Dove abiti?
B: Abito a Cortona.
A: A Cortona? Dov'è esattamente?
B: È una cittadina nell'Italia centrale, a diciassette chilometri da Arezzo, a sud di Arezzo.
A: E com'è Cortona?
B: Beh ... è una piccola cittadina in collina. È un centro storico e turistico, ma è tranquillo.
A: E che cosa c'è da fare, da vedere?
B: Non molto. Per i giovani dev'essere uno dei paesi più noiosi della zona. Ci sono due musei, il duomo e il Palazzo del Popolo, ma non c'è una piscina, non c'è un cinema e non ci sono discoteche.
A: Ti piace vivere a Cortona?
B: No, non mi piace proprio. E tu, dove abiti?

C The students adapt the dialogue to fit personal situations. They can refer to phrases listed under *La mia città* (page 20).

D The students listen to these unscripted recordings of Italians adapting this dialogue. After hearing each one twice, they pick out pieces of information which they heard and which interested them. They then listen again and comment on, e.g.

- the techniques and topics used to initiate conversation
- how the other person responded
- what the conversation shows about the personalities of the speakers
- what the conversation shows about the age and relationship of the speakers.

Conversazioni

Dialogo 1

- Senti Federico, dov'è che abiti tu?
- Abito a Ostia.
- Ostia. Dov'è esattamente?
- È una cittadina vicino a Roma, a venti minuti in macchina, sul mare.
- Ah ho capito. E com'è questo posto?
- È bello. Ehmmm ... ci sono molti giovani. Specialmente d'estate, ehmm ... si può uscire, andare in gelateria, passeggiare sulla spiaggia ...
- Praticamente a te piace vivere ad Ostia?
- Sì, molto.

Dialogo 2

- Lei, dove abita?
- A Fiesole.
- Ah Fiesole, in Toscana.
- Sì è un paese rinascimentale su una collina di Firenze.
- Uhmm. E da fare, da vedere, cosa c'è d'interessante?
- Beh ... da vedere c'è il bellissimo panorama, da fare è famosa l'estate fiesolana dove si organizzano concerti di musica classica, teatro e altre manifestazioni culturali.
- Dunque Le piace molto vivere a Fiesole?
- Ah sì molto e ne sono orgoglioso.

Dialogo 3

- Dove abiti tu?
- A Filacciano.
- A Filacciano? È dov'è esattamente?
- È un paesino nell'Italia centrale a quarantacinque chilometri a nord di Roma.
- E com'è questo Filacciano?
- Beh ... è una piccola cittadina in collina ... piuttosto tranquillo.
- Ma c'è niente da vedere o da fare?
- Da vedere c'è una bellissima torre del cinquecento e anche una chiesa del mille, una chiesa molto carina, affrescata. Da fare non molto, infatti i giovani preferiscono andare a Roma.
- E quindi ti piace vivere a Filacciano?
- Diciamo che tutto l'anno è piuttosto noioso ... è l'ideale per chi deve studiare o riposarsi.

Dialogo 4

- Mi scusi ma ... Lei dove abita?
- Ehmm ... abito a Camogli.
- Camogli si trova in Liguria?
- Bravo, è una cittadina nell'Italia settentrionale a circa cinquanta chilometri da Genova.
- Eh mi sa dire com'è Camogli?
- Il paesaggio è bellissimo. È un ... proprio un piccolo gioiello sul mare, circondato dalle montagne.
- Ma cosa si può fare, cosa c'è da vedere?
- Beh per i giovani non c'è molto. L'estate comunque è senz'altro il periodo migliore perché si può andare al mare. Il lungomare è bellissimo. Ci sono molti negozi di moda da vedere e la pasticceria dove si possono mangiare dolci buonissimi. Una volta all'anno c'è una grande festa .... la sagra del pesce.
- Ma quindi a Lei piace vivere a Camogli.
- Ah sì a me piace. Ci sto proprio bene. È un posto tranquillo. Sì, mi piace.

E The students practise asking and answering these questions, adapted to suit their own town. They then each interview five other students, using the same questions, and making brief notes of the answers. They compare the answers given by different people.

All' Ufficio Turistico (page 24)

Main aim: To practise obtaining information in a tourist office

A Make sure that everyone knows what to do.
Each student prepares a route for the first customers: they could do this in pairs. They then listen to the reply on tape and compare it with theirs.
When you have done this, and cleared up any problems, deal with the others in the same way.

📼 All'Ufficio Turistico

Numero 1

Hostess:	Buongiorno.
Man:	Buongiorno.
Hostess:	Dica ...
Man:	Dunque, ci piacerebbe vedere i monumenti più importanti ma ci è difficile camminare, e non possiamo fare troppa strada a piedi. Che cosa ci consiglia?
Hostess:	Allora, per primo Le do questa piantina. Noi siamo qui al numero nove, i monumenti più importanti sono qui, al numero uno, la cattedrale, al numero due la Pieve e Piazza Grande e poi, al numero tre, la chiesa di San Francesco.
Man:	Ho capito. Ma è lontano da qui?
Hostess:	Un po', sì. Io vi consiglio di prendere un taxi fino alla cattedrale. Cominciate la visita alla cattedrale. Poi potete andare a piedi alla Pieve di Santa Maria e in Piazza Grande. E poi di là, ci vogliono cinque minuti per arrivare alla Chiesa di San Francesco dove si vedono i bellissimi affreschi.
Man:	Va bene. Facciamo così, allora.
Hostess:	Benissimo.
Man:	Tante grazie.
Hostess:	Di niente. Buona visita!

Numero 2

Hostess:	Buongiorno.
Woman:	Buongiorno. Senta, avete una piantina di Arezzo con una lista dei monumenti, per favore?

Hostess:	Sì, ecco. Qui c'è la piantina e poi qui c'è una lista dei monumenti. Va bene così?
Woman:	Sì, grazie. Che cosa ci consiglia di fare? Abbiamo due ore a disposizione. Mia sorella deve completare questo questionario sui Romani per la scuola, e poi vorremmo comprare qualche souvenir, qualche regalo.
Hostess:	Ho capito. Un momento, allora ... Sì. Il questionnario è sui Romani?
Woman:	Sì.
Hostess:	Allora, secondo me dovete andare all'anfiteatro romano qui, e poi al museo archeologico ci sono moltissimi oggetti di origine romana. Il museo è qui al numero sei, proprio accanto all'anfiteatro.
Woman:	E per i regali?
Hostess:	Dunque ... ci sono due supermercati: la Standa, qui al numero diciassette, e l'UPIM qui. Poi i negozi più importanti sono tutti qui in Corso Italia, no?
Woman:	Corso Italia?
Hostess:	Sì. Qui troverete facilmente dei souvenir.
Woman:	Grazie delle informazioni.
Hostess:	Prego. E buona fortuna con il questionario.
Woman:	Grazie.

Numero 3

Hostess:	Buongiorno. Mi dica!
Woman:	Buongiorno. Avete una pianta di Arezzo, per favore, e un dépliant?
Hostess:	Sì. Tenga.
Woman:	Grazie. Senta, ci piacerebbe fare una piccola visita ma poi, verso mezzogiorno, vorremmo fare un picnic. Così i bambini possono almeno giocare un po'. C'è un posto dove possiamo fare un picnic?
Hostess:	Sì, sì. Allora, noi siamo qui al numero nove. Potete fare così, no? Prendete la via della Madonna del Prato e andate prima alla Chiesa di San Francesco. Poi andate qui alla Pieve di Santa Maria al numero due. Dietro la chiesa c'è Piazza Grande e poi da Piazza Grande potete andare su al parco, qui al numero tredici. Si chiama il Prato. Qui potete fare un picnic.
Woman:	Ho capito, grazie.
Hostess:	E poi al Prato c'è un bel panorama.
Woman:	Grazie.
Hostess:	Di niente. Arrivederci.
Woman:	Arrivederci.

B When they have heard all the answers, play all three once more. The students listen to decide what they think about the hostess, e.g.

- Does she know Arezzo well?
- Is she courteous and helpful?
- Is she good at her job?

C This would be a good time to do some more work on *Scoprite qualcosa di più* (pages 150-151).

Arezzo estate (page 25)

Main aim: To develop reading and writing skills on the topic of towns

A Help the students to learn how best to approach a text like this. They could find as quickly as possible the main topics dealt with, using titles and visuals. Another way could be to find the key words in each paragraph or advertisement and decide, as quickly as possible, what each paragraph and advertisement is about.

B Give some practice in quick scan reading by asking, e.g.

- Where does this suggest you go for a birthday treat?
- Where could you go to improve your Italian?
- What sort of a place is Crocodile?
- How much would it cost to go to the disco on Saturday? And on Wednesday?
- What could you see in Piazza Grande on 9th September?
- At what time does it start?
- Name two things which this article suggests you might buy at the shops.
- When can you go swimming in Arezzo?

C Ask the students to read the advertisements again and to list all the abbreviations they can find. They should try to give the full version of each abbreviation and to write it next to the abbreviation.

D The students now list down the left-hand side of a page in their exercise books 15-20 key words from *Informazioni turistiche* (pages 22-23). On the right-hand side of the same page, they now write the 15-20 key words from this item. They use these as a basis for comparing the two texts orally. Some students may go on to write a comparison of the two introductions to Arezzo, mentioning differences and what they have in common.

E Working in pairs or groups, the students should now produce a similar guide for young Italian visitors to their own town and region, with each group working on a different aspect. These could be corrected and collated to form an interesting and attractive guide which could be presented to the local tourist office. Similar guides produced by students in foreign languages have been printed by tourist offices and given out to tourists.

Ti piace abitare a Subbiano? (page 26)

Main aim: To develop listening skills, the ability to ask questions about where people live and the ability to understand the answers

A Work first on each set of questions.
Ensure that everyone understands them and can say them. In random order, give possible answers to the questions, adapting those in the Students' Book. The students listen and read out the question most likely to produce that answer.

B The students now compare the four sets of questions and discuss why, in Italian, questions asking for the same information use different words. To reinforce the point about which questions you can put to various people, present a range of photos cut from magazines. Choose photos of men and women, boys and girls. With each person, the students say which of the questions on this page they could ask. Try to maintain a brisk pace.

C Play each recorded interview. The students listen as they follow the text in their book. After each one, you could ask both about the content of the questions and answers and also about, e.g.
– the age of the interviewer and interviewee
– the relationship between them
– the attitudes expressed.

📼 Ti piace abitare a Subbiano?

Dialogo A
– Dove abiti esattamente?
– Abito a Subbiano, un paese vicino ad Arezzo, a tredici chilometri a nord di Arezzo.
– Da quanto tempo ci abiti?
– Da quindici anni; da quando sono nato.
– Ti piace abitare a Subbiano?
– Non molto. Non c'è molto da fare in un piccolo paese come Subbiano.

Dialogo B
– Dove abita?
– Abito a Siena.

– Abita in centro?
– Beh ... abito non lontano dal centro.
– È grande Siena?
– Sì, abbastanza. Ci sono circa sessantamila abitanti.
– E che cosa c'è da fare?
– Si può visitare il Duomo, il Palazzo Pubblico, la Torre del Mangia. Poi c'è Piazza del Campo; è una delle piazze più belle d'Italia. Ci sono molti bar, molti caffè e nei mesi di luglio e agosto si può anche vedere la festa del Palio.

Dialogo C
– Dove abiti?
– Anch'io abito a Siena.
– E che cosa c'è da fare a Siena?
– Tante cose; Siena è una delle più vive città della Toscana. Si può andare al cinema, si possono praticare molti sport, si può andare in piscina, andare a ballare. Ci sono poi molti ristoranti e molte pizzerie nelle quali si possono mangiare pizze buonissime.

Dialogo D
– Lei abita ad Arezzo?
– Sì, abito qui ad Arezzo.
– E da quanto tempo abita qui?
– Da più di trent'anni.
– E Le piace abitare ad Arezzo?
– Euh ... sì, moltissimo.
– Perché?
– Beh ... è una bella città. È la più bella città della Toscana. Ci sono molte cose da vedere. Ci sono molti negozi. Si può andare al cinema e poi a settembre si può guardare la festa che si chiama La Giostra del Saracino.

D Each student now prepares sets of questions to interview such people as other students, you, the assistant, students on teaching practice, a waiter in a local Italian restaurant, etc. about where they live. When you have checked their questions, they use them to conduct interviews: they should write notes in Italian about the answers and use these to write a brief account of the answers. It would help if you wrote a model on the board or OHP and left it there for them to consult, e.g.

Threlkeld - paese - 6 km - Keswick
8 anni
tranquillo
– Abita a Threlkeld, un piccolo paese a sei chilometri all'est di Keswick. Ci abita da otto anni. Gli piace moltissimo perché è un posto tranquillo.

E Give each student a copy of Copymaster 14. Make sure that everyone understands everything on it and what to do. Their task is to interview people in the class so as to put someone's name against each question. To ensure that the students use the correct question forms, do some preparatory question and answer work with the class.

Informatissimi! (Copymaster 15)

Main aim: To practise using superlatives

A Finish work on *Scoprite qualcosa di più* (page 151).

B Give each student a copy of Copymaster 15. The students are not expected to know the answers to all these questions before they work on the quiz. Much of the fun of such quizzes is, in fact, finding out new facts and figures, and, in this case, doing it in Italian!
Work on each question in turn. Read the question to the class and invite students to guess the answer. Do not confirm or correct their guesses, but rather use them to stimulate others to join in, e.g.

Teacher: Qual è la montagna più alta d'Italia?
Student: È il Monte Bianco?
Teacher: Allora, secondo Tom il Monte Bianco è la montagna più alta d'Italia. Sei d'accordo, Julie?

Before the students lose interest, confirm the right answer and go on to the next question.
To reinforce the language and the information, you could occasionally go back to some of the questions previously dealt with and put them to a few volunteers. You could also use some of the 'incorrect' answers to put similar questions, e.g.

– Il Monte Bianco è la montagna più alta di quale paese?
– Qual è l'isola più piccola di queste qui?

Answers:

  1 A
  2 C
  3 B
  4 D
  5 A
  6 C
  7 A
  8 C
  9 A
10 C

C The students make up similar quizzes of their own. They could be similar to this one, but based on their own country, or another country. More ambitious students could choose another topic, based on their own hobbies or using the 'Guinness Book of Records' (especially if the Italian version of this is available in a library, 'Il Guinness dei Primati').

D Make copies of Copymasters 16A and 16B so that one partner in each pair has A and the other has B. Students work in pairs along the lines suggested on the copymasters.

When they have finished, put the questions to various students for them to answer orally.

Grazie per la tua lettera (page 27)

Main aim: To practise reading and writing a letter about your town and region

A The students skim the letter to find, as quickly as possible, the answer to the questions in the introductory sentence to this item. Ask students who suggest answers to read aloud the words which contain the answer.

B Ask the students to read the letter to find the key sentences, the ones which contain the most important information. Encourage them to compare, and argue about, the sentences they have chosen, and to reach agreement.

C The students try to draw some conclusions from the letter, e.g.
- Does Mariella like her home town?
- Would they like to stay there? Why?
- In what ways is Castiglion Fiorentino different from your town?
- Would they probably get on well with Mariella? Why (not)?

D Ask the students to adapt orally the parts of the letter which describe Castiglion in order to describe their own town and region. Write the key words which they need on the board or OHP. Each student then answers the letter: this could be done as homework.

Arriva il gruppo italiano (page 27)

Main aim: To produce information about aspects of your own town and region to help Italian visitors to the area.

A Suggested activities:
- Using phrases and key words borrowed from leaflets and brochures received from Italy, students produce a brochure about their own town(s) mentioning: number of inhabitants, location, history, main sights locally and dates of construction if known, e.g. La Chiesa di All Saints, costruita nel 1452, aperta tutti i giorni dalle 9.00 alle 18.00.
- Town plan with main places of interest, leisure, shopping, landmarks, etc. labelled in Italian.
- Lists of discos, monuments, hotels, campsites, restaurants, pubs, cinemas, sports facilities, chemists. Name and address and phone number and opening hours in Italian.
- List of useful phone numbers: school, station, travel agent, etc. Information on opening and closing times.
- Markets: days and times.
- Travel information: buses, trains, coaches, taxis. Routes and timetables. Information on buying tickets.
- Record interviews with different people in class, talking about the town/village in which they live.
- Plan an itinerary/programme for a one-day visit by a group of Italians.
- Make a video of your own town including some commentary in Italian, prepared in advance.
- Prepare a programme for a one-week visit by an exchange school.

- Make a scrap book on your town: postcards, articles from local newspaper with headings translated into Italian.
- Lists of shops/supermarkets/places to buy presents, souvenirs, clothes, postcards, stamps, phone cards, etc.
- Suggestions for presents and souvenirs.
- Photos of places in town with captions in Italian.
- Poster using superlatives, with captions in Italian: 'la chiesa più antica di Bedford,' 'la via più importante,' 'il parco più bello' etc.

The materials produced could be sent to your class-link school as part of a materials exchange.

B Looking at page 27, the students write a list of the things advertised, using the key words in the advertisements. They then write these key words again, putting them into groups: each student can decide the criteria for his/her groups. They could write them all once more in the order of interest for them.

C Give each student a copy of Copymaster 17. Check that everyone understands all the questions. Give everyone time to prepare their answers and then get them to practise asking and answering the questions in pairs: the student asking the questions writes his/her partner's answers in Italian.

The students could now produce a set of questions to send to their partners in Italy, trying to improve on this set of questions.

They could all record their answers to these questions and send the cassette to Italy with their sets of questions.

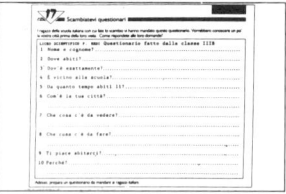

Adesso, tocca a te! (page 28)

Main aim: To demonstrate that the language of this unit has been mastered

Exercise 1
Language area: Talking about where you live
Skill area: Speaking

Each student in turn asks and answers these questions. If possible, record these. Encourage them to help each other as much as possible.

Exercise 2

Language area: Town and region
Skill area: Reading

Give the students a time limit for this: about five minutes should be enough for most students, but allow more or less in the light of your knowledge of your students.

Exercise 3

Language area: Town and region
Skill area: Reading

This practises the more advanced reading skills involved in drawing conclusions from a text. Give the students about five minutes for this, writing their answers in English.

Exercise 4

Language area: Information about a town
Skill area: Letter writing

Each student chooses one of these towns and writes for further information.

Exercise 5

Language area: Interests, pets, town and region
Skill area: Listening

Make sure that everyone realises what they need to listen for. Play the recording twice, allowing students to take notes when they wish to. They then write answers in English to the questions. You could allow anyone who wants to, to do this in Italian.

🔊 Adesso, tocca a te!

– Ciao! Sono Giovanni, il tuo partner per lo scambio. Grazie per la tua lettera e per le foto. Mi piace molto quella con te e il tuo cane. Invece di scrivere una lettera ho deciso di spedirti una cassetta.

Per cominciare, rispondo alle tue domande. Di hobby, ne ho molti. Faccio collezione di dischi e di materiale sulle Olimpiadi. Forse il mio più grande hobby è la chitarra. Suono la chitarra elettrica, e con due altri amici abbiamo formato un complesso, cioè un gruppo. Suono la chitarra ogni sera dopo la scuola. E tu, sai suonare uno strumento musicale? Che tipo di musica ti piace di più? Mi potresti mandare del materiale sulle Olimpiadi – materiale in inglese, ovviamente.

Come sai, il mio paese si chiama Lucignano. Dicono che è uno dei centri più interessanti della Toscana per via delle strade, a forma di cerchi concentrici, ma in realtà dev'essere uno dei paesi più tranquilli e più noiosi della zona. Non c'è niente per i giovani, e per questo, il sabato pomeriggio e durante le vacanze, ci piace andare in una delle città più grandi - Siena, Firenze o Arezzo. Lì, almeno si può andare al cinema, andare in piscina e trovare gli amici.

E tu, che cosa fai il sabato pomeriggio? Cosa c'è da fare dove abiti tu durante le vacanze? Scrivimi presto,
Ti saluto, ciao,
Giovanni.

Exercise 6

Language area: Interests, town and region
Skill area: Speaking

Allow the students to write the key words they wish to use to do this recording, but do not allow any fuller notes.

Ora sai (page 29)

Main aim: **To act as a summary and reference point for the main language of this unit**

Help the students to master this language and to increase their repertoire of techniques for practising and revising important language, using the following activities.

The students study this page for a few minutes and try to learn the key words. They then close their books and race to write ten words on a theme chosen by one of them, e.g. words to describe a town, words for places in a town, words for interesting activities.

In class, and then in pairs, play 'Question and answer tennis'. One team or player begins with a question about where you live, the other volleys back with the answer, the server replies with another question and so on. Points are scored when a team or player cannot think of a question or answer in ten seconds, when a question is on another topic or when a question or answer is incomprehensible!

The students try to learn the model letter. Their partners have a strip of paper which is 2cm. wide. They lay this across their partner's letter from top to bottom, choosing which part to cover up: the partner tries to write the letter in full.

Revision

1 Meals and buying food for a picnic (Book 2, Unit 3)
   Di + definite article (Book 2, Unit 3)

A Describe your favourite picnic meal and write the name of each dish on the board. Then ask the class to help you to produce a shopping list to include everything you need to produce this meal. Write the list on the board.

Invite a few students to describe their favourite picnic meals. Write any key words on the board and leave them there. The students now each write a menu for their favourite picnic meals and, under it, a shopping list containing everything they need. Encourage them to ask each other, and you, for help when they need it.

B   Give each student a copy of Copymaster 18. When everyone has written a description of what they have for breakfast, talk about the differences between what they have and the breakfast described in this article.

To create another conversational 'island of security' (see page 37) you could encourage the students to write down the key words in their corrected descriptions and, using only these, practise talking about what they have for breakfast. They finally do this without the key words.

2   Daily routine (Book 2, Unit 9)
Reflexive verbs: present tense (Book 2, Unit 9)

A   Organise a few minutes of verb circle practice, e.g.

– Mi alzo alle sette di mattina.
– Non mi lavo con acqua fredda.

B   Give each student a copy of Copymaster 19. Make sure first that everyone understands the letter. Then ask several students each to say one thing which they will say in their reply. Then ask several students each to say two things and then three things which they will write. Write the key phrases on the board and leave them there.

Each student now writes a reply to the letter.

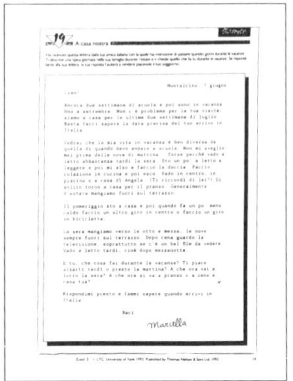

3   Talking about interests and personality (Book 3, Unit 2)

Make copies of Copymaster 20. Cut it into ten cards and put each set of ten cards into an envelope, preparing one envelope for each group.

The task is to decide who will sit where at Francesca's birthday party. The students should discuss criteria for a seating plan, e.g.

– should two Italians sit together?
– should two boys/girls sit together?
– should two people with similar interests/personalities sit together?

Present key expressions for this discussion on the board or OHP, e.g.

– Mettiamo X accanto a Y perché:

  X è _____ e Y è _____ .
  X ama _____ e Y ama _____ .
  X fa collezione di _____ e Y fa collezione di _____ .
  X suona _____ e Y suona _____ .

– Perché tutti i due:

  sono _____ .
  amano _____ .
  fanno _____ .
  suonano _____ .

Use these to get the discussion started between yourself and the class. The students then continue with, and complete, the task in groups.

4 Comparative adjectives (Book 2, Unit 2)

A Present the following table on the OHP:

Dove ti piacerebbe andare?

	moderna	vecchia	brutta	bella	interessante	viva			
Arezzo									
Roma									
Rimini									
Firenze									
New York									
Londra									
Parigi									

The students work on their own to tick the grid appropriately, but asking for help and advice when necessary. You could do a few on the OHP as a model, e.g.

– Com'è Roma? È bella?
– Roma è più bella di Parigi?
– Arezzo è più viva di Rimini?

Discuss each feature and tick the grid when it is agreed that this word or phrase accurately describes Arezzo. Put in the end columns any other words which the class can suggest to describe Arezzo.

There is space left for several more towns. The students put in here any towns they like and complete the grid for these towns. Then discuss with the students each feature and how the various towns compare, e.g.

– Secondo te (voi), di queste città, qual è la più bella?
– Arezzo.
– Davvero? Secondo me Roma è più bella di Arezzo. E tu, Alison, che ne pensi?

B Present this drawing on the board:

le mele   le pesche

With help from the students, write this caption to the drawing:

– Le mele pesano più delle pesche.

The students now produce their own drawings to illustrate the following.

1 Il formaggio pesa più del burro.
2 Il pesce pesa meno del salame.
3 Lo yogurt pesa meno degli spaghetti.
4 L'uva pesa più di del pane.
5 Le uova pesano più della torta.
6 I biscotti pesano meno del latte.
7 Due gelati pesano più di due pezzi di pizza.
8 Due cornetti pesano meno di due paste.

4ª Unità
IN ALBERGO

Main aims

~ To be able to get by in an Italian hotel
~ To be able to understand hotel guides and brochures

Materials

~ Tape
Quale albergo? (Teacher's Book page 50)
Una camera singola o doppia? (Teacher's Book page 51)
Che tipo di camera vogliono? (Teacher's Book page 51)
Per quante notti? (Teacher's Book page 52)
Sei arrivato! (Teacher's Book page 53)
La mia chiave, per favore (Teacher's Book page 54)
A che ora si mangia? (Teacher's Book page 56)
Non funziona! (Teacher's Book page 56)

~ Copymasters 21–26

Grammar in *Scoprite qualcosa di più*

~ Direct object pronouns after 'ecco'

Revision

~ Introductions and greetings (Book 1, Unit 1)
~ Buying ice creams, snacks and pizza (Book 2, Unit 4)
~ Talking about free-time activities (Book 2, Unit 10)
~ Present tense: 'io' and 'tu' forms (Book 2, Unit 10)
~ Talking about a town (Book 3, Unit 3)
~ Superlative adjectives (Book 3, Unit 3)

Vocabulary

A: Productive

aria condizionata
un asciugamano
la carta igienica
la chiave
con
da
la doccia
doppia
funzionare
il gabinetto
un letto
libero
la luce

mancare
matrimoniale
la notte
il passaporto
prenotare
il riscaldamento (centrale)
il sapone
una settimana
servire
i servizi
singolo
(con) vista sul mare

B: Receptive

un ascensore
l'autorimessa

caldo
cani ammessi

la Direzione
dopo
durare
fare delle passeggiate
la fine
freddo
il luna park
mi dispiace
niente
un opuscolo
il pallone
un parcheggio

una pensione
per quante notti?
un posteggio
prima di
privato
la sala giochi
senza
stasera

In albergo (page 30)

Main aim: To present the main objectives of this unit

A Before the students read this introduction, give them two minutes to skim over the pages for this unit in the book: their task is to work out as much as they can about the objectives of the unit. At the end of two minutes, ask the students to say what they think they will learn to do in this unit: involve as many students as possible.

B The students read the introduction and discuss it with you and each other. To help the discussion, you could ask, e.g.

– Siete già andati all'estero?
– Avete dormito in albergo?
– Avete avuto dei problemi?

C Write on the board some of the key words in this introduction, writing them in pairs, e.g.

un albergo, una pensione;   un bar, un ristorante.

Encourage the students to compare the words in each pair, e.g.

– Un albergo è più grande di una pensione.

D Working in pairs, or groups of four, the students could write a list, in English, of what they think they need to learn to cope with going to a hotel. Before the end of the work on this unit, they should check that they have learnt everything on their lists.

Segni convenzionali (page 30)

Main aim: To present and practise some of the most useful words associated with a hotel

A Read the introduction to this item and make sure that everyone understands it. Then read aloud the words with each symbol, reading them several times as the students look at them and listen. Ask students to explain what the words mean. When it is clear that everyone understands, read the word(s) again and encourage the students to repeat after you. From time to time, read a few which the students have already repeated, in random order. Then see how many the class can repeat, in random order, in 30 seconds. They then try to beat this score!

B The students read silently to themselves what the hotel manager says. You then read aloud the first sentence and ask someone to draw on the board the appropriate symbol. Repeat this with one or two more sentences. The students then write all the appropriate symbols in their books. When they have finished, encourage them to look at what their partners have drawn and to suggest any necessary corrections. When a student is having problems, his/her partner should try to help.

C The students look again at the symbols in the Students' Book. You read aloud any three captions; you then read them again, but changing one and reading a caption you did not say the first time. The students listen and try to say what you changed, e.g.

- La prima volta ha detto 'piscina' e la seconda volta ha detto 'tennis'.

Write this sentence on the board and leave it there as a model.
After a while, instead of saying three captions, you could say four and then five, adding one the second time - the students say which one you added.

D Ask the students to write down the six captions from this list which they find the most difficult to remember. They then try to learn them. You could suggest a technique for doing this, but allow them to use any technique which works for them. They could, for example, try to memorise the words, in pairs or threes. When they think they know them, they cover them up with a piece of paper and try to write the words on the paper. They then check what is on the paper with the original. If there are any mistakes, they repeat the process until they can do it correctly. They then repeat this with all six captions. When they have learnt their own six captions, they try to teach them to someone else so that this person will never forget them!

E The students look once more at the symbols. Ask if each one is clear. Invite the students to draw better symbols for those which are not clear. Make a wall display with these and use them, from time to time, for some oral work.

Le caratteristiche più importanti (page 30)

Main aim: **To practise some of the most useful words associated with a hotel**

A Referring to the list, the students write the most important features under the six categories suggested. They should first write only the key words for each one. Then, referring to their key words, they make up a sentence like the example. Finally, they write six full sentences.

B The students write down the six most important features of their ideal hotel, in order of importance. In pairs, they compare their lists and try to agree on a joint list. To prepare them for this, you could do this with one or two students and write a model on the board, e.g.

- Per me, un ascensore è molto importante.
- Sì, ma una piscina è più importante di un ascensore.
- Va bene. Sono d'accordo. Secondo te, un ristorante è importante?
- No, l'aria condizionata è più importante di un ristorante.

C Give each student a copy of Copymasters 21 A and B. Work first on the table to ensure that everyone understands it, e.g.

- Che cosa ha l'Albergo Adlon (ecc.)?
- Quale albergo è il più (il meno) caro?
- Perché?
- Quali alberghi hanno un campo da tennis (sono aperti tutto l'anno, ecc.)?
- Quali alberghi non hanno una piscina (non sono vicini al frontemare, ecc.)?
- Che cosa hanno in comune tutti gli alberghi? (per esempio una spiaggia, un ascensore)

The students read silently to themselves what all the people are thinking and make a note of the best hotel for each of them. They then ask you which is the best hotel for each person, e.g.

Qual è il miglior albergo per la nonna?

You reply, e.g.

- È l'albergo Canada. Eccolo.

You may get one or two wrong, in which case the students should correct you!

Answers:

il nonno:	Beny	il fratello:	Bettina
Jason:	Bertha	la zia:	Canada
la mamma:	Adlon	lo zio:	Aquileia
la sorella:	Cambridge	il papà:	Cambridge

Finally, each student writes a sentence for each person, along the lines of the model.

Quale albergo? (page 31)

Main aim: **To develop reading skills**

A Give each student a copy of Copymaster 22. Ask them to read the information about the Hotel San Marco and to check that the ticks and crosses on the grid are all correct. Then ask them to write in the ticks and crosses for the Hotel Anthony. Check these and clear up any problems. Then deal with each of the other hotels in the same way, stopping after each one to work on any difficulties. This way, the students should steadily improve as they proceed.

B Use this information to give some practice in scan reading. Ask for some details and encourage the students to race to find each one, e.g.

– How many people can get into the conference room at the San Marco? (400)
– What is the phone number of the Hotel Condor? (0421 91691)
– How many bedrooms are there in the Hotel Venezuela? (50)
– Which hotel has a panoramic restaurant? (Hotel Caravelle)
– How far from the beach is the Hotel Tahiti? (It is just next to the beach.)

C Play the unscripted recording of some people who have stayed at the Hotel Anthony and the Hotel San Marco. The students listen to see if what they say differs at all from what is claimed by the publicity. What conclusions do they draw about the publicity?

Quale albergo?

– Allora andiamo al Lido di Jesolo, che ne dici?
– Perché no, mi sembra una buona idea, ma non voglio andare all'Anthony questa volta. Tu lo conosci?
– Sì ci sono andata l'anno scorso, con mio marito, era molto stanco e voleva riposarsi ma non si poteva stare tranquilli lì. C'è stato rumore durante tutta la notte.
– Uhmm... allora andiamo al San Marco, lì si sta tranquilli. Ma non c'è la piscina. All'Anthony almeno c'è una piscina.
– Sì ma è così piccola che non vale la pena usarla. E poi possiamo sempre andare al mare per nuotare no?
– Uhm ... hai ragione. Sì allora andiamo al San Marco. Come ci andiamo? Ci andiamo in macchina?
– Sì d'accordo, poi c'è un grande parcheggio ci si trova sempre un posto.
– Eh sì meglio così. Ho sentito che all'Anthony c'è un gran parcheggio, coperto, ma è sempre pieno zeppo di macchine, non si trova mai un posto.

La mia camera ideale (page 32)

Main aim: **To present and practise some of the main words needed for talking about hotel rooms**

A Ask the students to study the drawings and the captions, and to try to work out what each caption means. Then read each caption aloud, two or three times, and ask students to say in English what it means. If anyone has any difficulty, encourage such strategies as using the visual clues or using similarities with English (e.g. 'tranquilla' - tranquil).

Also, when a student has worked out the meaning of a caption, ask him/her to explain the strategies which he/she used.

B Read aloud the captions in random order, reading each one several times to give the students every chance to hear it properly pronounced. The students listen and point to the appropriate symbol. Walk around as you do this and help any students who are having problems. The students could continue this in pairs.

C Use the symbols to play 'Loto'. Each student writes down any four of the captions. You read them out in random order and students tick their captions as they hear them. The first to tick all four reads his/her captions aloud so that you can check the claim. After one or two games with the whole class, the students can continue to play in groups of four, taking turns to be the caller.

D The students read the instructions and the example and then, working in pairs, describe their ideal hotel room.

E Play a game of 'Categorie' with the class (see Teacher's Book page 6). Write on the board: 'in una camera', 'in una pizzeria', 'in un ufficio turistico'.

You call out a series of words and the students choose one of the three places to indicate where they are most likely to find what you have mentioned. If they are correct, you go on to the next word. If not, you correct them before going on. See how many words the students can categorise in one minute. Then give them one or two opportunities to improve on their score. You could call out, e.g.

– doccia, cameriere, pianta, bar, focaccia, cartolina, birra, gabinetto, cono, servizi, tavolo, letto, dépliant, telefono, riscaldamento, gelato, balcone, televisione, insalata, aria condizionata, lista di monumenti.

F The students now test your memory! They ask about things which are illustrated on this page and also things which are not, e.g.
– C'è una camera singola?
– C'è una camera a quattro letti?

You reply without looking at the book. When you say that the thing is illustrated, you then immediately point to it and say, e.g.
– Eccola.

You then write on the board:
– Eccolo.
– Eccola.

You then ask, e.g.
– C'è una doccia?
– C'è un balcone?
– C'è l'aria condizionata?

The students choose one of the replies on the board and say it as they point to the appropriate picture. If anyone asks about which to use, explain.

Una camera singola o doppia? (page 32)

Main aim: To practise asking for different kinds of rooms in a hotel

A Read the introduction to the class and ensure that everyone understands. Then play the recording and ask the students to say what sort of room is asked for. Play it again, and ask the students to say in English what was said. Play it once more, stopping at the end of each sentence for the students to repeat. The students could then play-read this dialogue in pairs.

Una camera singola o doppia?

Receptionist: Buongiorno.
Customer: Buongiorno. Avete una camera?
Receptionist: Una camera singola o una camera doppia?
Customer: Una camera doppia, a due letti.

B Make sure that everyone understands what to do in the pairs exercise. You could demonstrate with an assistant or a student. They then make up dialogues of their own to match the drawings. Move around as they do this, listening and helping.

C Play the following recordings of *Che tipo di camera vogliono?* The students listen first to find out what sort of room each person asks for. Stop after each one to check the students' answers and to clear up any problems. Then play that dialogue again before going on to the next one.

Che tipo di camera vogliono?

Esempio

Customer: Buongiorno.
Receptionist: Buongiorno.
Customer: Avete una camera?
Receptionist: Sì. Una camera singola?
Customer: No, una camera doppia, con due letti.
Receptionist: Va bene, signore. Preferisce con bagno o con doccia?
Customer: Con doccia, per favore. Avete camere con gabinetto privato?
Receptionist: Certo. Tutte le camere hanno gabinetto privato.
Customer: C'è il telefono in camera?
Receptionist: Sì, signore, ma per telefonare fuori città deve chiedere alla Direzione.
Customer: Ho capito. Quanto costa?
Receptionist: Allora, una camera a due letti, con doccia ... centoventimila lire.
Customer: Centoventimila lire? Non avete una camera meno cara?
Receptionist: Abbiamo una camera senza doccia ...
Customer: Va bene, va bene, la prendo.

Dialogo 1

Customer: Buonasera.
Receptionist: Buonasera.
Customer: Ha una camera?
Receptionist: Per stasera?
Customer: Sì.
Receptionist: Una camera singola?

Customer:	Sì, singola, con bagno.
Receptionist:	Mi dispiace, le camere con bagno sono tutte prenotate.
Customer:	Peccato. Vorrei se possibile una camera tranquilla.
Receptionist:	Una camera tranquilla ... Abbiamo la numero 32. Dà sul giardino.
Customer:	Perfetto, grazie.

Dialogo 2

Receptionist:	Pronto? Albergo Riviera.
Customer:	Voglio una camera per due per il mese di agosto.
Receptionist:	Abbiamo camere a due letti, o se preferisce con letto matrimoniale.
Customer:	Con letto matrimoniale.
Receptionist:	Vuole una camera con servizi?
Customer:	Sì, con servizi. E con balcone e vista sul mare.
Receptionist:	Balcone e vista sul mare.
Customer:	C'è la televisione in camera?
Receptionist:	No, mi dispiace.
Customer:	Peccato.
Receptionist:	Abbiamo una bella sala televisione.
Customer:	Sì, sì, non importa ...

Dialogo 3

Receptionist:	Buonasera signorine.
Customer 1:	Buonasera.
Customer 2:	Buonasera.
Customer 1:	Ha una camera per stasera?
Receptionist:	Una camera a due letti?
Customer 1:	Sì, a due letti.
Receptionist:	Ci sono poche camere libere. Preferiscono con doccia o con bagno?
Customer 1:	Non so ... penso ...
Customer 2:	Con bagno, no?
Customer 1:	Sì, con bagno.
Receptionist:	Allora, la numero 53 è libera.
Customer 2:	C'è riscaldamento centrale nella camera?
Receptionist:	Sì signorina.
Customer 2:	E anche la radio?
Receptionist:	Eh no, mi dispiace, non c'è la radio.
Customer 1:	La prendiamo lo stesso.
Receptionist:	Va bene.

D After working through all the recordings along the lines suggested above, play them all again, stopping after each one to discuss the attitudes and moods of the speakers, as well as how these attitudes and moods were conveyed.

Per quante notti? (page 33)

Main aim: To practise asking for a room and saying for how long it is needed

A Ask the students to look at the calendars and ensure that everyone can understand, e.g.

– Cosa significa D (L, Ma, etc)?

Then ask them to try to work out what the captions mean and to explain them to everyone. Practise these key words, e.g.

– Quante notti ci sono in una settimana?
– Quante settimane ci sono in un mese?
– Quante notti ci sono in due settimane?
– Quante notti ci sono in agosto?
– Quante settimane ci sono in agosto?

B The students shut their books and you write on the board:

una camera?
doppia, a due letti.
quattro notti.
numero ventiquattro.

Say that these are the key words of a conversation and encourage them to try to create the conversation. Write on the board what they say. Then ask them to compare this with the one in the Students' Book. They should be very encouraged by how similar they are!

C The students follow the text in the Students' Book and listen to the recording. Then play the recording again, stopping after each sentence for the students to repeat.
They then do the pairs exercise, making up dialogues to match the calendars. After they have practised this for a while, give them five minutes to make up all five dialogues.

🛏 Per quante notti?

Receptionist:	Buongiorno.
Customer:	Buongiorno. Avete una camera?
Receptionist:	Una camera singola o una camera doppia?
Customer:	Una camera doppia, a due letti.
Receptionist:	Per quante notti?
Customer:	Per quattro notti.
Receptionist:	Sì .... camera numero ventiquattro.
Customer:	Grazie.

D Practise the key words again. You could read some words and ask the students to find a word, or words, with a similar meaning, e.g.

sette notti (una settimana)
quattro settimane (agosto)
due settimane (quattordici notti)
una settimana (sette notti)
quattordici notti (due settimane)
agosto (quattro settimane)
una camera doppia (una camera a due letti)
31 notti (agosto)

Una lettera ad un albergo (page 33)

Main aim: To learn how to write a letter reserving a room in a hotel

A Read aloud the instructions and the model letter. Ask students to explain, in English, what they should do and what the letter says. Encourage them to adapt the letter orally.

B You read the model letter, making some changes, e.g. the date, the sort of room, the number of nights.
The students stop you whenever you make a change and read the original.

C Present the following on the OHP or board. Encourage the students to complete them orally and then to write them.

```
                              Sheffield, 31 agosto


Spett. Direzione Hotel Venezuela
Via Bafile, 43,
30017 Lido di Jesolo

Spettabile Direz_____,

Vorrei pren_____ una cam_____ doppia con
bag____ per le notti del 23 al 27 sett_____.

In att____ di una Vostra cort____ risposta,
Dist_____ saluti,

Paula Earl

Ms. P. Earl,
4 Edgebrook Road,
Sheffield 7,
Inghilterra.
```

```
                              Perth, 8 ottobre

Spett. Direz_____ Hotel Condor,
Via Padova,
30017 Lido di Jesolo.


Spett_____ Direzione,

Vorr____ prenotare una camera sing_____ con
docc_____ ed una cam_____ doppia con
bagno per la nott_____ del 20 dicembre.

In attesa di una Vos____ cortese risp_____,
Distinti sal____,

Harry Parry

Mr. H. Parry,
15 Morningside Drive,
Perth,
W. Australia.
```

D The students now write the letter on behalf of Paul Williams. This could be done at home.

Sei arrivato! (Copymaster 23)

Main aim: To practise checking in at a hotel

A The students listen to the recording, then play-read the dialogue and adapt it, in pairs. Move around, listening and helping.

B Suggest a technique to help them to learn the dialogue. For example, they could take a strip of paper 2 cm wide and lay it over the dialogue, covering part of it. They try to read it, including what is covered. They then put the strip in another place and repeat this.

C Play the recording again and stop the tape from time to time. A volunteer tries to carry on the dialogue.

Sei arrivato!

Receptionist:	Buonasera.
Woman:	Buonasera, signora.
Receptionist:	Avete già prenotato?
Woman:	Sì.
Receptionist:	Il Suo nome, per favore?

Woman:	Leitner.
Receptionist:	Benissimo. Avete due camere con servizi al secondo piano. Avete un passaporto, per favore?
Woman:	Sì, eccolo.
Receptionist:	Grazie. Vi faccio vedere le vostre camere. Avete fatto buon viaggio?
Woman:	Non male, comunque è stato un po' lungo …

La mia chiave, per favore (page 34)

Main aims: To practise asking for the key for a hotel room

To practise the use of 'Eccola', etc

A Before starting on this item, revise the use of numerals. Here are two ways of doing so.

• Draw the following on the board:

1-10				
11-20				
21-30				
60-70				
90-100				
131-140				
250-259				

Each student copies this and writes a number in each empty square, choosing the four numbers in any horizontal line from the range indicated in the box on the left. Use these to play 'Loto'.

Remember to keep a record of the numbers you call out, so that you can check claims to have won and to avoid calling numbers twice.

• In pairs, both players try to say 99. They take turns to count, starting from 70, and saying just one or two numbers, always in sequence. No player is allowed to say more than two numbers, e.g.

    A: 90, 91
    B: 92, 93
    A: 94, 95
    B: 96, 97
    A: 98, 99.

So, player A wins. You could practise this for a while with students or an assistant before the students play in pairs, using 55 as the number and starting at 30.

After a while, the students could start at 99 and work backwards to, say, 70. Another variation would be to agree on a number which both players try to avoid saying, for example, 113.

B The students now look at this item in the Students' Book. When everyone understands what to do, call out a few of the numbers on the board of keys and the students write them down. After every two, stop and ask students to read back the numbers they have written.

Now play the recorded example. The students write the number of each key that is asked for. At the end, ask which keys are left, rationing any one student to one number so as to involve as many as possible.

C If necessary, have some more number practice; for example, four students stand at the board, each with a piece of chalk. Someone in the class says, e.g.

— Il numero 317, per favore.

The students at the board race to write the number asked for. Now play dialogues 1 to 4 while the students write the numbers asked for and then work out which keys remain.

La mia chiave, per favore

Esempio

Receptionist:	Buonasera.
Client:	Buonasera. Mi dà la mia chiave per favore.
Receptionist:	Che numero è?
Client:	417.
Receptionist:	417. Eccola.
Client:	Grazie.

Receptionist:	Buonasera signorina.
Client:	Buonasera. La mia chiave, per favore.
Receptionist:	È la 314, vero?
Client:	Sì, 314.
Receptionist:	Eccola.
Client:	Grazie.

Client:	Buonasera.
Receptionist:	Buonasera signor Donati. La Sua chiave… ?
Client:	Grazie … Scusi, questa non è la mia.
Receptionist:	Scusi tanto, signore. Che numero è la Sua?
Client:	103.
Receptionist:	103 … Ecco.
Client:	Grazie.
Receptionist:	Prego.

Dialogo 1

Receptionist:	Buonasera signore. Ha passato una bella giornata?
Client:	Molto bella, grazie. Mi dia la mia chiave, per favore, numero 311.
Receptionist:	311. Eccola.
Client:	Grazie.

Dialogo 2

Customer:	Anch'io vorrei la mia chiave, per favore.
Receptionist:	Certo signorina.
Client:	È numero 206.
Receptionist:	206 ... eccola.
Client:	Grazie.

Dialogo 3

Client:	Buonasera.
Receptionist:	Buonasera. Ha trovato la chiesa di Sant'Antonio?
Client:	Sì, che bellezza! È piccola ma perfetta.
Receptionist:	Ecco la Sua chiave, 103, sì?
Client:	103, grazie. Buonasera.
Receptionist:	Buonasera, signore.

Dialogo 4

Client:	La mia chiave per favore.
Receptionist:	Ecco signora.
Client:	Questa non è la mia, questa è la numero 417, la mia è la 418.
Receptionist:	Mille scuse, signora, ecco la Sua, 418.
Client:	Grazie.

D In pairs, the students make up dialogues based on the model in the Students' Book and point to the key asked for.

E This would be a good time to work on *Scoprite qualcosa di più* (pages 152-154).

F You could practise 'Eccolo', etc. in class, in one of the following ways.
- Using what is displayed in the classroom, or putting pictures up especially in different parts of the room, you could ask, e.g.

– Dov'è la pizzeria (la gelateria, il gelato, la birra, il dépliant)?

– Dove sono le cartoline (i tavoli, le focacce, i coni)?

The students point to what you have asked for and say, e.g.

– Eccolo, signora.

This will soon seem too easy. Then ask the students to do it with their eyes shut! They listen, point and reply with eyes shut, only opening their eyes when everyone is pointing and you say:

– Aprite gli occhi.

There may be some surprises!

- For this game, use a wall display with several pictures on, or one large picture with several things in it. Divide the class into two teams and number everyone in each team, using the same numbers so that, in each team, there is a student number 1, etc.

Call one of the numbers to alert the students. Then ask where something is, e.g.

– Dov'è la gelateria?

When you ask for something which is visible, the two students should race to point to it and say, e.g.

– Eccola.

However, they should avoid pointing when you ask for something which is not there. You can award, and subtract, points.

A che ora si mangia, per favore? (page 34)

Main aim: To practise asking when meals are served, and understanding the replies

A Revise understanding the time, in one of the following ways.
- Say a number of useful sentences which include a time, e.g.

– Il primo treno parte alle dieci e mezza.
– L'autobus arriva alle undici e un quarto.
– La banca apre alle otto.
– La posta chiude alle due meno un quarto.

The students listen and write the time you say. Check after each one and clear up any difficulties before going on.

- Play a game of 'Il gioco degli spazi' (see Teacher's Book 1, page 110) e.g.

1 Il ristorante chiude alle ____ . (quattro)
2 La posta apre alle ____ e ____ . (otto e mezza)
3 Il museo chiude alle ____ . (nove)
4 La pizzeria apre alle ____ . (sette)
5 La gelateria apre alle ____ meno un ____ . (dieci meno un quarto)
6 La scuola chiude all' ____ e ____ . (una e mezza)
7 Il giardino pubblico chiude alle ____ meno un ____ . (sette meno un quarto)
8 La biblioteca apre alle ____ e un ____ . (otto e un quarto)
9 Il centro sportivo chiude alle ____ . (undici)
10 Il luna park chiude alle ____ e ____ . (due e mezza)

B Now present this item to the students. Explain that they are going to hear two dialogues. In each dialogue a guest is asking about meal times. They must work out which hotel matches each dialogue.

Answers:
Dialogue 1 = Hotel San Lorenzo
Dialogue 2 = Hotel Astor

🎞 A che ora si mangia, per favore?

Dialogo 1

- Buonasera. Potrebbe dirmi a che ora si cena questa sera?
- Sì, dunque la cena si serve dalle otto alle nove e trenta.
- E la colazione domani mattina?
- Un attimo che controllo. Dunque la colazione dalle otto alle nove.
- E per quanto riguarda il pranzo?
- Dodici e trenta fino alle due.
- Grazie, arrivederci.

Dialogo 2

- Buongiorno, mi scusi se la disturbo, mi saprebbe dire a che ora viene servito il pranzo?
- Il pranzo viene servito dalle dodici all'una e trenta.
- E per questa sera la cena?
- La cena dalle otto alle nove e mezza.
- Domani mattina avrei intenzione di partire abbastanza presto, a che ora servite la colazione?
- La colazione viene servita dalle sette e mezza alle nove. Desidera altro?
- No grazie, arrivederci.
- Arrivederci.

C Explain to the students that they are going to play a deduction game. They take it in turns to ask the time of a meal. Their partner replies giving the meal time in one of the hotels. The person who asked the question has to identify the hotel. They can refer to the model dialogue in the Students' Book if necessary.

D For homework, each student could draw up a timetable, like those in the Students' Book, showing at what time they have these meals. In class, these can be used as the basis of an information-gap exercise, e.g.

A: A che ora fai colazione?
B: Alle sette e un quarto.
A: È presto! Io la faccio alle otto.

Non funziona! (page 35)

Main aim: **To practise reporting faults**

A Introduce this item and make sure that everyone understands the main words. You could do this in one of the following ways.

- Say that one of the things illustrated is not working. The students write the letter of the object to show that they understand.

- Talk about one of the objects illustrated. On some occasions, say that it is not working and on other occasions say that it is working. The students write the letter of the object and draw a cross over the letter if the object is faulty.

- The students choose any three of the objects and write the appropriate letters. Use these to play at 'Loto', with you saying, e.g.

  - Mi dispiace, ma la luce (il televisore, ecc.) nella mia camera non funziona.

The students can continue to play this in groups of four, taking turns to be the caller.

B The students work in pairs to make up dialogues based on the model in the Students' Book.

C The students listen to this recording of telephoned complaints in a hotel: their task is to spot the complaint which is logically impossible (the last one, since the phone is obviously working).

🎞 Non funziona!

Dialogo 1

Receptionist:	Pronto. Direzione.
Client:	Pronto. Può mandare qualcuno alla mia camera - numero 40? La doccia non funziona.
Receptionist:	Va bene. Camera 40. Vengo subito.

Dialogo 2

Receptionist:	Pronto. Desidera?
Client:	Pronto. Qui, abbiamo un problema. Siamo nella camera numero 4. C'è uno spettacolo che vogliamo guardare alla televisione. Ma il televisore non funziona. Potrebbe aiutarci?
Receptionist:	Certo, signora. Mando subito qualcuno.

Dialogo 3

Receptionist:	Pronto. Direzione. Desidera?
Client:	Allora, venga qui alla camera numero 53, subito, capisce. La luce non funziona, ed io voglio leggere il giornale.
Receptionist:	Senz'altro signorina. Vengo io fra cinque minuti.
Client:	Va bene - allora non se ne dimentichi, eh!

Dialogo 4

Receptionist:	Pronto.
Customer:	Pronto, mi scusi, ma come si fa per scendere? Siamo al dodicesimo piano e l'ascensore non funziona.
Receptionist:	Non si preoccupi, signore. Sarà bloccato qui sotto. Aspetti due minuti, poi provi di nuovo. Va bene?

Client:	Sì, va bene, grazie.
Receptionist:	Prego.

Dialogo 5

Receptionist:	Pronto. Direzione. Desidera?
Client:	Pronto. Qui è la camera numero 32. Fa molto caldo qui dentro. Le finestre non si aprono e l'aria condizionata non funziona. Che cosa devo fare?
Receptionist:	Abbia un po' di pazienza. Mando qualcuno per ripararla.
Client:	Grazie.
Receptionist:	Prego, signorina.

Dialogo 6

Receptionist:	Pronto. Desidera?
Client:	Che razza d'albergo è questo? Tutto è guasto. Non funziona nemmeno il telefono.
Receptionist:	Il telefono? Ma ...

D After listening to these recordings, each student writes four or five similar complaints, including one which is logically impossible. They read these to their partners who try to spot the impossible one. Some could be performed for the class.

E To practise 'Eccolo', etc, you could base some questions and answers on this page, e.g.

Teacher:	C'è una luce (ecc.) che non funziona?
Students:	Sì, eccola.

Manca un asciugamano (page 35)

Main aim: To practise saying that something is missing

A Read aloud the four captions a few times and ask the students to work out what they mean. When everyone understands them, read them in random order: the students repeat and point to the appropriate drawing. Increase the speed of this until it is going very fast.
You could play a game of Hangman ('Boia') using these expressions and variations on them. Draw a line on the board to represent each word of the sentence you have in mind. When a student guesses one of these words, write it in. When a student makes a wrong guess, draw a line of the gallows or the man.

In addition to the objects illustrated on this page, you could use, e.g.

– Manca una luce (il televisore, un letto, il bagno, la doccia, il telefono, il gabinetto privato).

The students could continue to play this in pairs.

B The students study the pictures and write what they think is missing from each one.

Answers:

1 soap
2 toilet paper
3 towel
4 water

Using the same pictures, the students could choose any two and write a list of five things which the two have in common and one difference. In pairs, they read their lists to each other and the partners try to say which the two pictures are.

Due cartoline (page 36)

Main aim: To develop reading and writing skills on the topic of a hotel

A Before the students look at the postcards, present the following on the board or OHP:

... albergo ... bello ... piscina ... camera ... balcone ... TV ... spiaggia ... caldo ... teatro.

Tell the students that these words come from a postcard and encourage them to guess the contents of the card and the mood of the writer.
Repeat the above with:

... delusa ... albergo ... spiaggia ... piccolissima ... sporca ... non è buona ... non funziona.

The students now read the cards and see how accurate their predictions were: this should confirm the point that it is not necessary to understand every word in order to get most of what matters in a text. Encourage the students to react both to the details and to the attitudes expressed in the cards.

B Orally, the students adapt the two cards, adding their own positive and negative comments. Write their ideas on the board.
The students then imagine that they are on holiday in one of the hotels on page 31 of the Students' Book. They write two cards from it to you, one very positive and one full of complaints.

C Give each student a copy of Copymasters 24 A and B. Start off by practising scan reading techniques. The students race to find the information you ask for, e.g.

1 How much does a double room, with bath or shower, cost? (Lit. 80.000)
2 How much does lunch cost? (Lit. 22.000/25.000)
3 How many people can get into the VIP lounge? (50-60)
4 How far from the motorway turn-off is the hotel? (5 km)
5 How far is it from the centre of Arezzo? (2 km)

6 What word is used to describe the bar? (piacevole)

7 What two words are used to describe the restaurant? (elegante e confortevole)

The students now read the information again and write the memo for their employer. You could then ask them what else they have found in the text which it would be useful to tell their employer.

Finally, the students find and underline or highlight the key words in the text about the hotel. They can discuss these in pairs and try to agree on what they are. The class then discusses what the key words are and where they are in the text. This should help them to build up an idea of how to find the key words quickly.

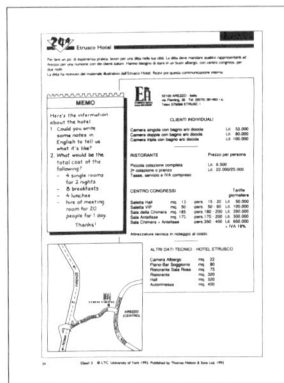

Adesso, tocca a te! (page 37)

Main aim: **To demonstrate that the language of this unit has been mastered**

Exercise 1

Language area: Asking for a room and about meal times
Skill areas: Listening and speaking

Present Copymaster 25 to the class on the OHP. Work through the example before giving Copymaster 26A to students A and Copymaster 26B to students B. As the students work on this role-play, move around, listening and noting any problems which will call for additional input and/or teaching.

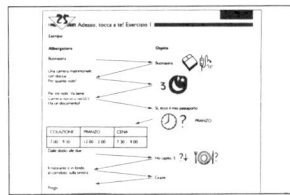

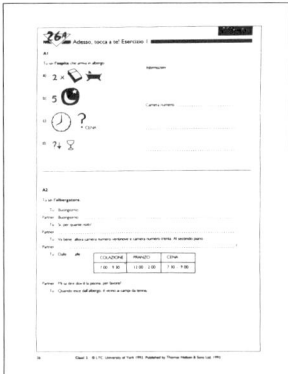
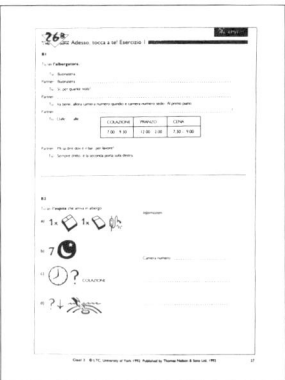

Exercise 2

Language area: Reporting faults and missing objects, in a hotel
Skill areas: Listening and speaking

In pairs, the students work on this along the lines suggested. Stress that this is not a competition, but a chance for them to help each other to master this point: each student is responsible for helping his or her partner to become really perfect at reporting faults and missing objects.

Exercise 3

Language area: Choosing a hotel
Skill areas: Reading

The students answer the English questions.

Exercise 4

Language area: Choosing a hotel
Skill areas: Reading and writing

Students answer the Italian questions, writing their answers in Italian if they can.

Ora sai (page 38)

Main aim: **To act as a summary and reference point for the main language of this unit**

A After the students have had the opportunity to study this (as a homework task, for example) they could work on it in pairs, in one of the following ways.

• Student A reads aloud one of the Italian phrases, or a variation of one, on this page. Student B covers up the Italian expressions and, looking only at the English, says which category Student A's phrase is from. After a few minutes, they change roles.

• Student A says one of the Italian phrases, or a variation. Student B listens and says, for each one, if it would be said by a tourist or a hotel manager.

B This game practises 'eccolo', etc.

I ladri

To ensure that plurals are practised, the teacher should encourage some items to be hidden in pairs, e.g. two exercise books together, two pens, etc.

The game is probably best played in groups of six or seven. Two people volunteer to be 'victims' ('le vittime'). They place on the table about ten different belongings (exercise books, text books, pens and pencils, coat, bag, etc.). They then leave the room. While they are out of the room, the other players distribute the items among themselves any way they like and hide them where they are sitting. Objects may not be put anywhere else, only in pockets, up jumpers, sat on, etc. For variety, sometimes one person could take almost all the objects, at other times everyone could have two each. To reinforce vocabulary, the hiding process can take place in Italian. ('Chi prende queste penne?' etc.) The 'victims' return and have to ask for their belongings back. They must ask one 'thief' at a time and name the object they want back. The thief must answer 'Non ce l'ho', 'Non li/le ho' or 'Eccolo/la/le/li' and return it/them. No lying is allowed. The key answers can be written on the board and left there as a model, as can the example below.

Esempio:

A: Susanna, hai la mia penna?
B: No, mi dispiace, non ce l'ho.
A: Gary, hai la mia penna?
B: No, mi dispiace, non ce l'ho.
A: Sheila, hai la mia penna?
B: Sì, eccola.
A: Grazie. (takes pen, and the other victim has a go)

Revision

1 Introductions and greetings (Book 1, Unit 1)

A Play 'Same or different?'
The students first write the numbers 1-15 in their books, one to each line. You read out two sentences: the students make a tick if they sound the same and a cross if they sound different. Read each pair three or four times and then check the answer before saying it again two or three times and then moving on to the next pair, e.g.

1 Mi chiamo Paolo. Mi chiamo Paola.
2 Come si chiama? Come ti chiami?
3 Ti presento Marco. Ti presento Marco.
4 Buongiorno signore. Buongiorno signora.
5 Buonasera professore. Buonasera professore.
6 Ciao ragazzi. Ciao ragazze.
7 Arrivederci. Arrivederci.
8 Dove abiti? Dove abita?
9 Abito a Roma. Abito a Roma.
10 Di dove sei? Di dove sei?
11 Sono inglese. Sono francese.
12 Hai un fratello? Ho un fratello.
13 Ho 14 anni. Ho 14 anni.
14 Come stai? Come stai?
15 Va bene? Va bene.

B Present the following on the OHP or board. They are examples of key sentences written as one word. The students re-write them, separating the words, and read them aloud.

– AbitoadArezzo.
– Buonaseraprofessore.
– CiaoCecilia.
– Cometichiami?
– TipresentoSnoopy.
– MichiamoRoberto.

When this becomes too easy, break up the sentences at odd places, e.g.

– Do vea biti?
– Tip reseent omi amam ma.
– Mic hiam oPa olo.
– Bu ongi or nopro fesso ressa.
– Comet ich i am i?
– Ioso noSt efano.

After some class practice along these lines, the students could all write brief introductions of themselves using these two techniques. They exchange these and try to write out correctly their partners' puzzles.

2 Buying ice creams, snacks and pizza (Book 2, Unit 4)

Part of knowing what a word means and how it can be used is knowing what other words it can be used with. Present the following on the OHP or board. Invite the students to tell you which words in each circle cannot be used to describe the word in the box. Cross out those which cannot be used. Then ask for others which could be added to the circle and write these in.

3 Talking about free-time activities (Book 2, Unit 10)

Present tense: 'io' and 'tu' forms (Book 2, Unit 10)

Students work in pairs to find four things their partner enjoys doing in their free time.

A Write on the board, e.g.

- Ti piace <u>fare</u> il bagno?
- Sì, <u>faccio</u> il bagno ogni giorno.
- Ti piace <u>guardare</u> la televisione?
- Sì, <u>guardo</u> la televisione ogni giorno.
- Ti piace <u>leggere</u> delle riviste?
- Sì <u>leggo</u> molto le riviste.
- Ti piace <u>andare</u> in discoteca?
- Sì, <u>vado</u> in discoteca ogni domenica.
- Ti piace <u>fare</u> delle passeggiate?
- Sì, <u>faccio</u> delle passeggiate ogni settimana.

Draw the students' attention to the infinitive forms and ask them to provide the infinitives to go with the following (looking in the Students' Book to find them, if necessary), which you write on the board:

faccio; gioco; mangio; vado; scrivo; leggo; ascolto; fai; scrive; scrivi; fa; aspetta; chiedi.

Write the infinitives on the board and leave them there for reference.

B Organise some verb circle practice for a few minutes, based on, e.g.

- Non ho prenotato.
- Voglio una camera singola.
- Leggo un opuscolo.
- Vado al parcheggio.
- Chiedo la chiave.

4 Talking about a town (Book 3, Unit 3)

A Present the following words on the board. Ask the students to list them according to how difficult they find them to pronounce, from the easiest to the hardest. Then ask them for their ideas for helping people to learn to pronounce the words they find difficult. The information about what they find difficult will be useful, as will their ideas for helping each other.

noioso	visitare	la chiesa
commerciale	la provincia	importante
la biblioteca	situato	il bocciodromo
il luna park	vedere	

You could also ask the students to list these, or other, words in order of difficulty for spelling, and encourage them to share their ideas for coping with the hard ones. This activity can be used regularly, with different sets of words.

B Play 'Lascia o raddoppia'.

You need a collection of counters or beads. Divide the class into four teams. Make a statement and choose a team to say if it is true or false, e.g.

Teacher: Un giardino pubblico è un grand'albergo.
Student: Falso.

When an answer is correct, give the team two counters. You now offer the team the chance to double its counters by responding to another sentence. If they do so correctly, they get two more counters. If they are wrong, they have to give back the two they won for the first sentence. Allow the teams to consult briefly so that every decision is a team decision. If a team decides 'passiamo', you move on to another team. After a team takes on a second sentence, successfully or not, you move on to another team. In order to maintain a fast pace, allow a maximum of twenty seconds for a response.

Possible sentences include:

- Roma è una piccola città.
- Arezzo è situata in collina.
- Birmingham è situata al mare.
- Miami è un paese tranquillo.
- Beverley è una brutta cittadina.
- La cathedrale di Lincoln è uno dei monumenti più distinti della città.
- Canberra è la città più turistica d'Australia.
- La biblioteca è il posto più interessante della città.

5 Superlative adjectives (Book 3, Unit 3)

Present on the board or OHP a number of sentences to be completed, e.g.

1 Secondo me, la cosa più _____ in una camera è un letto.
2 Il negozio più _____ della città è il supermercato.
3 Secondo me, la pizza più _____ è la Siciliana.
4 Lo sport più _____ è il calcio.
5 Il monumento più _____ di New York si chiama Empire State Building.
6 La più _____ piazza di Venezia si chiama San Marco.
7 Pisa è una delle città più _____ d'Italia.
8 Il giardino pubblico è il posto più _____ della città.

You could give a list of adjectives for the students to choose from, e.g.

grande, interessante, costruiti, bella, turistiche, tranquillo, famoso, deliziosa, rifatte, brutti, restaurate, importante.

5ª Unità
LE VACANZE

Main aims

~ To understand and give an account of a recent holiday
~ To understand and give opinions regarding journeys, accommodation, etc

Materials

~ Tape

Dove sei andato in vacanza? (Teacher's Book page 62)
Dove? Come? (Teacher's Book page 62)
Dove sei stato? (Teacher's Book page 63)
Inchiesta sulle vacanze in Toscana (Teacher's Book page 64)
Le vacanze degli amici (Teacher's Book page 66)
Com'è andato il viaggio? (Teacher's Book page 66)
Siamo rimasti proprio delusi (Teacher's Book page 68)
Adesso, tocca a te! (Teacher's Book page 69)

~ Copymasters 27–31
~ Selection of tourist brochures on Italian towns and regions

Grammar in *Scoprite qualcosa di più*

~ Perfect tense with 'essere'

Revision

~ Using Italian in the classroom (Book 1, Unit 2)
~ Talking about homes and their location (Book 2, Unit 5)
~ Present tense of -are verbs, 1st–3rd person singular (Book 2, Unit 5)
~ Travelling by train (Book 3, Unit 1)
~ Present tense of regular -are, -ere, -ire verbs (Book 3, Unit 1)
~ Direct object pronoun after 'ecco' (Book 3, Unit 4)
~ Booking hotel accommodation (Book 3, Unit 4)

Vocabulary

A: Productive

un aereo	perfetto
il disastro	rimanere
la discoteca	salire
divertente	sciare
fa	scorso
interessante	la settimana
il mare	la spiaggia
la montagna	la vacanza
il monumento	il viaggio
noioso	visitare

B: Receptive

l'Adriatico	il Mediterraneo
un aeroporto	il pullman
cadere	scomodo
la cartolina	lo ski-lift
così così	la torre
la gita	il traghetto
insomma	il turismo
un'isola	il/la turista

Le vacanze (page 39)

Main aims: To introduce the topic of past holidays

To provide students with some background information on resorts and places to visit in Italy

A Bring in a selection of tourist brochures on various Italian towns and regions. These are normally available from the Italian State Tourist Office, 1 Princes Street, London W1 (tel. 071-408 1254).

Find out how many of your students have already visited Italy. If there are any, ask them whether the place they visited is in any of the brochures. If not, ask them to say its name.

B Ask the students to look at the brochures and say what pictures some of the names conjure up in their mind. You could then say what pictures are conjured up in your mind by the place-names.

C Ask the students to read the introduction in the Students' Book and clarify words and phrases they do not understand. Ask them to read it again and to note down what they think the two main points of the text are. They should then compare and discuss with each other what they have written down.

D If you have the appropriate range of tourist brochures, ask the students to classify the places into three types of resorts: seaside, mountain, cultural (historic). See if they all agree.

E It would be useful to bring in a native speaker to answer queries they may have about holidaying in Italy.

F The students write lists of eight to ten questions which they like to ask people about their holidays, doing as many as they can in Italian and the others in English. Their task is then to ensure that, by the end of work on this unit, they can ask and answer, in Italian, all the questions on their lists.

Dove sei andato(a) in vacanza? (page 39)

Main aims: To say where you went on holiday and how you got there

To ask others for the same information

A The students read this item silently and then listen to the recording: their task is to decide what the gist, or main point, of the text is. Encourage them to use all the available clues: the text, the tone of the recording, the photos, the heading.

🔊 Dove sei andato in vacanza?

Dialogo 1

Boy 1:   Dove sei andato in vacanza l'anno scorso?
Boy 2:   Sono andato a Rimini.
Boy 1:   Come ci sei andato?
Boy 2:   In macchina.

Dialogo 2

Girl 1:   L'anno scorso, dove sei andata in vacanza?
Girl 2:   Sono andata in montagna, sulle Dolomiti.
Girl 1:   Ci sei andata in macchina?
Girl 2:   No, ci sono andata in treno ed in pullman.

Dialogo 3

Teacher: Dove sei andato in vacanza?
Boy: Sono andato negli Stati Uniti.
Teacher: Ci sei andato in aereo, immagino?
Boy: Sì, in aereo.

Dialogo 4

Teacher: Dove sei andata in vacanza quest'anno?
Girl: Non sono andata in vacanza quest'anno. Sono rimasta a casa. Ho dovuto fare una ricerca su Piero della Francesca.
Teacher: Ah, sei rimasta a casa. Ho capito.

B The students read the text again to find out how to ask in Italian: 'Where did you go on holiday?'. Encourage them to find the different ways of asking the question and to try to work out why these different forms exist.
Repeat the procedure with the answers.

C The students read and listen to each short dialogue again. After each one, ask them to summarise the contents in English.

D With their books closed, the students listen again to the recordings. After each one, they should say where the person went and how. Do this in Italian or English, depending on the students.

E Play the recording **Dove? Come?** introducing it, e.g.

– Un gruppo di giovani italiani sono ad una festa. Cominciano a parlare di vacanze: dove sono stati e come ci sono arrivati. Ascoltate bene. Dovete dire dove sono stati e come ci sono arrivati. Guardate l'esempio nel vostro libro.

Work on each dialogue in turn and try to clear up any problems as you go along.

🔊 Dove? Come?

Dialogo 1

Boy: Mirella, dove sei stata in vacanza quest'anno?
Mirella: Ho fatto una bellissima vacanza. Sono stata in Sardegna, sai.
Girl: In Sardegna? Che bello! Hai preso il traghetto?
Mirella: No, ci sono andata in aereo. È stata la mia prima volta in aereo.

Dialogo 2

Mirella: E tu, Roberto, sei andato via?
Roberto: Sì.
Boy: Dove sei andato?
Roberto: Sono stato in Inghilterra - a Londra.
Girl: Ah, hai visto la regina Elisabetta?
Roberto: No.
Boy: Ci sei andato in aereo?
Roberto: No, ho preso il treno. È stato un viaggio lungo e scomodo.

Dialogo 3

Roberto: E tu, Gianna?
Gianna: Sì, sì, sono stata in vacanza anch'io.
Girl: Dove?
Gianna: La mia famiglia non aveva mai visto Venezia: allora quest'anno ci siamo andati.
Boy: Ti è piaciuta?
Gianna: È bellissima. Però il viaggio in macchina è stato noioso.

Dialogo 4

Gianna: E tu, Sandra, dove sei andata?
Sandra: Beh, in vacanza veramente no. Però sono stata due giorni a Firenze con la scuola.
Boy: Ci siete andati in pullman?
Sandra: Sì, è abbastanza comodo ma avrei preferito prendere il treno. E Patrizia, cos'hai fatto tu? ...

F The class could suggest orally some variations on the questions and answers in this item, e.g.

– Ci sei andato in treno?
– Ci sei andata a piedi?
– Ci sono andato in macchina.

Write these on the board or OHP. Then ask the students to think about which of the questions could be put to boys and which to girls and then to do the same with the answers. In pairs, they could then practise stringing together the questions and answers, with one choosing a question and asking it and the other choosing an appropriate answer and giving it.

G You could ask several students now about where and how they went on holiday. Using this as a model, the students carry out a brief survey, asking each other where and how they went on holiday and making brief notes. Ask them to report to you on their findings.

H Now would be a good time to start work on *Scoprite qualcosa di più* (pages 154-158).

Dove sei stato(a)? (page 40)

Main aims: To say where you stayed on holiday, who you went with and what you did

To elicit the same information from others

A The students' confidence should be boosted by realising that they already know most of the words in this list. They have reached the point where they know many of the key words needed to do new jobs. To prove the point, ask them to read the list and to write down any Italian words which are new to them. They then compare their lists with each other. Other activities which could be used to help the students to learn the sentences in the list include:
* In speech bubbles, students write a dialogue using questions and answers from the list. They could act these in pairs. This activity could be used with other lists.

* Each student writes the two words on the list which they have found most difficult to learn. They then close the Students' Book. Choose a student to read aloud his/her two words: everyone writes these down. You, or the student, then write the words on the board. Repeat this with several students.
Instead of two words, the students could choose one sentence.

B Discuss which are the most interesting questions and why. The students now read, listen to and act in pairs the three dialogues in their book. They then answer the questions at the end.

🚌 Dove sei stato?

Dialogo 1

Maria: Ciao! Dove sei andato in vacanza?
Carlo: Sono andato in Francia.

Maria: Che bello! Dove sei stato?
Carlo: Sono stato in un piccolo albergo vicino a Cannes. È venuta anche mia sorella.
Maria: Per quanto tempo ci sei rimasto?
Carlo: Ci sono rimasto per due settimane.
Maria: E che cosa hai fatto?
Carlo: Sono andato in spiaggia, e anche in discoteca. E sono andato a fare delle spese.

Dialogo 2

Luigi: Ciao! Dove sei andata in vacanza?
Anna: A Roma.
Luigi: Dove sei stata?
Anna: In albergo.
Luigi: Per quanto tempo?
Anna: Una settimana.
Luigi: Che cosa hai fatto?
Anna: Sono andata a visitare i monumenti principali.

Dialogo 3

Paola: Dove sei andata in vacanza quest'anno?
Elena: Sono andata a Viareggio. La conosci? Mi è piaciuta moltissimo!
Paola: Dove sei stata?
Elena: In un centro di vacanze. C'erano tanti altri giovani!
Paola: Con chi sei andata?
Elena: Con alcune amiche di scuola.
Paola: E che cosa hai fatto?
Elena: Sono andata in spiaggia, mi piace nuotare, sai. Sono andata a fare dello shopping, e la sera sono andata in discoteca.

C The students look again at the list and decide who in the class each question could be put to and who could use each answer. This would be a good time to do some more work on *Scoprite qualcosa di più* (pages 154-158).

D Give each student in each pair either Copymaster 27A or Copymaster 27B. Make sure that everyone knows what to do and practise doing it with two or three students. As the students work on this in pairs, move around making sure that they are working along the right lines, listening and helping.

E This would be a suitable time to continue work on *Scoprite qualcosa di più*.

Inchiesta sulle vacanze in Toscana (page 41)

Main aim: To practise saying where you went, what you did and whether you enjoyed yourself

A Give the students sixty seconds to look at this and to work out what it is about and what their task is. Then, with the Students' Book closed, they speculate about the sorts of questions most likely to be asked and the sorts of information that people are likely to give. Do as much as possible of this in Italian.

Encourage the students to see that work of this kind is a good way of preparing to understand what they are about to hear. It is a technique which they can use with other listening exercises and tests.

B The students read the interview in the Students' Book and see if any of what they had predicted comes up. They then listen to the recording of the first three interviews on the tape and again see how their preparatory work prepared them to understand the interviews.

🔲 Inchiesta sulle vacanze in Toscana

Prima intervista

Interviewer:	Buongiorno, signori.
Young men:	Buongiorno.
Interviewer:	Sentite, sto facendo un'inchiesta sulle vacanze in Toscana. Vi posso fare alcune domande?
Young man:	Quali domande?
Interviewer:	Quando siete arrivati in Italia?
Young man:	In giugno ... vediamo, il trenta.
Interviewer:	Siete arrivati all'aeroporto di Pisa?
Young man:	No, no, siamo venuti in Italia in macchina, sa: con l'autostop.
Interviewer:	Allora, dove siete stati?
Young man:	Siamo stati dappertutto: Venezia ... Rimini ... Roma. Siamo stati un giorno anche a Pisa.
Interviewer:	Siete stati in albergo?
Young man:	No, troppi soldi. Siamo stati in pensione; ma abbiamo dormito anche in spiaggia.
Interviewer:	Che cos'avete fatto?
Young man:	Siamo stati in giro a guardare l'Italia. Che bel paese!
Interviewer:	E come siete venuti all'aeroporto?
Young man:	A piedi!
Interviewer:	Siete stati contenti della vostra vacanza?
Young man:	Sì, è stata favolosa, stupenda ... grandiosa.

Interviewer:	Grazie, buon viaggio.

Seconda intervista

Interviewer:	Buongiorno.
Mother:	Buongiorno.
Interviewer:	Sto facendo un'inchiesta sulle vacanze in Toscana. Vi posso fare alcune domande?
Mother:	Faccia pure.
Interviewer:	Quando siete arrivati in Italia?
Mother:	Il 13 luglio.
Interviewer:	Siete arrivati all'aeroporto di Pisa?
Mother:	Sì, siamo venuti qui in aereo.
Interviewer:	Siete venuti proprio a Pisa in vacanza?
Mother:	Sì, siamo stati proprio qui, ma abbiamo fatto delle gite nel resto della Toscana.
Interviewer:	Dove siete stati: in albergo?
Mother:	Sì, sì, un bell' albergo in centro.
Interviewer:	E che cos'avete fatto?
Mother:	Tante cose. Siamo saliti sulla Torre di Pisa. Siamo stati a Firenze a vedere tutto. Sa ... tutto quello che c'è da vedere a Firenze.
Interviewer:	E per venire all'aeroporto, siete venuti con il treno?
Mother:	No, abbiamo preso il pullman ... dal centro di Pisa.
Interviewer:	E siete stati contenti della vostra vacanza?
Mother:	Molto ... anzi moltissimo. Ma a mio marito non è piaciuta Firenze perché c'era troppa gente.
Interviewer:	Grazie.
Mother:	Di niente.

Terza intervista

Interviewer:	Buongiorno, signorine.
Young women:	Buongiorno.
Interviewer:	Faccio un'inchiesta sulle vacanze in Toscana. Vi posso fare alcune domande?
Woman 1:	Volentieri.
Interviewer:	Quando siete arrivate in Italia?
Woman 2:	Qualche giorno fa ...
Woman 1:	Il ventisei luglio.
Interviewer:	Siete arrivate all'aeroporto di Pisa?
Woman 2:	No, siamo andate a Firenze in treno.
Interviewer:	Siete rimaste sempre là?
Woman 1:	Quasi. Siamo venute qua due giorni fa.
Interviewer:	Siete state in albergo?
Woman 2:	No, siamo state da un'amica che studia a Firenze.
Interviewer:	Che cos'avete fatto?
Woman 1:	Abbiamo visitato Firenze, sa. Abbiamo fatto dello shopping sul Ponte Vecchio e da Gucci. E siamo state due giorni al mare, in spiaggia.

Interviewer:	E come siete venute all'aeroporto?
Woman 2:	Un'amica ci ha accompagnate in macchina.
Interviewer:	Siete rimaste contente della vostra vacanza?
Woman 1:	Sì, ci siamo divertite molto.
Woman 2:	Però, i ragazzi italiani ... insistono troppo! Non ti lasciano stare.
Interviewer:	Mi dispiace per i ragazzi italiani, ma grazie, e buon ritorno.

Quarta intervista

Interviewer:	Buongiorno.
Young man:	Buongiorno.
Interviewer:	Senta, sto facendo un'inchiesta sulle vacanze in Toscana. Le posso fare alcune domande?
Young man:	Sì, certo.
Interviewer:	Quando è arrivato in Italia?
Young man:	Sono arrivato il venti luglio.
Interviewer:	È arrivato all'aeroporto di Pisa?
Young man:	No, sono andato a Linate, all'aeroporto di Milano.
Interviewer:	E quanto tempo c'è rimasto?
Young man:	Sono stato a Milano due giorni, per affari. Poi, dieci giorni fa, sono andato a Lucca a trovare un'amica.
Interviewer:	È stato in albergo?
Young man:	No, sono rimasto dieci giorni in pensione.
Interviewer:	E che cosa ha fatto?
Young man:	La mia amica mi ha accompagnato in giro. Siamo andati a fare del windsurf sulla costa tirrenica. E siamo anche andati a mangiare in qualche ristorante tipico della Toscana.
Interviewer:	E per venire all'aeroporto, è venuto col treno?
Young man:	Sì.
Interviewer:	È stato contento della Sua vacanza?
Young man:	Sì, è stata formidabile. Mi sono riposato. Però, adesso, devo tornare al lavoro.
Interviewer:	Grazie. Buon viaggio.

C Give each student a copy of Copymaster 28. Work with them on the example to ensure that everyone knows what to do. Then play the next interview, check the students' replies and clear up any problems. Repeat this process with each other interview in turn.

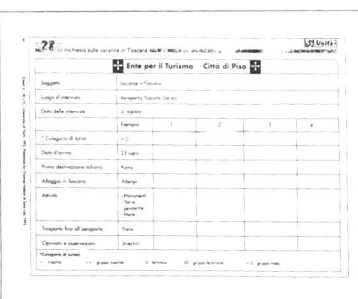

D The students look at the grids they have completed on Copymaster 28. They use their answers to summarise the first interview. If there are any disagreements, play the recording again to clear them up. You could repeat this with one or two other interviews.

E Ask the students to find in the interview on page 41 all the examples of the perfect tense. Can they explain all the forms used? Give whatever help they need to see how the 'siete' and 'siamo' forms work.

This would be an appropriate time to continue work on *Scoprite qualcosa di più* (pages 154-158).

Siamo state dappertutto (page 41)

Main aim: To send a friend a postcard, saying where you have been and what you have done

A Give the students thirty seconds to look at this and to work out what it is about and what their task is.
They then close the Students' Book and write down five or six words or expressions which they expect to find in the postcard. When they read the postcard, they tick all the words and expressions in their lists which are used: who predicted the best?

B The students read the card again to find out who wrote it. How do they know?

C Give the class thirty seconds to read the card again and to decide what the gist, or main point, of it is. When everyone is agreed on this, ask some questions to encourage scan reading, e.g.

- Where did the girls go on holiday?
- Name two places they have visited.
- Where is Viareggio?
- What did they do there every morning?

D Ask the class to adapt the card orally to what two boys who did the same things would write and then to what a brother and sister would write.

E You could continue work on *Scoprite qualcosa di più* (pages 154-158)

Vacanze a Parigi (page 42)

Main aim: To send a postcard to a friend saying where you have been and what you have done on holiday

A If you have not completed work on *Scoprite qualcosa di più* (pages 154-158), now would be a good time to do so.

B Give the class one minute to read this page and, using all the clues available (title, pictures, text, table), to find out what it is about. Discuss their conclusions.

C Play a game of 'Vero o Falso?'. Using the phrases in the table, and others introduced in this unit, make up some statements about the photos, some true and some false, e.g.

– Siamo andati a Parigi.
– Siamo stati in campeggio.

D The students study the table for three minutes and try to learn the words in it. They then use the photos to say what they did. Working on each photo in turn, they say as much about it as they can. Use a 'snowballing' technique to involve more students.

E As a collective exercise, the students dictate a postcard about this trip. You write what they describe, making any necessary corrections.

F Each student now writes the text for a postcard describing this class trip to Paris.

Le vacanze degli amici (page 42)

Main aims: To say what other people did for their holidays
To ask others for similar information

A Read the introduction with the class and ensure that everyone understands it. Students then read the two dialogues to find out as much as they can about Sheelagh's brother and sister. They report back in Italian.

B The students read and listen to both dialogues again: tell them to watch out for phrases that they can use to say what they have done. Then ask the students what they have done: they reply using phrases from these dialogues, adapted if necessary, e.g.

– Mary, sei andata in Spagna?
– Sì, sono andata in Spagna l'anno scorso.

🔊 Le vacanze degli amici

Dialogo A

Mirella:	E tuo fratello, Patrick, è andato in vacanza?
Sheelagh:	Patrick, sì, è andato in Spagna.
Mirella:	Con chi?
Sheelagh:	Ci è andato con la scuola.
Mirella:	Dove sono stati?
Sheelagh:	In albergo, vicino alla spiaggia.
Mirella:	Quanto tempo ci sono rimasti?
Sheelagh:	Due settimane. Ci sono andati con l'aereo.

Dialogo B

Mirella:	E Moira, è andata in vacanza in Spagna anche lei?
Sheelagh:	No, è andata in Svizzera.
Mirella:	Con chi?
Sheelagh:	Ci è andata con due amiche.
Mirella:	Dove sono state?
Sheelagh:	Sono state in pensione.
Mirella:	Quanto tempo ci sono rimaste?
Sheelagh:	Sette giorni.
Mirella:	Ci sono andate in aereo?
Sheelagh:	No, in traghetto e in treno.

C Give the students one minute to try to learn the first dialogue. They then cover it up and try to reconstruct the dialogue in pairs.
Repeat this procedure with the second dialogue.

Com'è andato il viaggio? (page 43)

Main aims: To ask others what kind of journey they have had
To say what kind of journey you have had

A Practise the phrases in the list, using a combination of familiar and new techniques, e.g.

• Present on the board or OHP the sentences in the list or variations on them. Underline half of them in red and the others in green. In pairs, the students each have two minutes only to copy one set. They then check their partners' work and try to help them to make any necessary corrections: their aim is to ensure that all their sentences are correct.

• Use the same list on the board or OHP, or a different list based on this one. Divide the class into two teams. A student from each team draws a ring round one word in the list for the students in the other team to copy. They then check each other's work to ensure that it is correct and count up the number of correct words in each team.

B Students look at the drawings and speculate on how they think the people described the journeys they had. A class consensus could be gathered before the students listen to the recording and compare their versions with how the Italians did the same task.

🔊 Com'è andato il viaggio?

Dialogo 1

Mother:	Ciao vieni caro, come stai?
Boy:	Ciao mamma, sto bene, grazie.
Mother:	Hai fatto buon viaggio?
Boy:	Sì, è stato perfetto. Il Concorde è un aereo stupendo.

Dialogo 2

Male cyclist:	Ciao Pietro. Eccoci!
Pietro:	Olà, salute. Ben tornati!
Female cyclist:	Ciao Pietro, dov'è mamma?
Pietro:	È in casa. Sentite, avete fatto buon viaggio?
Male cyclist:	Sì, è stato molto interessante.
Female cyclist:	È stato anche molto divertente.
Pietro:	Bene, entrate.

Dialogo 3

Mother:	Ciao Anna, vieni, vieni.
Anna:	Ciao mamma, come stai?
Mother:	Bene, e tu? Sei stanca, eh? Hai fatto buon viaggio?
Anna:	No, per niente. Si è rotto il pullman. Siamo rimasti per strada. È stato un disastro.
Mother:	Ahimè, poveretta!

Dialogo 4

Carletto, Antonia:	Ciao, nonna, come stai?
Grandma:	Ciao Carletto, ciao Antonia. Come state? Io sto benissimo. Avete fatto buon viaggio?
Carletto:	Veramente, nonna, il viaggio è stato noioso.
Antonia:	È vero. Però, siamo contenti di vederti, nonna.

Dialogo 5

Father:	Benvenuto, Fulvio. Vieni … Hai fatto buon viaggio?
Fulvio:	Ciao papà. Sì, sì, non c'era male.
Father:	Vieni. Tua madre sarà contenta di rivederti.

Dialogo 6

Mother:	Ciao cara, ben tornata. Come stai?
Girl:	Sono stanca, mamma.
Mother:	Come mai? Non hai fatto buon viaggio?
Girl:	Tutt'altro. È andato tutto male!
Mother:	Poveretta! Dammi la valigia, dai!

C The tape could be exploited further by getting pairs to reconstruct the dialogues they have heard. A few prompts could be provided.

Concorso lettori (page 44)

Main aim: **To develop reading and writing skills on the topic of a day on holiday**

A To develop skimming techniques, give a brief description of three or four of the letters: the students read them as quickly as possible to find the letter you have summarised, e.g.

– This woman went to the mountains. She had a lovely day with her children and grandchildren.

– This boy visited all the main cities of Italy in one day. How did he do it?

– This boy went on a day trip which was a disaster.

– This girl took her parents skiing and she won't be doing it again!

B You could continue the above exercise in Italian, e.g.

– Questa ragazza ha conosciuto il suo ragazzo ideale in spiaggia.

– Questa signora è arrivata in ritardo ad un appuntamento molto importante.

– Questa ragazza ha fatto brutta figura a causa dei suoi genitori.

– Questo ragazzo è andato in gita con la scuola, ma tutto è andato male.

This time, when a student finds the letter, ask the class to read it again and to pick out the main points in it.

C Each student selects one letter and then picks out three to five key expressions in it; the expressions which convey the most important information. They then try to teach these to a partner.

D Work with the class on the activities suggested under the letters.

E Give each student a copy of Copymaster 29. Make sure that they all understand the information that Christine is looking for. They then look for this and prepare to explain it all in English, as Christine would do to her parents.

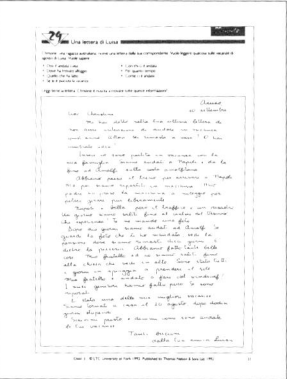

Statistica vacanze (page 45)

Main aim: **To develop the ability to understand and use the perfect tense**

A Organise a few minutes of verb circle practice, e.g.

– Sono andato a Rimini.

– È stato in albergo.

– Non siamo rimasti a Parigi.

B Give the students just one minute to get the gist of this item. Then ask questions to develop their ability to scan, e.g.

– How many Germans (Spaniards, etc.) went to Rimini last year?
– How many Danes (Greeks, etc.) went to Rimini this year?

After a short while, switch to using Italian for this.

C Give the students time to read the ten statements and to decide whether each is true or false. Then read each one aloud and invite students to say if it is true or false. When a statement is false, encourage the students to correct it.

D Present on the board or OHP six to eight incomplete sentences, e.g.

– L'anno scorso ci sono stati 65.011 turisti dall' ...

The students complete these orally. They could then copy and complete them in their exercise books.

Siamo rimasti proprio delusi (page 45)

Main aim: To develop listening skills on the topic of problems encountered on holiday

A The students practise anticipating what people will say. They look at the pictures and guess the sorts of things that the people concerned will say. They could write these in their exercise books: on the left they could write a summary, in English or Italian, of what they expect the people to say and, on the right, some of the Italian words and expressions they expect to hear.

B Play each recording twice so that the students can compare their predictions with what happened. Discuss the results and use this as an opportunity to encourage the students and to help them to improve their anticipation techniques.

🔊 Siamo rimasti proprio delusi

Numero 1

Presenter: E adesso, gentili telespettatori, vi presento un ragazzo di sedici anni, che si chiama Mauro Bontempi. A febbraio, Mauro è partito, con dei compagni di scuola, a fare una breve vacanza di sci. Sentiamo quello che ci racconta Mauro.

Mauro: È andato tutto male. Il viaggio è stato lungo e noioso ed è piovuto sempre. Poi, la prima mattina, ci siamo alzati presto, abbiamo indossato tutta la roba da sci, e via, ma ci aspettava una brutta sorpresa. Non c'era neve! – e in ogni caso lo skilift era chiuso e siamo dovuti tornare in albergo. È stato così, per tutti e cinque i giorni. Che delusione! Ci siamo rimasti proprio male.

Numero 2

Presenter: Che tristezza, Mauro! ... E adesso una famiglia. I Graziani ed i loro quattro figli sono andati al mare. A voi il signor Franco che vi dirà il resto ... Prego, venga, venga.

Franco Graziani: L'anno scorso, abbiamo deciso di prendere un appartamentino al mare: di quelli dove si fa tutto da soli. Come ha detto Lei, eravamo in sei, ma sa quale è stata la prima cosa che abbiamo visto? Beh, di mobili non c'era quasi niente: un tavolo ... piccolo ... un tavolino insomma, e due sedie, sì, dico bene, due! Abbiamo dovuto mangiare per terra; fare il picnic in casa! Però, sono stati gentili. Ci hanno lasciato un piatto e una tazza.

Presenter: E le posate? Coltelli, forchette?

Franco Graziani: Macchè. Non ce n'erano per niente!

Numero 3

Presenter: Una storia non proprio piacevole ... Ora abbiamo una giovane coppia, Marco e Linda. È Linda che vi parlerà. A Lei.

Linda: Grazie. Solo un mese fa, io e Marco siamo andati via qualche giorno per riposarci. Un giorno abbiamo voluto fare una scampagnata. Allora, abbiamo preso una macchina a noleggio. Eravamo per strada da un'ora, un'oretta, quando ... Boum! ... si è sentito questo rumore orrendo, tremendo. Naturalmente siamo scesi subito. C'era del fumo dappertutto, e per di più, c'era una gomma a terra. Un disastro! Ci sono volute quattro ore per tornare al deposito macchine. E sa che cosa ci hanno detto? Che la colpa era nostra!

Numero 4

Presenter: Grazie, Linda. Speriamo che vi rimborsino ... E per terminare, vi presento gli Aliboni: madre, padre e figlioletto. Portavoce questa volta è la signora Aliboni ... Signora, prego.

Signora Aliboni: Anche noi siamo stati al mare. Parlo dell'anno scorso. Siamo stati in un albergo molto noto. Il primo choc è stato la camera ... piccolissima, anzi minuscola. E poi, in questa camera c'era un letto solo; un letto matrimoniale, per tre persone! Secondo il dépliant tutte le camere avevano vista panoramica. Però, da noi si vedeva ... un parcheggio ... vastissimo! Insomma, non funzionava niente. Il televisore era rotto, e non funzionava neanche la doccia. Siamo rimasti proprio delusi.

C Encourage the students to say who was most disappointed and why: they should justify their choice.

Adesso, tocca a te! (page 46)

Main aim: To demonstrate that the language of this unit has been mastered

Exercise 1

Language area: Holidays
Skill area: Listening

Encourage the students to familiarise themselves thoroughly with the task before they listen: this will help them to listen for what they need to understand.

Adesso, tocca a te!

You:	My parents are going to the States next month.
Friend:	I wish I could go.
Woman:	Scusi, giovanotto. Capisco un po' l'inglese ma non lo parlo. Lei parla italiano?
You:	Sì, signora.
Woman:	Parlavate dell'America? Sono tornata da lì due giorni fa. Ci sono stata in vacanza con mio marito.
You:	Le è piaciuta, signora?
Woman:	Sì, moltissimo. Siamo andati da New York fino in Florida in macchina.
You:	Quanto tempo ci siete rimasti?
Woman:	Una ventina di giorni ... sì, venti giorni.
You:	E come ci siete arrivati dall'Italia?
Woman:	Ci siamo andati in aereo. Infatti, abbiamo preso il Concorde a Parigi ... È meraviglioso, sa. Le hostess sono così gentili. È stato un viaggio perfetto.
You:	E ha detto che vi sono piaciuti gli Stati Uniti?
Woman:	Sì, come ho detto, siamo andati in macchina dal nord fino al sud. La notte siamo stati nei motel. Sa, costano poco e ce ne sono tanti.
You:	Ed il mangiare americano - Le è piaciuto?
Woman:	A me, sì, è piaciuto. Però, mio marito e il fast food ... non vanno d'accordo!
You:	Ah, molto interessante, signora.
Friend:	What was she saying? ...

Exercise 2

Language area: Holidays
Skill area: Reading

Again, make sure that the students study carefully the questions before they read the letter.

Exercise 3

Language area: Holidays
Skill area: Speaking

Encourage the students to work on this in a co-operative way, to help each other as much as possible and to take responsibility for their joint performance.

Exercise 4

Language area: Holidays
Skill area: Writing

Each student writes a card, using as much of the model as he/she wishes.

Ora sai (page 47)

Main aim: To act as a summary and reference point for the main language of this unit

After the students have worked on this alone, or in pairs, to make sure that they know everything in it, you could help them to consolidate this, e.g.

● They cover up the English. You call out the English equivalent of some of the Italian examples and the students race to find them and read them aloud. Then do this with variations of the examples e.g.

– I went to the seaside.
– We went there by plane.
– We stayed in a hotel.
– I stayed there for a week.

When the students realise how this works, they could continue this in pairs. Point out that this is a technique they could use regularly to help each other to learn and revise key words.

● The students study the English summaries and make sure that they could ask for, and give, all the information mentioned. They then all interview three people in the class (including you and the assistant) to get all this information from them.

Revision

1 Using Italian in the classroom (Book 1, Unit 2)

A Before the students come in, put a number of classroom objects (e.g. pens, pencils, erasers, books) and a few other small objects (e.g. keys, a glass, a cassette) under a cloth. Then play 'Bumps under the cloth'. Point to each bump in turn and ask:

– Che cos'è?

The students all write what they think it is or, e.g.

- Non lo so.
- Non mi ricordo.

Take the cloth away and ask students to identify each object. If more practice is needed, you could cover the objects again and play Kim's Game, e.g.

- Quante penne (matite, ecc.) ci sono?
- Di che colore è il libro?
- Dove sono le chiavi?

B You could organise a game of 'Il gioco degli spazi', e.g.

- Non ho _____ .
- Ha il mio _____ ?
- Hai la mia _____ ?
- Posso andare in _____ ?
- Può parlare più _____ ?
- Non è molto _____ .

2 Talking about homes and their location (Book 2, Unit 5)

A Present on the board or OHP some word puzzles, e.g.

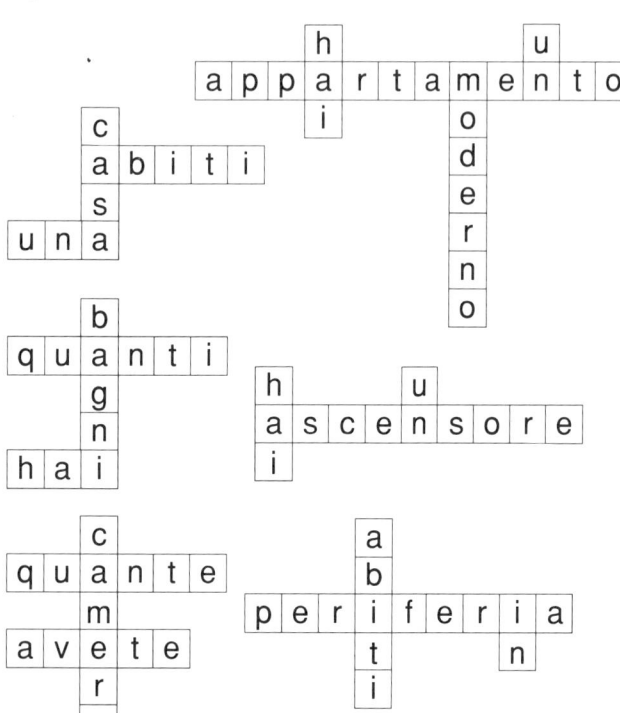

Tell the students that these are all questions about where people live. They work out what each question is, write it down and then write an answer. In pairs, they then put the questions to each other and answer them in turn.

B Give each student a copy of Copymaster 30. Working in pairs, they race to tick the expressions which are identical in each list and to put a cross by those which are different. After each list, they stop and check. Whoever has the more mistakes loses, even if he/she finished first. Speed only counts when neither has any mistakes or when both have the same number of mistakes.

3 Present tense of '-are' verbs (Book 2, Unit 5)

A Organise a few minutes of verb circle practice, e.g.

- Abito in campagna.
- Affitto un appartamento.
- Lavoro in giardino.

B Present the following questions on the board or OHP:

1 Dove abita Lei?
2 Chi ami?
3 Quali materie studi a scuola?
4 Che cosa mangi?
5 Scusi, quando mi porta il vino?
6 Da quanto tempo parla l'italiano?

The students read the questions and write the name of two people to whom they could put each one.
They then write how they would answer these questions.
In pairs, they practise asking and answering these questions.

4 Travelling by train (Book 3, Unit 1)

Present this dialogue on the board or OHP:

Tu: Scusi, quando parte il prossimo treno per Milano?
Bigliettaio: C'è un treno alle undici e trenta, signore.
Tu: Allora, due per Milano, andata e ritorno, seconda classe.
Bigliettaio: È un treno rapido, signore. C'è un supplemento di 2.000 lire.
Tu: D'accordo. Quant'è?
Bigliettaio: Sono 44.000 lire.

Tu: Ecco. Scusi, dov'è il deposito bagagli?
Bigliettaio: Dritto, poi a sinistra, e c'è un cartello.
Tu: Grazie. Dove posso aspettare il treno?
Bigliettaio: La sala d'attesa è vicino al deposito bagagli.
Tu: Grazie.
Bigliettaio: Prego.

The students play-read this in pairs and try to learn it. Then replace the full dialogue with this gapped version, containing just the key words:

Tu: ___ , quando ___ ___ ___ ___ ___ Milano?
Bigliettaio: ___' ___ ___ ___ ___ undici ___ trenta, ___.
Tu: ___ , due ___ ___ , andata ___ ___ , seconda ___.
Bigliettaio: ___ ___ ___ rapido, ___. ___' ___ ___
             ___ ___ 2.000 ___ .
Tu: ___' ___. Quant' ___?
Bigliettaio: ___ 44.000 ___.
Tu: ___. ___ , dov'è ___ ___ ___?
Bigliettaio: Dritto, ___ ___ ___ , ___ ___ ' ___ ___
             cartello.
Tu: ___. ___ ___ aspettare ___ ___ ?
Bigliettaio: ___ ___ ___ ' attesa ___ vicino ___ ___ ___.
Tu: ___.
Bigliettaio: ___.

The students practise acting the dialogue, with only the key words as cues. This technique can be used with other topics. It can help to overcome the problems (of pronunciation and intonation, for example) often associated with reading dialogues, and the stumbling and forgetting often associated with trying to manage without any text. Use only the key words in the gapped version so that if the students emphasise these it will not sound too unnatural.

5 Present tense of regular '-are', '-ere' and '-ire' verbs (Book 3, Unit 1)

A You could work again on some of the explanations and exercises in *Scoprite qualcosa di più* (pages 154-158). The students should find these very easy now and this should be a source of encouragement.

B Organise a few minutes of verb circle practice, e.g.

- Compro due biglietti per Roma.
- Leggo l'orario dei treni.
- Parto con il treno delle due.

C Play a game of 'La frase magica'. You write a simple sentence on a piece of paper and give one to each student. When the students have seen their sentences they must keep them secret. In pairs, they begin a conversation. Each student

tries to steer the conversation in a direction which will allow him/her to bring in his/her sentence in a sensible way. The first to do so is the winner.
Sentences could include, e.g.

- Mia sorella dorme in una camera piccola.
- Guardo la televisione in soggiorno.
- Vendiamo il nostro appartamento.
- Scrivo con una penna rossa.
- Prendo una camera in albergo.
- Il treno parte fra cinque minuti.
- Il treno arriva con trenta minuti di ritardo.
- Compro due biglietti di andata e ritorno.
- Lasciamo le valigie al deposito bagagli.
- Ti do questa matita.
- Mangiamo in cucina.
- Aspettiamo il treno nella sala d'attesa.
- Gioco a tennis nel parco.
- Do il mio compito al professore.
- Lavoro in giardino.
- Pago il conto dell'albergo.
- Parliamo italiano.
- Mangio sempre nella sala da pranzo.

6 Direct object pronoun after 'ecco' (Book 3, Unit 4)

A In pairs, and individually, the students revise *Ora sai* on page 47 of the Students' Book. As they do so, move around listening. Keep a note of the most commonly used techniques. Report back on this and discuss your findings with the class.

B Divide the class into two teams. Keeping up a very fast pace, ask where things in the class are, e.g.

- Dov'è la porta?
- Dove sono i poster?
- Dov'è il televisore?
- Dove sono le finestre?
- Dove sono i libri?
- Dov'è il registratore?

The first student to point to the object(s) and to reply correctly wins a team point, e.g.

- Eccolo.

You could, while maintaining the fast pace, occasionally ask for something which is not in the class, e.g.

- Dov'è la macchina?
- Dove sono gli alberi?
- Dov'è il professore/la professoressa?
- Dov'è la casa?

7 Booking hotel accomadation (Book 3, Unit 4)

A Present the following on the board or OHP.

Students copy this in the middle of a page in their exercise book. Give them five minutes to write on each hook a word connected with a hotel. If necessary, let them consult the Students' Book.

In pairs, they compare the words they have written, e.g.

— one reads aloud his/her words and the other underlines on his/her list all the words they have in common;
— the same student reads his/her words again and the other writes any words which he/she does not have;
— they count up the number of different words they have written.

B Work with the class on Copymaster 31 along the lines suggested.

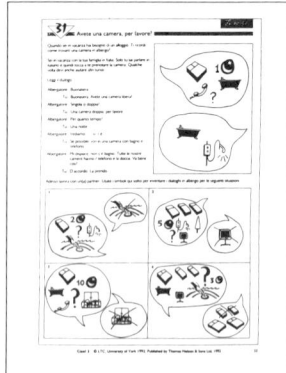

6ª Unità
ALLA STAZIONE DI SERVIZIO

Main aims

~ To be able to buy petrol
~ To be able to ask for essential services
~ To be able to check your route
~ To be able to buy drinks, snacks and maps, etc

Materials

~ Tape
Il pieno, per favore (Teacher's Book page 74)
Mi può controllare l'olio, per favore (Teacher's Book page 75)
Sono cortesi? (Teacher's Book page 76)
Che cosa comprano? Quanto spendono? (Teacher's Book page 76)
È questa la strada per Arezzo? (Teacher's Book page 77)
Non si sente (Teacher's Book page 78)
Quanto è lontana Arezzo? (Teacher's Book page 78)
Adesso, tocca a te! (Teacher's Book page 79)

~ Copymasters 32–35

Grammar in *Scoprite qualcosa di più*

~ Indirect object pronouns

Revision

~ Obtaining information about places in town and opening times (Book 1, Unit 3)
~ Definite articles: il, l', la (Book 1, Unit 3)
~ Buying presents and souvenirs (Book 2, Unit 6)
~ Agreement of adjectives (Book 2, Unit 6)
~ Interests and personality (Book 3, Unit 2)
~ Comparative adjectives (Book 3, Unit 2)
~ Talking about a recent holiday (Book 3, Unit 5)

Vocabulary

A: Productive

la benzina	la gomma
una bibita	una lattina
le caramelle	normale
una cartina della regione	l'olio
chiedere la strada	il parabrezza
controllare	il pieno
un distributore	la pressione delle gomme
fare benzina	senza piombo
i fazzoletti di carta	una stazione di servizio
il gasolio	super

B: Receptive

un(') automobilista	l'incrocio
la benzinaia	la nafta
il benzinaio	ne manca un po'
il bivio	il semaforo
un(a) giornalista	sporco

Alla stazione di servizio (page 48)

Main aim: **To present the main aims and some of the key language of this unit**

A Ask the students to read this page to find out the goals of the unit. Then discuss with them when they will find this useful.

B The students look at the photos on this page and look for any similarities or differences between this Italian petrol station and petrol stations where they live. Encourage and help them to make these comparisons in Italian. After some minutes of this, they should read the next section in the Students' Book to see if this confirms their first impressions.

Le stazioni di servizio in Italia (page 48)

Main aims: **To develop reading skills**

To present information about petrol stations in Italy

A Before the students read this, their curiosity should be aroused by work on the photos on this page. When they have read this page, ask, e.g.

— if their ideas have changed at all
— what they have found out about Italian petrol stations.

B Practise scan reading techniques by asking the students to answer, as quickly as possible, such questions as:

— Are most petrol stations self-service?
— What is the person who serves you called?
— What is 'senza piombo'?
— What do vehicles with diesel engines use?
— Give two ways of buying petrol.
— Name two things sold in the shops.
— Give the name of one Italian petrol company.

C Practise some higher level reading skills by asking, e.g.

— What four sorts of fuel can you buy?
— Find two Italian words for diesel fuel.
— How would you ask for petrol?
— How much in (your local currency) do Italians normally spend when buying petrol?

D The students could be encouraged to draw cultural conclusions based on this information, e.g. to consider why there are not many self-service petrol stations and what effects this may have on employment and costs.

E Give each student a copy of Copymaster 32. They first tick using a pencil. Then go over the quiz orally, discussing each question. Invite several students to complete the sentence. The students then complete the quiz. If possible, give a small prize to the best replies.

Answers:

1	falso
2	falso
3	vero
4	falso
5	falso
6	falso
7	vero
8	vero
9	falso
10	falso

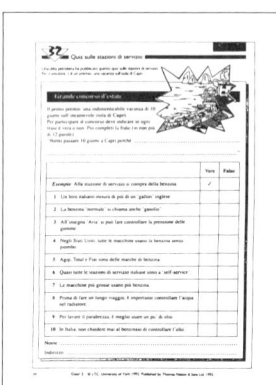

F Ask the students to choose the ten words on this page which they think are the most useful. They write and illustrate these in their books and then compare the words they have chosen.

Il pieno, per favore (page 49)

Main aim: To practise buying petrol

A The students read the dialogues silently and then ask about anything they do not understand. Praise students who ask questions. When everyone understands everything, play the recordings: the students listen and follow the texts in their book. Play the tape again, stopping after each sentence for the students to repeat: let them refer to their books as they do this. They then play-read the two dialogues in pairs.

Il pieno, per favore

Dialogo 1

Client:	Buongiorno.
Attendant:	Buongiorno.
Client:	Mi dà trentamila lire di benzina senza piombo, per favore? ... Tenga ...
Attendant:	Grazie, signora.
Client:	ArrivederLa.
Attendant:	ArrivederLa. Buon viaggio.

Dialogo 2

Attendant:	Buonasera.
Client:	Buonasera. Mi fa il pieno di super, per favore ...
Attendant:	25.400 L. signore.
Client:	Ecco.
Attendant:	Grazie. Buon viaggio.
Client:	Grazie. Arrivederci.

B Work on the substitution table with the class: see how many different requests they can make up from it in two minutes. They could then try to improve on this score.

C In pairs, the students adapt the two dialogues to make up more of their own. Make sure that both students play both roles.

D Base a memory game on the cartoon. Give the students one minute to study it and then ask them questions about it which they try to answer with the Students' Book shut, e.g.

- Si vende super (benzina senza piombo, gasolio) qui?
- Dov'è la toilette?

The students then open the Students' Book and answer the same questions.

E Spend a few minutes revising numbers:

- Write on the board some 'magic crosses', e.g.

	1.000				3.000		
3.000	5.000			7.000	9.000	2.000	
	4.000						

					12.000		
25.000	30.000	5.000		14.000		16.000	
	10.000				18.000		

The students tell you what number to write in each empty square. (The number in the middle is the sum of the two other numbers in the row.) They can then do more of their own in pairs.

- Play 'Chinese Whispers' (see Teacher's Book page 6) Pass a number along each row. Each student whispers the number to the next one and then writes down the number. At the end the starting number is compared with the one at the end. If they are different, ask students to read the numbers they wrote. You will then find where changes were made.

Mi può controllare l'olio, per favore? (page 49)

Main aim: To practise asking for other essential services at a petrol station

A The students study the pictures and the tables. You could then:

• Make up some sentences based on the tables and ask the students to say which picture each sentence goes with, e.g.

– Mi può controllare l'acqua, per favore.

– Numero due.

– Manca un po' l'olio.

– Numero uno.

• Ask the students to make up, and read aloud, as many sentences as they can for each picture, using the tables. They then read the model dialogue silently, listen to the recording as they follow the text, then listen and repeat. In pairs, they then play-read the dialogue, reading both roles. Work on the first set of symbols with the class so that everyone understands what they represent and how to use them. Draw other combinations on the board and ask a pair of students to demonstrate how to make up a dialogue based on them. The students can then work on the four sets of symbols that follow.

🎞 Mi può controllare l'olio, per favore?

Client:	Buongiorno. Mi può controllare l'acqua, per favore?
Attendant:	Certo signore ... l'acqua va bene. Vuole altro?
Client:	Mi può controllare anche l'olio?
Attendant:	Sì ... un momento ... Ne manca un po'. Adesso va bene.
Client:	Quanto Le devo?
Attendant:	4.200 lire, per favore.
Client:	Ecco. Grazie mille. Arrivederci.
Attendant:	Arrivederci. Buon viaggio.

B The technically minded may like to know that tyre pressures in Italy are measured in kg/cm². To help them to cope with this, you could present the table below on the board, omitting the kg/cm² figures. Invite students to guess these and write in their guesses. Then write the correct figures, saying them aloud as you do so and comparing the two, e.g.

– Il numero giusto è (molto) più grande (meno grande).

Tyre pressures								
lb/sq.in.	20	22	24	26	28	30	32	34
kg/sq.cm.	1.41	1.55	1.69	1.83	1.97	2.11	2.25	2.39

Now would be a good point to begin work on *Scoprite qualcosa di più* (pages 158-161).

Scusi, mi può lavare il parabrezza? (page 50)

Main aim: To practise asking for services at a petrol station

A The students read the text to themselves and ask about anything they do not understand. You could then ask, e.g.

– Secondo voi, chi è più cortese?
meno cortese?

Encourage several students to answer each question and encourage them to disagree with each other. Do not, at this stage, say who is right.

Each student writes the five sentences in what they think is the right order, starting with the most courteous. You then reveal the correct order and give any necessary explanations.
It would be a good idea to clarify the following points:

– the usefulness of 'scusi' and 'per favore'

– the shorter the request, the more rude it sounds

– 'mi può' and 'mi potrebbe' are the same, but 'mi potrebbe' is slightly gentler/more polite

– that 'over-the-top' politeness is inappropriate and might seem rude.

Students could start collecting useful 'formule di cortesia', e.g.

– Disturbo?

– Non si disturbi.

– Non doveva disturbarsi.

It is important they understand the context for each of them.

B Give each student a copy of Copymaster 33. Before playing the recording, ensure that everyone understands what they are to do. After each dialogue, ask, e.g.

– Com'è stata la cliente?

Clear up any problems and play the dialogue again before going on to the next one.
When they have heard all the dialogues, the students decide which client was the most and least polite. Ask various pairs which they have chosen for each. If there is any disagreement, play the recordings again and see if agreement can be reached.

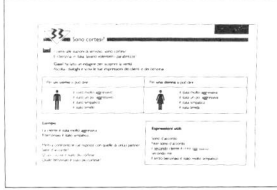

🔊 Sono cortesi?

Dialogo I

Woman: Mi faccia il pieno di super.
Attendant: Certo, signora. Le serve altro?
Woman: Lavi il parabrezza.
Attendant: D'accordo, signora. Subito.

Dialogo 2

Man: Il parabrezza è sporco. Non vedo niente. Me lo lavi?
Attendant: Sì, signore.
Man: Basta così ... ho fretta ... devo andare.
Attendant: Sì, signore. Buon viaggio, signore.

Dialogo 3

Attendant: Dica.
Woman: Scusi, mi potrebbe controllare l'olio e la pressione delle gomme?
Attendant: Vuole anche della benzina?
Woman: Sì. Mi metta ventimila lire di normale, per favore.
Attendant: Sì ...
Woman: Per cortesia, mi può lavare il parabrezza?
Attendant: Ma guarda questa ... prima l'olio poi le gomme ... adesso che vuole?!

Dialogo 4

Attendant: Buongiorno, signore. Cosa Le posso dare?
Man: Mi potrebbe fare il pieno di normale, per cortesia?
Attendant: Certo, signore. Le serve altro?
Man: Se non disturbo, il parabrezza è un po' sporco.
Attendant: Ma signore, glieLo lavo. Un attimo che prendo uno straccio.
Man: Grazie.
Attendant: Non c'è di che, signore.

Dialogo 5

Man: Buongiorno. Mi dia quarantamila lire di gasolio, per cortesia.
Attendant: Faccio il pieno?
Man: No, no, grazie. Basta quarantamila.
Attendant: Quarantamila. Va bene.
Man: Devo andare un attimo alla toilette. Mi potrebbe lavare il parabrezza, per favore?
Attendant: Uffa!
Man: Signorina. Lasci stare. Faccio io.

C The students look again at page 49 of the Students' Book. Ask them to adapt orally the expressions there to ask for other jobs to be done, e.g. checking the oil, water and tyres, and buying petrol.

Each student then prepares a request and reads it aloud. The others have to say what he/she wants and how politely he/she has asked for it, e.g.

– Kate ha chiesto al benzinaio di controllare l'olio ed è stata abbastanza/molto cortese.
– Tony ha chiesto al benzinaio di controllare l'acqua ed è stato abbastanza/molto scortese.

Avete delle caramelle? (page 50)

Main aim: To practise buying sweets, drinks, maps, etc. at a petrol station

A The students read *Avete delle caramelle?* on page 50 of the Students' Book and ask about anything they do not understand. Several students volunteer to identify all the items illustrated in ten seconds. They then work in pairs to adapt the dialogue to buy three different things.

B Students write two headings in their exercise books: 'articoli' and 'costo totale'.
Play the recording *Che cosa comprano? Quanto spendono?* as often as students need. They note down what each person buys and how much they spend in all.

🔊 Che cosa comprano? Quanto spendono?

Dialogo I

Client: Buongiorno.
Assistant: Buongiorno. Desidera?
Client: Avete delle bibite?
Assistant: Sì, quante lattine vuole?
Client: Tre lattine, per favore ... Vorrei anche una cartina della regione.
Assistant: Certo. È tutto?
Client: Mi dà anche due pacchetti di caramelle ... Grazie ... Quant'è?
Assistant: Tre lattine, una cartina, due pacchetti di caramelle ... Novemilaottocento lire, signore ... Grazie ... Arrivederci.

Dialogo 2

Client: Buongiorno.
Assistant: Buongiorno.
Client: Due pacchetti di patatine, per favore.
Assistant: Ecco. Millecinquecento lire ... Grazie.
Client: Buongiorno.

Dialogo 3

Client:	Vorrei due litri di olio, per piacere, e questa cartina automobilistica.
Assistant:	Questa qui?
Client:	Sì. Quanto costa?
Assistant:	Seimila lire.
Client:	Va bene, la prendo. Quant'è in tutto?
Assistant:	Due litri d'olio ... la cartina automobilistica ... dodicimila lire, per favore.
Client:	Tenga.
Assistant:	Grazie. Ecco il resto.
Client:	Grazie. Arrivederci.

Dialogo 4

Client:	Buongiorno. Avete dei fazzoletti di carta?
Assistant:	Certo signore. Da duemila o da ottocento?
Client:	Un pacchetto da ottocento ...
Assistant:	Vuole altro?
Client:	Sì, prendo questa lattina di coca cola e anche un pacchetto di caramelle.
Assistant:	Bene, questo fa mille per la coca cola, milleottocento le caramelle ... tremilaseicento lire. Grazie.
Client:	Grazie. Buongiorno.

Dialogo 5

Client:	Buongiorno signore. Senta, avete delle cartine della regione?
Assistant:	Ho queste qui da quattromila lire.
Client:	Sì, va bene, ne prendo una ... grazie.
Assistant:	È tutto?
Client:	Sì ... no. Mi dà quattro pacchetti di patatine. Quanto Le devo?
Assistant:	Tremila e quattromila ... sono settemila lire. Grazie.

Dialogo 6

Client:	Buongiorno. Mi dia un litro d'olio, per favore.
Assistant:	Un litro d'olio, ecco signora.
Client:	Avete delle bibite?
Assistant:	Sì, c'è la coca cola, la fanta ...
Client:	Due lattine di coca cola e tre lattine di fanta ... Grazie.
Assistant:	Basta così?
Client:	Quanto costano queste caramelle?
Assistant:	Queste sono da milleduecento lire.
Client:	Le prendo, grazie. Quant'è in tutto?
Assistant:	Tremila ... cinque ... otto ... novemiladuecento lire, signora ... duecento, cinque, diecimila.
Client:	Grazie.
Assistant:	Grazie a Lei. Buon viaggio.

Quanto è lontana Arezzo? (page 51)

Main aim: **To practise asking the distance to somewhere and understanding the answer**

A Give each student a copy of Copymaster 34. Make sure that everyone understands it and knows what the main task is, i.e. to work out the meaning of the four words from what they hear.
Play the recording *È questa la strada per Arezzo?* once or twice.

Ask what each word means, and also ask students how they worked it out.

Use the map to practise asking the way and giving directions. You and the students could ask each other for directions to Perugia, the motorway to Rome, etc.

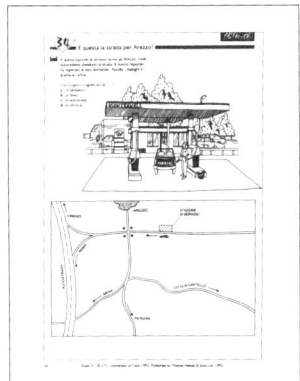

🔊 È questa la strada per Arezzo?

Dialogo 1

- Scusi, è questa la strada per Arezzo?
- Sì, giri a destra al semaforo.
- Grazie.
- Prego.

Dialogo 2

- Scusi, è questa la strada per Firenze?
- Sì, vada sempre dritto al semaforo, poi al bivio giri a destra. Dopo un po', arriva in autostrada.
- Grazie tanto.
- Di niente.

Dialogo 3

- Scusi, è questa la strada per Siena?
- No, giri a sinistra al semaforo, e poi all'incrocio giri a destra.
- A sinistra al semaforo, a destra all'incrocio?
- Esatto.
- Grazie. Buongiorno.

B Write the following incomplete dialogues on the OHP or board and introduce them, e.g.

– Alcuni turisti chiedono la strada. Guardate bene la cartina (Copymaster 34) e completate le domande e le risposte.

1 – Per favore, è questa la _____ per Firenze?
– Sì, vada sempre _____ . Dopo il semaforo c'è un bivio.
– Al _____ giri a _____ .
2 – Scusi, è questa la strada per Arezzo?
– Sì, giri a _____ al _____ .

C While the students look at the map on Copymaster 34, they listen to the following recording *Non si sente*. Introduce it in this way:

– A questo punto, un camion ha cominciato a fare molto rumore. Non si sente tutto. Potete indovinare le parole che mancano?

Stop the tape after each interruption by the lorry and ask the students to say what the missing words are. At the end of each dialogue, play it again without pauses and let the students try to say the missing words above the lorry noises. Repeat this to give them a chance to improve.

🔊 Non si sente

Dialogo 1

Client:	Mi scusi, è questa la strada per Perugia?
Attendant:	Sì, giri a sinistra al semaforo, poi vada sempre (dritto).
Client:	A (sinistra) al semaforo, poi sempre dritto?
Attendant:	Esatto.
Client:	Grazie.

Dialogo 2

Client:	Scusi signorina, è questa la (strada) per Roma?
Attendant:	Sì, vada sempre dritto. Dopo il (semaforo) c'è un bivio. Al bivio giri a (sinistra).
Client:	Grazie.
Attendant:	Prego.

Dialogo 3

Client:	Per favore, è questa la strada per Città di (Castello)?
Attendant:	No, deve girare a (sinistra) al semaforo e ancora a sinistra all'incrocio.
Client:	Scusi, può ripetere? Non si sente.
Attendant:	Giri a sinistra al (semaforo) e ancora a sinistra all' (incrocio).
Client:	Va bene. Grazie.
Attendant:	Buon viaggio!

D The students look at page 51 of the Students' Book. Before they try to complete the dialogues, revise the numbers they will need: as they look at the map, call out some of the numbers on it, saying each one several times while the students look for it and point to it.

They could also do some mental arithmetic by completing such sums as:

23 più 17 fa ...
20 più 18
24 più 12
43 più 33
69 più 20
19 più 32

When they have prepared their answers, they could play-read them in pairs. They then listen to the recording of *Quanto è lontana Arezzo?* and check the answers given.

🔊 Quanto è lontana Arezzo?

Dialogo 1
– Scusi, quanto è lontana Città di Castello?
– Circa diciotto chilometri.

Dialogo 2
– Per favore, mi sa dire quanto dista Arezzo?
– Trentotto chilometri, circa.
– Grazie.

Dialogo 3
– Scusi, mi sa dire quanto è lontana Bibbiena?
– Bibbiena è molto lontana, una cinquantina di chilometri.

Dialogo 4
– Buonasera. A che distanza siamo da Perugia, per favore?
– Da Perugia? Circa sessanta chilometri.
– Grazie.
– Di niente.

E You and the students ask each other about distances from one place to another on the map. When this gets too easy, try doing it without looking at the map!

This would be a suitable time to continue work on *Scoprite qualcosa di più* (pages 158-161).

Adesso, tocca a te! (page 52)

Main aim: To demonstrate that the language of this unit has been mastered

Exercise I

Language areas: Buying petrol and other goods; asking the way
Skill areas: Listening and speaking

Work on the example with the class to ensure that everyone knows what to do. The students then help each other to make up similar dialogues based on the other four drawings.

Exercise 2

Language area: Understanding directions
Skill area: Listening

Give each student a copy of Copymaster 35.
Then play the recording *Come si fa per andare ad Arezzo?*. The students have to follow the directions they are given, on the map, and mark the road to Arezzo. Play the tape twice.

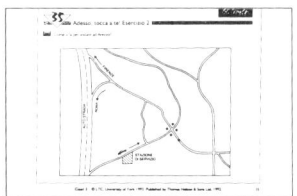

📻 Adesso, tocca a te!

Tourist:	Scusi, per favore, come si fa per arrivare ad Arezzo?
Attendant:	Arezzo? Allora, signorina, vada sempre dritto, sempre dritto, fino al semaforo. Al semaforo deve girare a destra. Poi c'è un incrocio. All'incrocio giri a sinistra, poi dopo un chilometro, al bivio, giri ancora a sinistra.
Tourist:	Allora, sempre dritto fino al semaforo, poi a destra, poi a sinistra e ancora a sinistra?
Attendant:	Esatto. Non dimentichi di girare a sinistra all'incrocio.
Tourist:	Grazie.
Attendant:	Di niente. Buongiorno.

Ora sai (page 53)

Main aim: To act as a summary and reference point for the main language of this unit

A The students look at the Italian expressions and read out to you, e.g.

- expressions they would probably hear when in Italy
- expressions they would probably say
- expressions they would probably read
- expressions they would probably say if they worked at a petrol station.

B Invite the students to pick out and tell you, e.g.

- the words here which they really like the sounds of
- the words which they found easy to learn
- the words which they found hard to learn
- the three words they consider to be most useful
- any words or phrases from the unit which are not here and which should be.

C Call out, in random order, the English equivalents of words and phrases in the list. The students race to find the Italian words and to say them to you. They could continue this in pairs.

Revision

I Obtaining information about places in town and opening times (Book 1, Unit 3)

A Use your foreign language assistant for this, or a student on teaching practice, if possible. He/she asks for advice from the class on the best places locally to buy certain things and at what times the shops recommended are open, e.g.

Assistant:	Vorrei comprare una cartina della regione.
Student:	Devi andare ad una stazione di servizio.
Assistant:	C'è una stazione di servizio qui vicino?
Student:	Sì. Ce n'è una a 200 metri da scuola.
Assistant:	Da che ora è aperta? Chiude a che ora?

The assistant/student could be briefed to ask for certain items, e.g.

Vorrei comprare una lattina di coca cola
dei fazzoletti di carta
un ombrello
una sciarpa
degli orecchini

B Draw on the OHP or board a simple plan of your town centre. Add to it some of the places which would interest Italian visitors. Invite the students to suggest other places and to say when they are open.

2 Definite articles: il, l', la (Book 1, Unit 3)

A One way for students to learn which article to use with each noun is for them to listen carefully to hear what Italians say. They can practise doing that now.

Divide the class into two teams. One team should stand (or put up their hands) whenever they hear 'il'. The others respond in the same way when they hear 'la'. No one moves when they hear 'l''.

You then say, with good pace, some important sentences containing one, or more than one, of these words, e.g.

- Il benzinaio può controllare la pressione delle gomme.
- Può anche lavare il parabrezza.
- Scusi, mi può controllare l'olio, per favore?
- Dov'è il mercato?
- Mi sa dire dov'è il campeggio?
- Dov'è la spiaggia, per favore?
- Mi piace la sciarpa rossa.
- Preferisco l'ombrello blu.
- Quanto viene la T-shirt?
- Ti piace la cintura nera?

B Present this grid for the students to copy:

	il	la	l'
1			
2			
3			
4			
5			
6			
7			
8			
9			
10			

They then listen to the sentences you read out and put a cross in the right box to show whether 'il', 'la' or 'l'' was used, e.g.

1 In Italia, la benzina si vende al litro o alla lira.
2 Buonasera. Mi fa il pieno di super, per favore.
3 Abbiamo visitato la città, il duomo e il battistero.
4 Ci sei andato con la scuola?
5 La mia professoressa d'inglese mi ha dato il tuo nome e indirizzo.
6 I miei sport preferiti sono il tennis, la pallavolo e il canottaggio.
7 Quanto viene l'ombrello nero?
8 Mi sa dire dov'è l'ufficio postale, per favore?
9 L'ufficio informazioni si trova in Via Cavour.
10 È questo l'autobus che va a Fiesole?

3 Buying presents and souvenirs (Book 2, Unit 6)

You could play 'Kim's game' with the class. Display 15–20 possible presents, or pictures or flashcards of possible presents. Talk about these for two to three minutes, identifying each item and writing the Italian for all of them on the board or OHP. Give the class two minutes to study the words and objects, then cover both. Give them three minutes to write down everything they can remember. Then show the words and objects again for two minutes, cover them and give the students two more minutes to add to their list.

4 Agreement of adjectives (Book 2, Unit 6)

Introduce the game 'La parola magica'.
You give a word to a student, written on a piece of paper. This student has to ask questions to get a partner, a group or the class to use the 'magic word' as often as possible in two minutes, without knowing what the word is.
To train the class to play this game (which is an excellent way of encouraging a flexible and creative use of language) do two or three with yourself asking the questions and anyone from the whole class answering. For these first two or three games, tell the class the word in advance. Then do two or three more without telling them what the word is until after each game. After this, two or three students can take over from you and take turns to put questions to the class. Words which could be used are:

bello	buono	sportivo
piccolo	verde	brutto
grande	bianco	serio
caro	interessante	perfetto
giovane	simpatico	

5 Talking about interests and personality (Book 3, Unit 2)

A The students write, in large green letters on a page of their exercise books, the word 'Sì'. In large red letters, they write on another page the word 'No'.
You ask a lot of questions about what they are like, or like doing: they hold up the appropriate word to reply. The replies will, of course, differ. Try to make this move quickly. Your questions can include, e.g.

- Ti piace andare al cinema?
- Ti piace giocare a calcio?
- Ti piace giocare a tennis?
- Ti piace giocare a pallavolo?
- Ti piace giocare con il computer?
- Ti piace ascoltare la musica?
- Ti piace guardare la televisione?
- Ti piace fare collezione di francobolli?
- Ti piace cucinare?

- Ti piace sciare?
- Sei timido(a)?
- Sei socievole?
- Sei maturo(a)?
- Sei sensibile?
- Sei allegro(a)?
- Sei calmo(a)?
- Sei simpatico(a)?
- Sei studioso(a)?
- Sei serio(a)?
- Sei sportivo(a)?

B Mime an activity which you like and which the students should know the Italian for. They guess, e.g.

- Ti piace guardare la televisione?

The first student to guess correctly can come and mime something which he/she likes doing. This game can continue in pairs.

C Present on the board a circle, e.g.

Ask the students to guess what goes in the other half, i.e. 'magro'. When someone guesses this, write it in. Then ask what goes in the following circles:

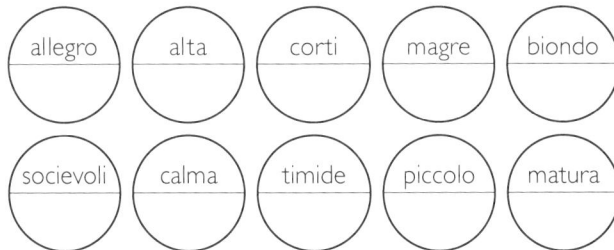

Each student should try to make up more to try on their partners and you.

6 Comparative adjectives (Book 3, Unit 2)

A Play a game of 'Vero o Falso?' The students say if each of your sentences is true or false, e.g.

- La Sicilia è più grande dell'Inghilterra.
- La Torre Pendente di Pisa è più alta della scuola.
- Una bicicletta è più rapida di una macchina.
- Un supermercato è più utile di un museo.
- Il calcio è più divertente di chimica.
- Mickey Mouse è più bello del professore di francese.
- Una discoteca è più grande di una piscina.
- Roma è più vecchia di Milton Keynes.
- Un gatto è più studioso del professore di spagnolo.

- Italiano è più facile di fisica.
- L'Italia è meno grande di America.
- L'Australia è meno grande di Scozia.
- Un pullman è meno comodo di una bicicletta.
- Il tennis è meno noioso di geografia.
- Il computer è meno utile di un gelato.
- Un castello è meno grande di un appartamento.
- Le vacanze sono meno divertenti della scuola.
- Un ombrello è meno caro di una maglia.
- Un treno è meno rapido di un aereo.
- Disegno è meno creativo di matematica.

B The students copy the words for these means of transport, listing them in order of speed:

la macchina	la bicicletta
il treno	l'autobus
l'aereo	il traghetto
il pullman	

Ask someone to read aloud the list he/she has written and encourage the others to question and disagree, e.g.

- Non sono d'accordo. Un pullman è meno rapido di una macchina.

Let the students decide who is right and who needs to correct their list.

The students could write similar lists for TV programmes (going from the most boring to the most interesting), places in town (going from the smallest to the biggest) and famous personalities (going from the least to the most good-looking).

7 Talking about a recent holiday (Book 3, Unit 5)

A Play a game of 'Ripetete se è vero'. You say some of the things you did last weekend, yesterday evening, or on a recent holiday. After each sentence, any student who did the same thing repeats what you said. The others remain silent. You could occasionally say to someone who remains silent, e.g.

- Non sei andata al cinema, ieri?

B Organise a few minutes of verb circle practice, e.g.

- Sono andato al mare.
- Non sono andato a Rimini.

C Present this grid, empty except for the letter E. Challenge everyone to write in it all the parts of 'essere' in five minutes, including the infinitive.

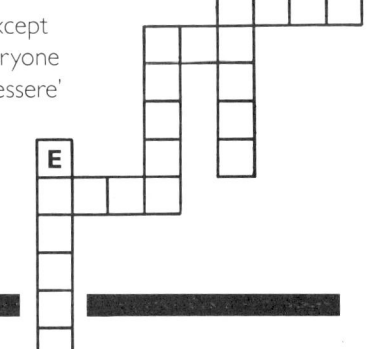

Main aims

~ To understand information about campsites
~ To book in at a campsite
~ To find your way around the site
~ To understand signs and notices
~ To settle the bill
~ To book accommodation at a campsite in advance

Materials

~ Tape
C'è ancora posto? (Teacher's Book page 85)
Si arriva (Teacher's Book page 86)
Dal nove al diciannove luglio (Teacher's Book page 87)
Al campeggio Rialto (Teacher's Book page 90)
Adesso, tocca a te! (Teacher's Book page 92)

~ Copymasters 36–40

~ A supply of lists of campsites, guide books and maps
  showing the location of campsites in Italy

Grammar in *Scoprite qualcosa di più*

~ Potere: present tense

Revision

~ Understanding and giving directions (Book 1, Unit 4)
~ Al, alla, all' (Book 1, Unit 4)
~ Irregular plurals of nouns (Book 2, Unit 7)
~ Town and region (Book 3, Unit 3)
~ Indirect object pronouns (Book 3, Unit 6)

Vocabulary

A: Productive

un adulto	una macchina
all'ombra	una piazzuola
un bambino	un posto
un campeggio	potere
un camper	prenotare
il campo da tennis	una settimana
il campo giochi	i servizi
fermarsi	sistemarsi
il locale ritrovo	lo spaccio
lontano da	una tenda

B: Receptive

il blocco servizi	una prenotazione
il campo da bocce	la presa luce
il gestore	la ricevuta
una guida	silenzio
in fondo	il tempo/per quanto tempo?
il lavandino	l'ufficio direzione
potabile	

In campeggio (page 54)

Main aim: To introduce the main objectives of this unit

A Ask if anyone in the class has been camping in Italy and, if so, to talk about it. You and the rest of the class could ask questions.

B Ask if anyone else has been camping anywhere else. Encourage them to talk about it so that those who have not camped get some idea of what is involved.

C Read through the introduction to the unit with the class. Make sure that everyone understands it and then ask, e.g.

– Trova una frase che ti da voglia di andare in un campeggio in Italia.

You could also ask the students to suggest other reasons why they would enjoy camping in Italy.

D Encourage the class to look at, and to talk about, the photo. Then ask them to work, in pairs or groups, to write a list of what they want to be able to say and understand to prepare for a camping trip to Italy. Take these in and study them: try to teach everything the students wish to know.

I campeggi in Italia (page 54)

Main aim: To find out how and where to find out about campsites in Italy

A The Touring Club Italiano (TCI) in conjunction with Federcampeggio, produces a guide book entitled 'Campeggi e villaggi turistici in Italia'. This is published yearly. It lists all sites approved by these organisations.

'I migliori campeggi d'Italia' in the series 'Tutto Turismo' is published by: Domus spa
Via Achile Grandi 5/7
20089 Rozzano (MI)

Federcampeggio produces a map showing and giving details of campsites, region by region.

Campsites listed by TCI/Federcampeggio are given a star rating (1-4 stars) on the basis of standards laid down by regional laws.

Discounts are usually available to TCI and FIC members and to holders of the International Camping Card or Carnet Camping International. In Britain, this is available through the AA.

B Give the students five minutes to read and study this information. Then allow them to ask you any questions about it and give them two more minutes to study it. They then close the Students' Book and try to answer your questions, e.g.

1 What is 'Campeggi e villaggi turistici in Italia'?
2 If you write to 'Federcampeggio', what will they send you?
3 Where can you get a list of campsites from?
4 How many campsites are there in Perugia?
5 Which one is open all year?
6 What is the address of the 'Ente Provinciale per il Turismo' in Arezzo?
7 What does Tom Eldridge ask for?
8 Who is he going camping with?

After you have discussed the students' answers and cleared up any problems, let them have two more minutes to read this information again.

C Ask the students to study the details of the sites in Perugia and, using the information given, describe them in as much detail as possible, in English. This will introduce them to the main symbols used.

D The students study the letter and answer your questions, e.g.

– Che cosa richiede Tom Eldridge?
– Con chi va in campeggio?
– Dove abita?

They then adapt the letter to say, e.g.

– I intend to go camping with my family.
– Please send me a list of the campsites near Assisi.

Com'è il campeggio? (page 55)

Main aims: To familiarise the students with some key vocabulary associated with talking about, and understanding details of, campsites

To develop communication strategies using visual clues

A Ask someone who has been camping what facilities there were. Write a list on the board in Italian.

Now look at the symbols shown here. Ask how many facilities on the Italian list are also on the list on the board.

B Encourage the students to deduce the meanings of the symbols, using the visual clues. Then ask if they can draw better symbols. Then, in pairs, they ask if their partners can tell them in Italian what their symbols represent.

C Each student writes the ten features which they would choose for their ideal site. They then see if their partners can guess which ten features they have chosen. They could also compare their lists with someone else's and then try to persuade him/her to change the features which they consider to be unimportant, e.g.

– È più importante avere uno spaccio che un ristorante.

D Ask the students which features they would look out for when selecting sites for these people.

a A family with two small children.
b An elderly couple.
c Some young people with no means of transport.
d A family where one child is allergic to animals.

Ask them to say which features are

a essential
b useful
c optional.

E Each student writes any four of the facilities in this list. You then play 'Tombola', with you reading the facilities in random order.

I campeggi in Toscana (page 55)

Main aim: To be able to understand essential information about campsites as set out in guide books

A The students practise scan reading to find the answers to your questions, e.g.

– Al Piano Orlando, quanto si paga la doccia calda?
– A che distanza dalla Verna c'è un distributore di benzina?
– Alla Fonte del Menchino c'è posto per quante persone?
– Al Capanno c'è posto per quante tende?

B Describe the needs of different campers. The students study this information and choose the best site for each, e.g.

– A mio zio piace la pesca, il nuoto. Gli piace anche giocare a calcio.
– Mia zia cerca un campeggio con spaccio, giochi per i bambini e docce calde.
– Il vostro professore vorrebbe fare una vacanza tranquilla; per quello sta cercando un campeggio dove non ci sono giochi per bambini.

C Give the class four minutes to study this information and then play a game of 'Vero o Falso?'

I   Il campeggio Il Capanno è più grande del campeggio La Verna.
2   Il Fonte del Menchino è aperto dal 15 giugno.
3   A Piano Orlando non ci sono posti all'ombra.
4   Ci sono più docce alla Verna che al Fonte del Menchino.
5   Non c'è molto da fare al Capanno.
6   Alla Verna non c'è uno spaccio in campeggio.
7   È una buona idea prenotare il posto alla Verna e al Capanno.
8   C'è un distributore di benzina a un chilometro di Piano Orlando.
9   Alla Verna e al Capanno non si vende gas liquido.
10 Una doccia calda al Fonte del Menchino costa 400 lire.

D You could base some question and answer work on this information to revise and practise superlatives and comparatives, e.g.

—   Qual è il campeggio più grande?
—   Qual è il campeggio più piccolo?
—   In quale campeggio ci sono più docce?
                                        lavandi?
                                        gruppi servizi? ecc.

E The teacher describes a number of facilities on a campsite. The students say which site it is. They could then play the same game in pairs, e.g.

Teacher: In questo campeggio c'è un bar. C'è un locale ritrovo. Vendono gas liquido. C'è un ristorante a un chilometro.
Student: È a Piano Orlando.
Teacher: Sì. Hai ragione. Adesso, tocca a te!

F Give each student a copy of Copymaster 36. This could be done as homework.

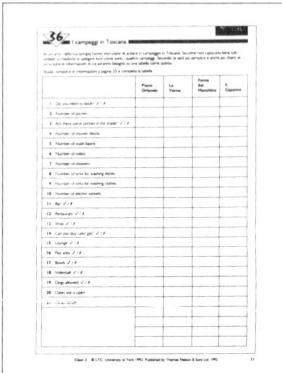

G The students now read the postcard and work out which site Michele and Fabrizio went to.

Encourage them to adapt the card orally to describe other things they could have done at the Fonte del Menchino site, and then at another site. Write on the board the key expressions.
Able students could now imagine that they are at one of the other sites: they write a card saying what they have done there and what they plan to do tomorrow.

Listino prezzi (page 56)

Main aim: To present and practise the key language needed for booking in at a campsite

A Present the following on the board or OHP. The students work out the meaning of the words which are underlined, e.g.

—   Costa 4.500 lire al giorno per persona.
—   Per una tenda costa 6.000 lire al giorno.
—   La presa elettricità costa 2.500 lire al giorno.
—   Per una roulotte o un camper paghi 7.000 lire.
—   I bambini pagano soltanto 3.500 lire al giorno.
—   Se avete la macchina dovete pagare 2.500 lire.

Check that everyone understands the words which are underlined. Then ask them to point at the symbols as you mention them, e.g.

—   Ho una tenda, ma mi piacerebbe avere una roulotte.
—   Un camper è più utile di una macchina.
—   Le tende costano di meno dei camper.
—   Gli adulti pagano più dei bambini.
—   È più importante avere una macchina che avere la presa elettricità.

B Base some question and answer work on this table, e.g.

—   Quanto costa per una roulotte (tenda) al giorno?
—   Che cosa costa 2.500 lire al giorno?
—   Devo pagare il posto per la macchina?

When this seems too easy, ask the students to answer with the Students' Book shut!

C Think of one of the symbols in this item. Draw on the board one line only to begin a drawing of this symbol. Give the class one guess only to say what it is. If they are right, complete the drawing and say, e.g.

—   Sì, avete ragione. È una tenda.
—   Guardate, ecco la mia tenda.

If they are wrong, draw one more line and give them another guess.
The students can soon continue to play this game in pairs.

C'è ancora posto? (page 56)

Main aim: To introduce and practise the main language associated with arriving, and registering, at a campsite

A Work on this list using techniques which you have previously found successful. Additional activities could include, e.g.

• The students copy all the words in this list which contain a given sound, e.g.

'o' as in 'tempo'
'e' as in 'persone'
words with both sounds.

• They start with one sentence in the list and then change it by changing one word, seeing how far they can go, e.g.

– Per una notte.
– Per due notti.
– Per tre notti.
– Per tre settimane.

• They start with a short sentence and make it as long as possible. e.g.

– C'è ancora posto?
– ... per due persone?
– ... con una tenda?
– ... e una macchina?

• You, and then individual students, read a sentence from the list. The other students say whether a camper or the warden would be most likely to say it.

B The students listen to the recordings of *C'è ancora posto?*. After each one, they say:

a what the problem is
b how well the camper deals with it.

C'è ancora posto?

Dialogo 1

Warden:	Buonasera.
Woman:	Buonasera. Senta, c'è ancora posto qui in campeggio?
Warden:	Lei ha la prenotazione, signora?
Woman:	No, mi dispiace, non abbiamo prenotato. Ma vorremmo un posto per una notte soltanto.
Warden:	E che tipo di posto volete?
Woman:	Un posto per una macchina, una tenda e una roulotte, per quattro persone.
Warden:	Mi dispiace, ma veramente non abbiamo abbastanza posto. Per un posto così, bisogna prenotare.
Woman:	Ho capito. Mi sa dire se c'è un altro campeggio qui nella zona?
Warden:	Beh, ce n'è uno a Poppi. Può sempre provare lì.
Woman:	Senta, posso telefonare da qui? Così sento se hanno posto.
Warden:	Certo. Il telefono è lì. Le do la linea.
Woman:	Grazie.

Dialogo 2

Warden:	Buongiorno.
Woman:	Buongiorno. Senta, si può avere un posto per una macchina e una roulotte per tre notti?
Warden:	Un momento. Avete la prenotazione?
Woman:	No.
Warden:	Vediamo, allora. Per tre notti ha detto?
Woman:	Sì.
Warden:	Mi dispiace, c'è un posto, ma è libero soltanto due notti. Tutti gli altri posti sono già prenotati.
Woman:	Non importa. Possiamo prendere il posto per due notti?
Warden:	Certo.
Woman:	E poi vedremo dopo domani per la terza notte.
Warden:	OK. Mi può dare un documento, per favore?
Woman:	Tenga.
Warden:	Grazie.

Dialogo 3

Warden:	Sì, mi dica.
Man:	Buongiorno. C'è ancora posto qui in campeggio per una macchina, una tenda e una roulotte, per due notti?
Warden:	Avete una tenda e una roulotte?
Man:	Sì.
Warden:	Beh, allora, no, mi dispiace ma in questo campeggio le roulotte e le tende non si mettono insieme. Ci sono due aree separate.
Man:	Come? Non è possibile sistemare la tenda insieme alla roulotte? È incredibile!
Warden:	Mi dispiace, ma è il regolamento che dice così. Così c'è più posto intorno alle roulotte.
Man:	Non ho mai sentito una storia così stupida. Andiamo in un altro campeggio.
Warden:	Buongiorno.

Dialogo 4

Man:	Buongiorno.
Warden:	Buongiorno. Mi dica.
Man:	Senta, vorrei un posto per due tende, per quattro persone, per una notte, per favore. C'è ancora posto?

Warden:	Per due tende, ha detto?
Man:	Sì.
Warden:	Mi dispiace, ma in questo campeggio abbiamo soltanto posti per roulotte. Non c'è area tende.
Man:	Come? Non prendete tende?
Warden:	No. I posti sono tutti per roulotte fisse.
Man:	Ho capito. C'è un altro campeggio qui vicino dove accettano tende?
Warden:	Sì. C'è il campeggio Il Rocolo a Colle della Trinità. Lì avranno posti per tende.
Man:	Grazie.
Warden:	Prego. Buongiorno.

Dialogo 5

Man:	Buonasera.
Warden:	Buonasera. Desidera?
Man:	Avete ancora posto qui in campeggio?
Warden:	Dipende. Avete la roulotte?
Man:	Sì, vorremmo un posto per una roulotte e una macchina. Quanto costa al giorno?
Warden:	Dunque, il posto macchina costa quattromila lire al giorno e il posto roulotte viene diecimila.
Man:	Quattordicimila lire al giorno? E quanto si deve pagare per persona?
Warden:	Seimila lire per un adulto.
Man:	Ma è un po' troppo caro. Grazie lo stesso. Arrivederci.
Warden:	Arrivederci.

Dialogo 6

Woman:	Buonasera.
Warden:	Prego.
Woman:	Senta, ho prenotato un posto per un camper per una settimana. Il nome è Agostini.
Warden:	Agostini. Un momento che guardo sul registro. Un camper ... Agostini ... mi dispiace ma non abbiamo una prenotazione in quel nome.
Woman:	Ma ho scritto una lettera di prenotazione alcune settimane fa.
Warden:	Guardi, la prenotazione non c'è.
Woman:	Avete posto per un camper lo stesso?
Warden:	Un momento. Sì, c'è posto, ma per quanto tempo?
Woman:	Per una settimana.
Warden:	Allora, vi posso dare il numero quindici per quattro giorni e poi dopo, dovete cambiare di posto per gli ultimi tre giorni.
Woman:	È l'unico posto che rimane?
Warden:	Sì.
Woman:	Va bene, lo prendiamo. Vuole un documento?
Warden:	Sì, grazie.

C In pairs, the students ask and answer questions about prices on the 'listino prezzi', following the model. You could do some first, with the class, to get them going.

Si arriva (page 57)

Main aims: To introduce and practise the key language associated with booking in at a campsite
To develop listening skills

A First work on the dialogues. You could, for example, say the English equivalent of a key sentence: the students then race to find the Italian equivalent and read it aloud. After a while, you could say the English equivalent of a variation of one of the sentences and the students adapt it, e.g.

- For five (six) nights.
- Two adults and three (four) children.
- We've got a tent and a caravan (campervan).

B The students listen to the three dialogues and follow the scripts in the Students' Book.

The students then listen a second time and fill in the information which the warden would record in the campsite register on Copymaster 37. Stop after each dialogue and correct it together in Italian.

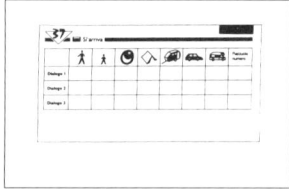

🔊 Si arriva

Dialogo 1

Warden:	Buonasera.
Woman:	Buonasera. C'è ancora posto qui in campeggio?
Warden:	Sì. Per quanto tempo?
Woman:	Per una settimana.
Warden:	Sì. E per quante persone?
Woman:	Quattro. Due adulti e due bambini.
Warden:	Va bene. Avete la tenda?
Woman:	No, abbiamo una macchina e una roulotte.
Warden:	Allora, piazzuola numero ottantacinque, accanto al campo gioco.
Woman:	Ho capito. Grazie.

Dialogo 2

Warden:	Buonasera.
Man:	Buonasera. Senta, avete ancora posto per una macchina e due tende, per favore?
Warden:	Vediamo. Per quanto tempo?
Man:	Possiamo fermarci due notti? Siamo in quattro.
Warden:	Sì, c'è posto.
Man:	Quanto costa al giorno per persona?
Warden:	Seimilacinquecento lire per persona, e poi tremilaottocento per una tenda e tremilaottocento per la macchina.
Man:	Ho capito.
Warden:	Ha un documento, per favore?

Dialogo 3

Warden:	Buonasera.
Girl:	Buonasera. C'è posto per un camper per quattro notti, per favore? Siamo in tre.
Warden:	Avete la prenotazione?
Girl:	No, mi dispiace.
Warden:	Non importa, c'è posto. Vi posso dare la piazzuola numero quattordici, in fondo, a sinistra.
Girl:	Senta, quanto costa al giorno?
Warden:	Dunque ... costa seimilacinquecento lire al giorno per persona e seimilacinquecento lire per il camper.
Girl:	Ah. Vuole un documento?
Warden:	Sì, grazie.

C In pairs, the students practise the dialogues.
Student A reads the part of the warden in the Students' Book and Student B uses the information on the grid on Copymaster 37 as a prompt.
They then change roles.
The students could be asked to calculate the totals which each person will have to pay on departure. Tell them that the charge for a caravan is the same as for a campervan, and that for a child it costs 4.000 lire.

D Give another copy of Copymaster 37 to each pair of students.

They take turns to play the parts of the warden and the camper. The warden interviews the camper and notes down the information given on the blank registration form.

Dal nove al diciannove luglio (page 58)

Main aim: To develop listening skills on the topic of camping

A To prepare the students for this, you could, e.g.

- Work on the calendar, making sure that everyone knows what each of the letters stands for by asking questions, e.g.
  - Il venti (31, 17, ecc.) luglio, che giorno è?
  - Se arrivi il nove luglio, in che giorno arrivi?
  - E che giorno parti?

- Make sure that everyone understands the listening task and then, to prepare for this, ask them:
  a to list, in Italian, some of the things they would hope to hear
  b to list, in Italian, some things which would make it difficult to make friends.

Dal nove al diciannove luglio

Dialogo I

Warden:	Buonasera.
Girl:	Buonasera. Ho prenotato un posto per cinque notti ...
Warden:	Sì, il Suo nome?
Girl:	Morelli.
Warden:	Morelli? Ah, sì. Ecco. Due persone per cinque notti. Avete la tenda?
Girl:	Sì.
Warden:	E la macchina?
Girl:	No, no. Siamo venuti col treno. Senta, possiamo sistemarci vicino alla piscina?
Warden:	No, mi dispiace. Se avete soltanto la tenda, vi metto a destra dello spaccio. Lì, non ci sono macchine.
Girl:	Ho capito.
Warden:	Avete i documenti?
Girl:	Sì. Tenga.

Dialogo 2

Warden:	Buongiorno.
Woman:	Buongiorno.
Warden:	Sì, dica.
Woman:	Abbiamo prenotato un posto per due settimane, dal dodici al ventisei luglio per quattro adulti.
Warden:	Per quattro persone ha detto?
Woman:	Sì esattamente quattro.
Warden:	Sotto che nome?
Woman:	Gala, con una elle sola.
Warden:	Sì. Che cosa avete?
Woman:	Eh, abbiamo una tenda e un camper ehm, è importante un posto con attacco luce.
Warden:	Sì, sì, certo, non si preoccupi ... l'attacco luce. Dunque Le posso dare il numero diciassette.
Woman:	Uhm, numero diciassette. Dove si trova esattamente?
Warden:	È qui, vicino alle docce, vede sulla mappa?

Woman:	Vicino alle docce. È un bel posto?
Warden:	Sì certo, signora, non sì preoccupi.
Woman:	Benissimo, allora posto numero diciassette vicino alle docce, intesi?
Warden:	Sì.
Woman:	Vuole un documento?
Warden:	Sì, grazie.
Woman:	Benissimo, ecco.
Warden:	Grazie.
Woman:	Sì, ecco la mia carta di identità.

Dialogo 3

Warden:	Buonasera.
Man:	Buonasera. Senta volevo sapere se avevate un posto per cinque persone.
Warden:	Sì, un po' ... Beh dipende, per quante notti?
Man:	Sette notti.
Warden:	Sì, sette notti. Allora dal, dal dodici al diciannove, giusto?
Man:	Dal dodici al diciannove, esattamente.
Warden:	Per quante persone ha detto?
Man:	Cinque, due adulti e i miei tre figli di quattordici, dodici e nove anni.
Warden:	Sì. Avete la tenda?
Man:	Sì. Abbiamo una tenda e una roulotte.
Warden:	Vi occorre l'attacco luce?
Man:	Sì, vogliamo l'attacco luce, sì. E abbiamo anche la macchina.
Warden:	Uhm, va bene. Posto numero, vi posso dare il numero ventisette che è vicino al campo giochi e al campo di pallavolo.
Man:	Uh, un po' rumoroso però, no?
Warden:	Beh, no beh è un buon posto per voi soprattutto per i vostri bambini così possono conoscerne altri, giocare, divertirsi.
Man:	Sì, sì. Ma io avrei preferito un posto tranquillo, magari all'ombra.
Warden:	E va bene, vediamo il ... vediamo Le posso dare il numero ventitre, è dall'altra parte del campeggio.
Man:	Ah, perfetto, sì sì ...

Dialogo 4

Boy 1:	Salve.
Warden:	Buonasera.
Boy 2:	Ciao.
Boy 1:	Un posto, il posto.
Warden:	Il posto? Per quante notti?
Boy 1:	Due notti.
Warden:	Per due notti, da quando dal dodici al quattordici allora?
Boy 1:	Sì, sì, dal dodici al quattordici.

Warden:	Sì, quanti siete?
Boy 1:	Eh ... quattro.
Boy 2:	Sì, sì, quattro.
Warden:	E avete la tenda?
Boy 1:	Sì, sì, abbiamo una tenda.
Boy 2:	No, abbiamo due tende.
Warden:	Due tende?
Boy 1:	Ah sì, due.
Warden:	Mah, eh ...
Boy 1:	È una macchina.
Warden:	Eh però non abbiamo posto per due tende. Eh ... è già prenotato qui.
Boy 1:	Ma, ma noi abbiamo prenotato. Ecco la conferma.
Warden:	Eh perché non me l'ha detto prima? Dia qui, dia qui. Ecco qua, allora dobbiamo ricominciare di nuovo. Quattro persone.
Boy 1:	Sì, quattro persone.
Warden:	Due notti.
Boy 1:	Due notti.
Warden:	Dal dodici al quattordici luglio, due tende più la macchina.
Boy 1:	Sì.
Boy 2:	Sì.
Warden:	Allora, trovatevi un posto nell'area tende, dall'altra parte della piscina, vicino al campo bocce.
Boy 1:	Ho capito, ho capito.
Boy 2:	Andiamo, va.
Boy 1:	Va bene. Ma è lontano?
Warden:	No, no, è qui, è qui. È proprio dall'altra parte della piscina.
Boy 1:	Va bene. Arrivederci.
Warden:	Buongiorno, grazie.
Boy 2:	Ciao.

B Once the students have recognised all the campers by the impressions they make of themselves, ask the students to say which camper they think they would be most likely to make friends with. They should explain their choice both in terms of the camper's personality and in terms of the length of time they will both be staying at the site, e.g.

– Secondo me sarà possibile fare amicizia con la prima campeggiatrice perché è gentile e simpatica e lei rimane cinque notti.

La ricevuta del campeggio (page 58)

Main aim: To practise booking in, and finding one's pitch, at a campsite

A Spend a few minutes quickly revising the list on page 56 of the Students' Book, e.g.

- After two minutes to study the list, the students cover up the Italian: they listen as you read the Italian sentences, in random order, and find and read aloud the English.
- Reverse the above, with you reading English sentences and the students, looking only at the Italian, choosing and reading out the Italian equivalents.

After a little classwork, both the above activities can be continued by the students in pairs.

B The students compare the bill (San Michele Lago) and the dialogue, picking up any differences. (They ask to stay for three nights but the warden only records one night on the bill.) In pairs, they then play-read the dialogue correcting any mistakes so that the dialogue fits the bill. Students who finish first could write out the dialogue, clearing up the mistake.

C In pairs, the students make up similar dialogues based on the other two receipts.

Dove possiamo sistemarci? (page 59)

Main aim: To present and practise the language associated with asking for a pitch in a particular place

A Before the students make up as many questions as they can in one minute, you will probably need to revise 'al, alla, all', ai', etc. e.g.

- The students look back in the Students' Book, choose any sentence and read it aloud. You say in which setting this sentence would probably be used, e.g.

Student: Mi può fare il pieno di super, per favore?
Teacher: Al distributore di benzina.
Student: Uno per Roma, andata e ritorno.
Teacher: Alla stazione.

The students decide if your answer is correct.
After a while, they could continue this in pairs.

- See how many different places on a campsite the students can correctly say they need to go to in one minute, e.g.

— Devo andare allo spaccio.

When you first play this, you could write some places on the board, e.g.

le docce	i gabinetti	il locale ritrovo
il bar	i lavapanni	la discoteca
lo spaccio	il ristorante	la piscina
il campo giochi	i lavapiatti	

Do this several times to give the students a chance to improve their score. Whenever anyone makes a mistake, stop and correct the mistake. After a while remove the words from the board.

B It would also be a good idea, before working on this activity, to revise 'del, dell'', etc., e.g.

- Cut, from magazines, pictures of things to eat and drink which your students know. Write a list of these on the board, leaving a space in front of each one, e.g.

___ latte	___ panini
___ frutta	___ caramelle
___ carne	___ spaghetti

Ask the students to say which word should go in front of each of these to show that there is some of it. You, or the students, write the missing words on the board.
Invite a student to the front. Show him/her one of your pictures. He/she mimes eating or drinking what is in the picture. The students try to guess what it is.   You could point out that 'dal, dalla', etc. works in exactly the same way.

C Work on the item in the Students' Book. Make sure that everyone understands each caption. To help them to learn the captions, you could use the nine pictures to play 'Noughts and crosses'. The students indicate where they would like a nought or a cross to go by saying the appropriate caption.

D Practise orally asking for a pitch in different ways. Then get the students each to write as many ways of doing this as they can in five minutes, before comparing their lists with each other.

E This would be a suitable point at which to begin work on *Scoprite qualcosa di più* (pages 161-164).

Al campeggio Rialto (page 59)

Main aims: To provide practice in understanding where to pitch a tent and find a plot at a campsite

To practise asking where facilities on a campsite are

A Make sure that everyone understands what to do. Discuss the campsite plan with the class. Point out, for example, that certain areas are reserved for caravans, and that others are reserved for tents. The students then write down what they would say to each of the four groups of campers, using the example to help them.

B In pairs, the students compare what they have written. Encourage them to make any changes they wish as a result of their discussions. Then play the tape, stopping after each one for the students to discuss similarities and differences between their suggestions and each recording. Play each recording once more after the discussion, before moving on to the next one.

🔊 Al campeggio Rialto

Dialogo 1

Warden: Buonasera.
Camper: Buonasera. Ho prenotato un posto per un camper, per tre notti, al nome di Luchetti.
Warden: Luchetti?
Camper: Sì.
Warden: Ah sì, due persone per tre notti ... Dunque, vi posso dare una piazzuola nell'area roulotte, vicino ai servizi.
Camper: È vicino al bar? Vicino alla discoteca?
Warden: No, no, è un posto all'ombra, in fondo. Andate sempre dritto, passate il primo blocco servizi e prendete il secondo viale a sinistra. Il posto è sulla sinistra.
Camper: Ho capito. Grazie.

Dialogo 2

Warden: Ciao!
Camper: Buongiorno. Senta, ha posto per quattro persone? Abbiamo due tende.
Warden: Per quanto tempo?
Camper: Per una notte.
Warden: Per una notte, sì. Allora ... potete sistemarvi nell'area tende vicino alla piscina, o se preferite c'è ancora posto accanto al campo di pallavolo.
Camper: Possiamo metterci accanto alla piscina?
Warden: Certo. Vediamo ... piazzuola numero quattordici.
Camper: Vuole un documento?
Warden: Sì. Grazie.

Dialogo 3

Camper: Buonasera. C'è ancora posto per un camper e una tenda, per favore?
Warden: Per quanto tempo?
Camper: Per cinque notti ... Siamo in quattro.
Warden: Un momento ... sì, sì, c'è posto. Mi può lasciare un documento?
Camper: Sì. Tenga ... E dove possiamo sistemarci?
Warden: Mm ... vi posso mettere nell'area roulotte vicino al campo di bocce ... prendete il viale qui a sinistra, ci sono dei posti subito dopo il blocco servizi, sulla destra.
Camper: Allora qui a sinistra?
Warden: Sì. In fondo c'è il campo da bocce e un blocco servizi. Prendete il viale sulla sinistra.
Camper: Sulla sinistra ...?
Warden: Sì. E il posto libero è sulla destra. Dietro il blocco servizi.
Camper: Ho capito. Grazie.

Dialogo 4

Warden: Buonasera.
Camper: Buonasera. Mi sa dire se c'è ancora posto?
Warden: Per un camper?
Camper: No, no ... per una tenda.
Warden: E una macchina?
Camper: No, siamo venuti coll'autobus.
Warden: Per quanto tempo?
Camper: Per una notte.
Warden: Una sola ... Dunque una tenda, due persone, una notte ... Ah ... suoni la chitarra?
Camper: Sì.
Warden: Lo sapete che dopo le undici c'è il silenzio?
Camper: Sì, sì.
Warden: Va bene. Allora potete sistemarvi nell'area tende qui davanti. C'è posto lì, a sinistra del bar.
Camper: Perfetto. Le lascio la carta d'identità?
Warden: Sì, grazie.

C To revise way-finding phrases, explain to the students that you are standing at the entrance to the campsite where 'Siete qui' is written. Describe your route to one of the facilities on the site in Italian. The students listen and work out where it is that you end up, e.g.

Teacher: Vado sempre dritto. Prendo la prima a sinistra e poi la prima a destra. È sulla sinistra.
Student: Il campo giochi.
Teacher: Sì, bravo(a)!

Write key phrases associated with giving directions on the board or OHP for the students to refer to. They can then play this game in pairs. You could suggest that they change the starting point from time to time.

D The students work in pairs and take turns to ask where different facilities are located.
Write this model on the board or OHP:

Student A: (Covers key) Scusi, mi sa dire dov'è la piscina?
Student B: Sì, è qui (points to F on map) accanto al campo giochi.

Only Student B may look at the key to the map.

E As a homework, each student could design and label their perfect campsite. They could compare these in class.

F Divide the class into groups of six and give each group a copy of Copymasters 38 A and B. In each group, each student has a different card. Students must not show each other their cards. Everyone knows where the 'Ufficio Direzione' is (F). The example is based around the 'Ufficio.' Each student knows where one other facility is located. The students circulate, asking each other where the remaining five places are located:

they write these on their plans. They assume that they are standing outside the 'Ufficio'; the spot is marked with a dot on each map. If the person answering knows where the place is, he/she gives directions from the dot.

The aim is to be the first student to locate all six places on the campsite, and to write them on the plan.

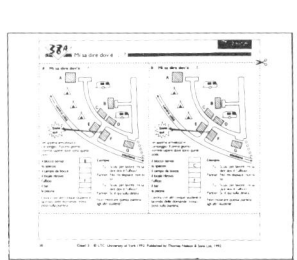 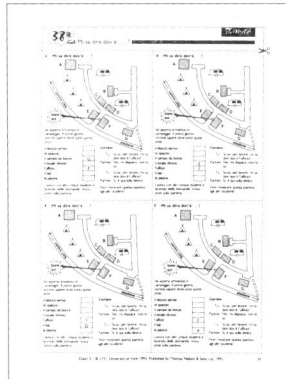

Il regolamento del campeggio (page 60)

Main aims: To develop communication strategies useful for understanding signs and notices

To discuss the need for rules and regulations in places frequented by large numbers of people

A Once the students have studied the signs, you could describe situations (in English, or in Italian), e.g.

The people in the next door tent have got their radio on and are talking loudly. It's 10.30 p.m. What would/could you do?

B You could make up 'Vero/Falso' statements based on the signs, e.g.

– Si può suonare la chitarra la mattina.
– Si può ascoltare la radio alle 6.30 di mattina.

Students correct them orally and then in writing.

C Using the table, the students make up at least one sentence which is compatible with the sentiments of each sign. When you have corrected these and cleared up any problems, give the students five minutes to write ten sentences, each based on the table: they should include two silly or impossible sentences. They read their sentences to each other and try to spot their partners' silly sentences.

D The students adapt the signs here to suit other places, times, etc., e.g.

– Silence from 9 a.m. until noon.
– No bikes allowed in the school from 9 a.m. until 10 a.m.
– Drinking water.

They could then design useful signs in Italian for local businesses (e.g. campsites, hotels, youth hostels).

E Continue to work on the exercises in *Scoprite qualcosa di più* (pages 161-164).

Mi può fare il conto, per favore? (page 60)

Main aim: To practise asking for and paying the bill at a campsite

A Read this with the class and ensure that everyone understands. If anyone asks what a word means, suggest questions they could ask themselves to try to work out for themselves the meaning, e.g. Does the word look like a word in English? Does the word look like another word in Italian? Play-read the dialogue with a student and then get the others to play-read it in pairs.

B Ensure that all the students can use Italian numbers accurately and fluently, e.g.

• Write a sequence of numbers on the board, saying each one once or twice as you write it, e.g.
500, 1000, 1500, 2000, 2500, 3000, 3500. Then rub one off and ask, e.g.

– Che numero manca?

The student who gives you the answer comes to the board, writes in the missing number and rubs out another.

• Write a list of digits vertically on the board, e.g.
9, 4, 1, 3, 8, 2, 6, 7, 5, 0.

Time the class while ten different students read these digits, saying one each. Write their score on the board, e.g.

– 40 secondi.

Then write another digit in front of each of those on the board and time ten students saying them. Repeat this with a third, and then a fourth, row of digits, producing on the board, e.g. 1239, 3454, 1111, 2563, 9168, 8222, 1246, 4567, 8765, 2550.

C The students now work in pairs to make up dialogues based on the situations outlined in **A** and **B** on page 60. The student playing the part of the warden prepares the bill for his/her partner using Copymaster 39, before beginning the dialogue. They change roles for the second situation. Move around, listening and helping. Keep a note of any common problems and work on these with the class later.
After a while, encourage the students to listen to each others' dialogues. They should notice how similar they are. This makes again the important point that in many common situations

what is said is highly predictable. This knowledge is a great help in preparing to listen to, or to take part in, such situations.

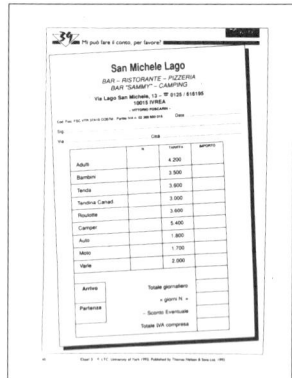

È meglio prenotare il posto (page 61)

Main aim: **To practise writing a letter to book accommodation on a campsite**

A The students read this to themselves and ask about anything which they cannot understand. They could be asked to produce a gapped letter and pass it on to another student to complete. Ration the students to seven gaps each, each of one word.

B The students could be asked to adapt the model orally, changing as many words as possible. This could be done adopting a snowballing technique.

C Background information: members of Federcampeggio/TCI can book using the forms supplied at the back of the guide book.

D Work with the class on the campsite advertisement. They could list the good and bad features of the site for different people, e.g.

- an old granny who hates sport and noise
- a girl who likes dancing but is afraid of the dark
- someone who likes visiting art galleries and swimming.

Allo spaccio (page 61)

Main aim: **To practise shopping on a campsite**

A The students work on this in pairs, making up as many sensible conversations as they can.

B Each student could write a dialogue based on this table and also illustrate it. This could be done at home.

Adesso, tocca a te! (page 62)

Main aim: **To demonstrate that the language of this unit has been mastered**

Exercise 1
Language area: Asking for information about campsites
Skill area: Writing

Allow those students who need it to look once more at the letter on page 54 before they try this. Remind everyone to be careful about where they write their address and the address of the information office.

Exercise 2
Language area: Campsites
Skill area: Reading

When students have written their lists individually, they could compare their lists in pairs to ensure that they have missed nothing.

Exercise 3
Language area: Talking about a campsite
Skill areas: Speaking or writing

This exercise practises drawing conclusions from a text. Students could explain their reasons in Italian or in English.

Exercise 4
Language area: Booking a place at a campsite
Skill area: Writing

Again, allow anyone who needs to, to look at the letter on page 61 before they try to write this letter. They will learn more from getting it right than from getting it wrong!

Exercise 5
Language area: Arriving at a campsite
Skill area: Listening

Before the students listen, encourage them to predict the sorts of things the people will talk about and the sorts of words they are likely to use. This is a strategy which they should develop and which will help them in tests and in life.

🔊 Adesso, tocca a te!

Warden:	Buongiorno.
Camper:	Buongiorno. Ho prenotato un posto per un camper per una settimana, al nome di Sella.
Warden:	Un momento che guardo. Ah sì ... Sella, tre adulti e un camper dal tre al dieci agosto.
Camper:	Esatto.
Warden:	Allora, vi do la piazzuola numero trentuno.
Camper:	L'attacco luce, c'è?

Warden: Sì, sì, tutti i posti hanno la luce elettrica. Dunque ... vede il locale ritrovo lì davanti?

Camper: Sì.

Warden: Prenda il viale sulla destra. La vostra piazzuola si trova sulla destra, un po' prima del blocco servizi.

Camper: Questo viale qui, allora? Sulla destra?

Warden: Esatto.

Camper: Senta, c'è uno spaccio qui in campeggio?

Warden: Sì, sì. È qui, accanto all'ufficio, e poi c'è un supermercato più grande in centro. Le do questo dépliant con tutte le informazioni sul campeggio e la zona intorno a Desenzano.

Camper: Grazie.

Warden: Di niente.

Exercise 6

Language area: Registering at a campsite
Skill area: Speaking

The students work on this in pairs, playing each role in turn. Make them feel responsible for their own and their partners' performances: jointly they should aim to do it perfectly. Try to record some. Play these back later and mark them with help from the class: in this way, all students develop a better understanding of the criteria for assessment.

Exercise 7

Language area: Paying the bill at the campsite
Skill area: Speaking

Work on this along the lines suggested for Exercise 6.

Ora sai (page 63)

Main aim: To act as a summary and reference point for the main language of this unit

Continue to use the *Ora sai* to help the students learn how to learn. Use various techniques to help the students learn this key language, discuss each technique with the students and encourage them to build up a repertoire of techniques which they find effective and enjoyable, e.g.

- Alone, and in pairs, the students choose – and say or write – phrases they would use, e.g.

- when arriving at a campsite
- when leaving a campsite
- in a campsite office
- in a campsite shop.

- The students choose – and say or write – phrases they would, e.g.

- hear – see – say – write.

- In class and in pairs, you could play a game of 'Hangman' using sentences from this list.

- You could organise a game of 'Il gioco degli spazi' (see Teacher's Book 1, page 110) using sentences based on those in this list, e.g.

- C'è posto per due _____ e una _____ per _____ notte?

Revision

1 Al, alla, all' (Book 1, Unit 4)

The students copy and complete the following sentences from the board. They look in the Students' Book for a photo or drawing which goes with each sentence, and they write the page number after the sentence.

1 Per avere delle informazioni sulla città, bisogna scrivere _____ Ente per il Turismo.
2 La discoteca Principe è vicino _____ stazione.
3 Se vuoi vedere dei vasi greci, devi andare _____ Museo Archeologico.
4 Ti piacerebbe andare _____ Giostra del Saracino?
5 Andiamo _____ parco Crocodile!
6 Questa persona si trova _____ stazione di servizio.
7 Si può sempre chiedere la strada _____ benzinaio.
8 La toilette si trova accanto _____ negozio.
9 _____ incrocio deve girare a sinistra.
10 Quando arriva _____ semaforo, giri a destra.

2 Irregular plurals of nouns (Book 2, Unit 7)

Divide the class into groups of four. Make one copy of Copymaster 40 for each group. Stick it onto card and cut each card into 24 squares. Put the squares into a separate envelope for each group.

The students lay the cards face down. They take it in turns to turn up two cards. If they turn up a label and picture which match, they keep the cards and have another go. If they turn up two cards which do not match, it is the next student's go. The aim is to collect more matching pairs than anyone else. If a student claims two cards which do not in fact match, the others can challenge him/her. The student who claimed them in error misses a go.

3 Town and region (Book 3, Unit 3)

A Ask the students to revise *Ora sai* on page 63 of the Students' Book, using their favourite techniques. Ask a few to say which techniques they used and why they like these techniques.

Then ask them to think of a way to test their partners' knowledge of these *Ora sai* phrases and vocabulary, and then to test each other. Ask them again to say which techniques they used, and why.

B Play a game of 'Doppio o passi'. You need a collection of counters or beads. Divide the class into four or five teams. Make a statement about your town or region, and choose a team to say if it is true or false, e.g.

Teacher: Un parco è un tipo di scuola.
Student: Falso.

When an answer is correct, give a team two counters. You now offer a team the chance to double its counters by responding to another statement. If they do so correctly, they win two more counters. If they are wrong, they have to give back the two they won for the first statement. Allow the teams to consult so that each decision is a team decision. If a team decides to pass, 'passare', you move on to another team. After a team takes on a second sentence, successfully or not, you move on to another team. In order to maintain a fast pace, allow a maximum of 20 seconds for a response. Possible sentences include:

– Alla biblioteca trovi molti libri.
– Se vuoi andare dalla polizia, devi andare in questura.
– I principali negozi si trovano in Grape Lane.
– La chiesa più importante è quella di St. Barnabas.
– A Whitchurch ci sono due musei.
– C'è un distributore di benzina in Heath Road.
– Qui a Whitchurch ci sono tre licei.
– La strada più lunga della città è Market Street.
– Il monumento più famoso della zona è Holmes Park House.
– A Whitchurch c'è il mercato ogni martedì.
– Se vuoi giocare a tennis devi andare alla pista di pattinaggio.
– Non ci sono discoteche qui a Whitchurch.

If this activity proves popular, you could use it to practise other topics.

C Play a game of 'Noughts and crosses'.
Present a frame like this on the board or OHP:

campeggio	farmacia	città
distributore di benzina	nella strada	regione
ufficio turistico	mercato	albergo

Divide the class into two teams. They take turns to choose a topic and to answer a question on it. When they reply correctly, they can draw a nought or a cross on that square. Questions could include, e.g.

– Mi sai dire se c'è un campeggio qui vicino?
– Hai mal di testa. Che cosa chiedi al farmacista?
– Vuoi andare al duomo ma non conosci la strada. Che cosa dici ad un passante?
– Manca l'olio. Che cosa dici al benzinaio?
– Avete fame e volete comprare un po' di frutta. Che cosa chiedete al venditore al mercato?
– Mi puoi dire in italiano come si dice 'a single room with a shower'?
– Partite dal campeggio stamattina. Chiedete il conto.

4 Indirect object pronouns (Book 3, Unit 6)

Write the following list on the board or OHP.

piace a me	→	mi piace
piace a te	→	ti piace
piace a Laura	→	le piace
piace a Roberto	→	gli piace
piace a noi	→	ci piace
piace a voi	→	vi piace
piace a loro	→	gli piace

After the class has studied these for a few minutes, rub out the indirect object pronouns and see if students can fill in the gaps orally. To reinforce this, students can work in pairs, one student reading e.g. 'piace a Roberto' and the other saying 'gli piace', before swapping round.

Then divide students into groups of four, labelling them A, B, C and D in each group. Ask A to interview B for one minute about his or her likes and dislikes, and C to interview D. Then A must report what he or she has found out about B to C and D and C must report about D to A and B. The person interviewed should correct and prompt where necessary. Finally, ask the groups of four to find three things which they all like and three things they all dislike, and to report these back to the whole class. In this way students will have practised ti, mi, le, gli, ci.

8ª Unità
SMARRITO, RUBATO, TROVATO?

Main aims

~ To be able to understand lost and found advertisements, and relevant signs and notices
~ To be able to understand procedures involved in a lost property office and a police station
~ To be able to report and describe articles lost, stolen or found

Materials

~ Tape
Cosa devo fare? (Teacher's Book page 96)
Scusi … cosa devo fare? (Teacher's Book page 96)
Lavori nell'ufficio (Teacher's Book page 97)
Ma questo non è il mio! (Teacher's Book page 98)
Dove? Quando? (Teacher's Book page 99)
Ho perso … (Teacher's Book page 100)
Il Suo cognome? (Teacher's Book page 101)
Adesso, tocca a te! (Teacher's Book page 102)
I canadesi arrivano ad Arezzo (Teacher's Book page 104)

~ Copymasters 41–43

Grammar in *Scoprite qualcosa di più*

~ Perfect tense with 'avere'

Revision

~ Travelling by bus (Book 1, Unit 5)
~ School (Book 2, Unit 8)
~ Fare: present tense (Book 2, Unit 8)
~ Hotels (Book 3, Unit 4)
~ Direct object pronouns after 'ecco' (Book 3, Unit 4)
~ Camping (Book 3, Unit 7)
~ Potere + infinitive (Book 3, Unit 7)

Vocabulary

A: Productive

a che ora apre?	un orologio
a che ora chiude?	pelle
argento	perdere (perso)
contiene	plastica
una gattina	trovare
lasciare	ufficio oggetti smarriti
una macchina fotografica	una valigia
mi hanno rubato	vecchio
nuovo	i vestiti
oro	

B: Receptive

accidenti!	una lauta mancia
anello	meno male
annuncio	la questura
che fortuna!	una ricompensa
che peccato!	ripassare
che rabbia!	ritrovare
il comune	scrivere
una denuncia	smarrire

Smarrito, rubato, trovato? (page 64)

Main aim: To introduce the main aims of this unit

The students read the introduction to themselves and ask about anything they do not understand. Use their questions to help them to develop communication strategies to work out the meaning of words in context.

Ask a few students to summarise the introduction. Encourage others to respond and to express their opinions about how useful the aims are. Each student could write down, in English, expressions they would like to learn in Italian for when they lose something: as usual, they should check that they have learnt these before the end of the unit.

Cosa devo fare? (page 64)

Main aim: Finding the right lost property office

A Explain, in Italian, the three sorts of lost property offices in Italy and their different functions, e.g.

L'ufficio oggetti smarriti
Se perdi qualcosa in una stazione, in un aeroporto, o in una città turistica, vai all'ufficio oggetti smarriti. Chiedi all'impiegato di aiutarti a ritrovare quello che hai perso.

Il comune
Se perdi qualcosa e non trovi un ufficio oggetti smarriti, vai in comune. Qui, chiedi all'impiegato di aiutarti.

La questura
Se sei certo(a) di aver perso qualcosa, o se qualcosa ti viene rubato, vai in questura. Lì, chiedi ad un poliziotto di aiutarti a fare una denuncia.

The students can ask you to repeat and to explain again. You can then ask questions so that they can show that they have understood, e.g.

– Hai lasciato una borsa sul treno. Dove vai?
– Hai lasciato un ombrello in un caffè. Dove vai?

– Hai perso un orologio costoso in città. Dove vai?
– Ti hanno rubato il portafoglio in città. Dove vai?

B The students read this page to themselves and ask about anything they cannot understand. They listen to the recording and follow the text as they listen. Then they close the Students' Books and listen again: after each dialogue, ask several students each to tell you one fact that they heard.

🔊 Cosa devo fare?

Dialogo 1

Woman: Scusi, ho perso il mio ombrello. Cosa devo fare?
Waiter: Deve andare all'ufficio oggetti smarriti, signora.
Woman: A che ora apre l'ufficio?
Waiter: Alle otto.
Woman: Ho capito. Grazie.
Waiter: Prego.

Dialogo 2

Boy: Scusi, ho trovato questa macchina fotografica. Cosa devo fare?
Woman: Deve andare in comune.
Boy: A che ora chiude il comune?
Woman: Alle sei.

Dialogo 3

Man: Mi hanno rubato il portafoglio. Cosa devo fare?
Policeman: Deve andare in questura per fare una denuncia.
Man: Scusi, mi sa dire dov'è la questura?
Policeman: Ma è proprio qui davanti!
Man: Ah sì. Grazie.
Policeman: Prego.

C Each student chooses and writes down ten key words and expressions from the three dialogues. In pairs, they teach their ten key expressions to their partners.

D The students listen to the next four dialogues. Play each one twice. After each, the students write the two pieces of information required. Check their answers, sort out any problems, confirm the right answers and play the dialogue again before going on to the next one.

🔊 Scusi . . . cosa devo fare?

Dialogo 1

Girl: Scusi, mi hanno rubato la borsa. Cosa devo fare?
Woman: Che disgrazia! Devi andare subito in questura.
Girl: Ma, è lontano?
Woman: Macchè? È qui, in fondo, a sinistra.
Girl: Meno male, grazie.
Woman: Prego.

Dialogo 2

Boy: Mi scusi, signora. Ho lasciato la mia tenda nel treno. Cosa devo fare?
Woman: Devi andare all'ufficio oggetti smarriti. È qui, accanto al bar.
Boy: Grazie. Mi sa dire a che ora chiude per favore?
Woman: Sì, certo - fra poco - alle sei e mezza, penso.
Boy: Grazie.
Woman: Non c'è di che.

Dialogo 3

Woman: Scusi, ho trovato questa bella maglia. Mi saprebbe dire che cosa devo fare?
Man: Sì, signorina, deve andare in comune.
Woman: È lontano?
Man: Mica tanto. Due cento metri, sempre dritto.
Woman: A che ora apre, per favore?
Man: Apre verso le otto e un quarto, se non mi sbaglio.
Woman: Grazie.
Man: Prego, signorina.

Dialogo 4

Boy: Signorina, signorina, mi può aiutare? Ho perso il mio zaino ... l'ho lasciato lì, mentre giocavo a calcio ... ora non lo trovo più.
Woman: Non ti preoccupare. Devi andare all'ufficio oggetti smarriti. Se qualcuno ha trovato il tuo zaino te lo daranno subito.
Boy: Ma ... è tardi ... a che ora chiude?
Woman: Chiude alle sette. Abbiamo tempo. Dai, ti accompagno.

E Each pair makes up a new dialogue by adapting those on page 64. They then change roles and do another one.

Tutto trovato (page 65)

Main aims: To develop reading skills

   To practise some of the key vocabulary of this unit

A Give the students three minutes to study the five drawings and to learn the names of the objects. To help them, read out four of the words in random order: the students listen and then tell you what you have not mentioned. After a few examples with the class, the students could continue this in pairs.

B With the Students' Book closed play a memory game based on the drawings, e.g.

– Ci sono due cani (etc)?
– C'è una borsa (etc)?
– Il numero cinque, che cos'è?

C Give the students two minutes to read the instructions. Ask one or two to tell the class what they need to do. Help them to plan the most efficient strategy for achieving this. For example, you could take each item in turn and scan the advertisements to find out what, if anything, is said about it.

D The students read the advertisements again to find the details of items which are not illustrated.

All' ufficio oggetti smarriti (page 65)

Main aim: To present some of the key language of this unit

A Work on the lists using techniques which have previously proved successful. To help the students to start to feel confident with these expressions, you could, e.g.

• ask them to pick out and say all the questions that would be asked if you reported losing a pair of glasses (a bag, a watch, a wallet)

• ask them to say which expressions they could use to describe an umbrella (a Walkman, a keyring, a watch, a pair of glasses, a wallet)

• describe one of the objects in the illustration: the students listen and say what it is.

B Ask some students to play-read the model dialogue. Give everyone a minute to prepare a dialogue on picture 1 and then act it out with a few students, with you playing the role of the clerk. Repeat this process with picture 2. In pairs, the students make up dialogues for all four pictures, taking turns to play the role of the clerk. Move around, listening and helping.

Un po' di confusione (page 66)

Main aim: To practise explaining that something has been lost or stolen

A Give the students two minutes to read this. Then ask someone to explain what they have to do. The students then write the two sentences which go together.

B You read aloud sentences 1 to 6. A student reads aloud which of sentences a to f goes with each sentence you read out. The others check their answers and correct as necessary.

C In pairs, the students make up a dialogue based around each pair of sentences, making each one as long as possible.

D Play a game of 'Confabulation': give a pair of students a piece of paper with a suitable sentence written on it, e.g.

– Ho perso la mia macchina.

– È di pelle, e molto vecchia.
– Porta l'indirizzo di un mio amico.
– Non so quanto vale.
– È rossa e gialla.

They have to make up a dialogue which uses their sentence as naturally as possible: the others listen and try to guess the sentence which was given to the pair.

Lavori nell'ufficio (page 66)

Main aim: To practise describing lost property

A Before working on this item, revise the list on page 65, e.g.

• The students pick out words and phrases they could use to describe a case (a bag, a purse, a watch, etc.).

• They categorise as quickly as possible words and phrases which describe 'un orologio', 'una borsa', 'un ombrello', e.g.

– è rosso(a) (bianco(a), nero(a), vecchio(a), nuovo(a), grande)
– è di plastica (di pelle, d'oro, d'argento)
– è metallico(a)
– è un(a) Rollex (un(a) Gucci)
– porta il mio nome (il mio indirizzo)
– vale 100.000 lire (vale poco)
– contiene dei soldi (il mio passaporto, delle chiavi).

B Work on this page along the lines suggested in the Students' Book. Each student will need a copy of Copymaster 41.

🔊 Lavori nell'ufficio

Dialogo 1

Boy:	Buongiorno. Ho perso la mia borsa.
Employee:	Buongiorno. Com'è la borsa?
Boy:	È grande e bianca.
Employee:	E di che cos'è?
Boy:	È di plastica.
Employee:	Che cosa contiene?
Boy:	Contiene i miei vestiti.
Employee:	Porta il Suo nome?
Boy:	Sì, e anche il mio indirizzo.
Employee:	Ho capito, allora vado a vedere se l'abbiamo.
Boy:	Grazie.

Dialogo 2

Girl:	Buongiorno. Spero proprio che Lei mi possa aiutare. Sono venuta qui perché ho perso la mia borsa.
Employee:	Buongiorno, sì, vediamo. La borsa com'era?
Girl:	Ma piccola, una piccola borsa. Era di pelle.
Employee:	Ah. E cosa conteneva?
Girl:	Conteneva il passaporto e delle chiavi.
Employee:	Uhm. E aveva scritto da qualche parte il nome o l'indirizzo?
Girl:	No, purtroppo no, sono stata proprio irresponsabile a non scrivercelo.
Employee:	D'accordo, un attimo vado a vedere se qualcuno l'ha trovata.
Girl:	Grazie.

Dialogo 3

Girl:	Buongiorno. Senta ho perso un portafoglio. Non può mica aiutarmi per caso?
Employee:	Oh che peccato. Di che cos'è il tuo portafoglio?
Girl:	Era tutto nuovo di plastica.
Employee:	Un portafoglio nuovo di plastica. Di che colore?
Girl:	Mah era blu e rosso.
Employee:	E che cosa conteneva, tanti soldi?
Girl:	Erano cinquantamila, cinquantamila lire.
Employee:	Eh insomma certo, una bella somma. Eh, c'era anche il tuo indirizzo dentro il portafoglio?
Girl:	Sì, c'era il nome e l'indirizzo, tutti i dati, non l'avete mica trovato per caso?
Employee:	No, non penso. Comunque per sicurezza vado a vedere. Aspetta un attimo.

Dialogo 4

Man:	Buongiorno.
Employee:	Buongiorno, mi dica.
Man:	Scusi io ho perso la mia valigia. Era una vecchia valigia.
Employee:	Sì. Di che cosa era?
Man:	Di pelle, pelle marrone.
Employee:	Ho capito, e che cosa c'era dentro?
Man:	Mah c'erano dei vestiti ed era alquanto piena, allora c'era una cinghia per tenerli insieme.
Employee:	Sì, e il Suo nome era sulla valigia?
Man:	Il mio nome sì, ma l'indirizzo no.
Employee:	Ho capito. Allora una vecchia valigia di pelle con dei vestiti dentro, c'era il Suo nome ma non il Suo indirizzo.
Man:	Esatto.
Employee:	Aspetti, vado a vedere, un attimo.
Man:	Grazie.
Employee:	Prego.

Dialogo 5

Woman:	Senta, scusi, sono disperata. Mi hanno rubato la borsa.
Employee:	Si calmi. Com'è la borsa?
Woman:	È grande, è blu.
Employee:	E di che cosa è?
Woman:	È di plastica.
Employee:	Che cosa conteneva?
Woman:	Contiene tutto, la spesa, anche il portamonete, e dentro c'erano duecentomila lire. E dentro il mio portamonete c'era anche il mio nome e il mio indirizzo.
Employee:	D'accordo, d'accordo, un attimo vado a vedere se l'abbiamo.
Woman:	Grazie mille.

Ma questo non è il mio! (page 67)

Main aim: To practise describing lost property

A Make sure that the key vocabulary is known by your students. You could draw silhouettes of an umbrella, a watch, a camera and a wallet, cut them out and project them on the OHP. The students have to try to identify them.

List the following on the board:

un orologio, un ombrello, un portafoglio, una macchina fotografica, una gattina, degli occhiali, un cane.

The students list them in order of usefulness, first for a holiday in Italy and then for survival on a desert island. Get them to justify their lists.

B Work on this page along the lines suggested.

🔊 Ma questo non è il mio!

Luca:	Buongiorno.
Employee:	Buongiorno.
Luca:	Ho perso un ombrello.
Employee:	Non ho sentito. Può ripetere?
Luca:	Ho perso il mio ombrello.

Employee:	Ho capito. Com'è?
Luca:	È rosso e nero, ed è abbastanza grande.
Employee:	È questo?
Luca:	No, mi dispiace. Il mio ombrello è più piccolo.

Dove? Quando? (page 67)

Main aim: **To explain when and where something was lost**

A Work on the list using previously successful techniques. Before leaving it, you could ask the students to cover up the Italian phrases and give you the English equivalent of variations on the phrases in the list, e.g.

– Dove ha lasciato la borsa (l'orologio, la valigia, etc.)?

They then cover up the list and give you the Italian for, e.g.

– I left it on the bus (plane, boat).
– I lost it yesterday morning (afternoon).

B The students listen to the recording of the dialogue and follow the text. Give them three minutes to try to learn the text. They then close the Students' Book and listen to the recording again: use the pause button to stop the tape and see who can carry on the dialogue. In pairs, they then adapt the dialogue as suggested.

🔊 Dove? Quando?

Tourist:	Buongiorno.
Employee:	Buongiorno. Posso aiutarLa?
Tourist:	Sì. Ho perso il mio orologio.
Employee:	Dove l'ha lasciato?
Tourist:	L'ho lasciato alla stazione, credo.
Employee:	Quando l'ha perso?
Tourist:	Ieri sera, verso le nove.
Employee:	Allora, vediamo … abbiamo un orologio, un Casio. È il Suo?
Tourist:	Ah, sì, che fortuna! È il mio, grazie.

C Give a volunteer a piece of paper with a text describing something that has been lost and when and where it was lost, e.g.

– Questa persona ha lasciato il suo ombrello in treno, stamattina verso le undici.

This student mimes the lost object and the others guess until they identify it. This is repeated for the time and place. You could repeat this with other volunteers, e.g.

– Questa persona ha perso il suo portafoglio nell'autobus ieri sera alle dieci. Il portafoglio contiene 200.000 lire.

– Questa persona ha lasciato una valigia in un tassì alle 7.00 stasera.

– A questa persona hanno rubato la macchina fotografica in centro città verso mezzanotte.

D This would be a good time to start work on *Scoprite qualcosa di più* (pages 165-167).

Emozioni! Emozioni! (page 68)

Main aims: **To develop reading skills**
To meet and understand examples of the Perfect Tense

A Work on this along the lines suggested. Give the students a few minutes to read the descriptions and to prepare their responses. Then ask a student to read aloud each description and invite several to respond appropriately.

B To develop listening skills and the ability to respond quickly, say a few more descriptions and invite students to respond, e.g.

6 Hai visto un biglietto da 100.000 lire sulla spiaggia. Ti sei fermato(a) per prenderlo, ma viene portato via dal vento. Che cosa dici?

7 Ti hanno rubato l'orologio nella stazione centrale. Sei andato(a) in questura, ma non è stato ritrovato. Hai lasciato il tuo numero di telefono. Due ore dopo ti telefonano per informarti che hanno ritrovato l'orologio. Che cosa dici?

8 In città hai visto una donna anziana che portava con molta difficoltà le borse della spesa. Hai offerto di aiutarla ma lei ti ha detto di andare via. Che cosa dici?

9 Sei passato(a) davanti al cinema ed hai visto che danno un buon film. Hai lasciato i soldi a casa. Un amico è arrivato e ti ha pagato l'entrata. Che cosa dici?

10 Cominciavi a fare il bagno, ed hai sentito qualcuno bussare alla porta d'entrata. Sei sceso(a) per vedere chi era, ma non hai visto nessuno. Sei tornato in bagno e c'è dell'acqua dappertutto. Che cosa dici?

C You could continue to work on *Scoprite qualcosa di più* (pages 165-167).

D This is a more difficult and imaginative exercise. A student expresses one of the emotions on this page. You and the other students try to work out what has happened.

Buongiorno. Posso aiutarLa? (page 69)

Main aim: Role-play for lost property

A Give the students a few minutes to read this and to prepare the role-play. Make sure that everyone knows how to prepare to perform such role-plays, e.g.

*   by finding quickly the things they are confident about and rehearsing those.
*   by looking for clues for things they are not sure about (e.g. lost, wallet).
*   by finding other ways to express what they can't find the words for (e.g. a look and a sound of relief).

B They practise this role-play in pairs, playing each part in turn. Each student helps his/her partner to perform as well as possible and they keep practising until both are satisfied that they can do it perfectly. Listen to their polished performances and praise appropriately.

C Each pair makes up a different dialogue. This is a co-operative effort and each pair is jointly responsible for producing the best possible dialogue and performance.

D Continue work on *Scoprite qualcosa di più* (pages 165-167).

Ho perso . . . (page 69)

Main aim: To develop listening skills

A Help the students to practise preparing for such listening tasks by anticipating what people are likely to say. For each item, ask them to write down words and phrases which they expect to hear. Discuss how accurate their predictions were, why they were sometimes inaccurate and how they can improve.

B The students listen again and discuss the three questions. They suggest ways in which the people could perform better.

C Continue work on *Scoprite qualcosa di più* (pages 165-167).

📼 Ho perso . . .

Dialogo 1

Girl:	Buongiorno.
Employee:	Buongiorno.
Girl:	Ho perso il mio ombrello.
Employee:	Sì di che colore?
Girl:	È piccolino, nero.
Employee:	No guardi, mi dispiace, non abbiamo nessun ombrello nero, piccolino.
Girl:	Va bene, grazie mille.
Employee:	Buongiorno.

Dialogo 2

Employee:	Buongiorno, mi dica.
Man:	Buongiorno, mi scusi, spero mi possa aiutare. Ho perso la valigia ieri sera alla stazione.
Employee:	Ho capito me la potrebbe descrivere?
Man:	Sì, era una grossa valigia di pelle. E aveva anche il mio nome.
Employee:	Sì.
Man:	Mi chiamo Pietro Colonna.
Employee:	C'era anche l'indirizzo?
Man:	Ah, sì. 22 Piazza Santa Croce, Firenze.
Employee:	D'accordo. Bah, senta è proprio fortunato eh, l'abbiamo ritrovata proprio adesso ce l'hanno riportata.
Man:	Ma è fantastico. La ringrazio. Lei è veramente gentile.

Dialogo 3

Employee:	Buongiorno, mi dica.
Man:	Buongiorno, senta ho lasciato l'ombrello in treno. Non l'avete mica trovato?
Employee:	Mi dica un po', com'è questo ombrello?
Man:	È uno di quelli molto grandi, bianco e azzurro.
Employee:	Aspetti un attimo che vado a vedere se ce l'hanno portato. È questo qui?
Man:	Ah, sì, grazie. È proprio questo.
Employee:	Prego, arrivederci.
Man:	Arrivederci. Tante grazie.

Dialogo 4

Employee:	Buongiorno.
Woman:	Buongiorno.
Employee:	Posso aiutarLa?
Woman:	Sì. Spero proprio di sì. Ho perso la mia borsa.
Employee:	Che tipo di borsa è?
Woman:	È una borsa grande.
Employee:	E cosa conteneva?
Woman:	Conteneva il mio libro, eh ... 'Il Gattopardo', sa 'Il Gattopardo' di Lampedusa, le mie chiavi e il portafoglio.
Employee:	E cosa c'era dentro il portafoglio?
Woman:	Dentro il portafoglio c'erano tutte le mie carte di credito, i miei soldi, esattamente cinquantamila lire in contanti, e una fotografia di mio marito.
Employee:	No, non è stata ancora trovata.
Woman:	Non l'avete ritrovato? Ehum ... in ogni caso, senta, se lo ritrovate, contattatemi immediatamente. Vi lascio il mio numero di telefono.
Employee:	Sì, certo.
Woman:	Grazie dell'aiuto, arrivederci.
Employee:	Prego. ArrivederLa.

Dialogo 5

Girl:	Buongiorno.
Employee:	Buongiorno mi dica.
Girl:	Ho perso una piccola borsa nera.
Employee:	Che cosa conteneva questa borsa?
Girl:	Le mie chiavi.
Employee:	Attenda un attimo, vado a vedere.

Dialogo 6

Man:	Buongiorno.
Employee:	Buongiorno. Posso aiutarLa?
Man:	Sì.
Employee:	Mi sa dire cosa ha perso?
Man:	Uh, una valigia.
Employee:	Una valigia. Mi sa dire s'è grande, piccola?
Man:	Ehh, piccola.
Employee:	Piccola. Di che cosa è fatta? Pelle, finta pelle, plastica?
Man:	Pelle.
Employee:	Pelle. Di che colore è? Bianca, rossa, verde, nera?
Man:	È rossa.
Employee:	Eh ... va bene. Mi sa dire che cosa contiene questa valigetta? Non so, degli abiti?
Man:	Sì eh ... degli abiti.
Employee:	Degli abiti. Qualcos'altro? Una macchina fotografica?
Man:	Eh, eh una macchina fotografica.
Employee:	Che marca è questa macchina fotografica?
Man:	Kodak.
Employee:	Ah, una Kodak. Un attimo che vado a vedere.
Man:	Va bene.
Employee:	No, mi dispiace. Non c'è nessuna valigetta di questo tipo.
Man:	Uhm, va bene.
Employee:	Arrivederci.

Il Suo cognome? (page 70)

Main aim: **To practise asking and answering questions in a lost property office**

A The students practise anticipating again and then listen to the recording.

🚌 Il Suo cognome?

Male employee:	Buongiorno signorina. Posso aiutarLa?
Young woman:	Sì, spero, ho perso il mio portafoglio.
Male employee:	Ho capito. Allora devo compilare un modulo. Quando l'ha perso?
Young woman:	Ieri sera.
Male employee:	A che ora?
Young woman:	Mm ... verso le sette, penso.
Male employee:	Ore diciannove ... e com'è il portafoglio?
Young woman:	Beh ... è nero, di pelle ...
Male employee:	E che cosa contiene, per favore?
Young woman:	Contiene 100.000 lire, in biglietti da 10.000.
Male employee:	Quanto vale il portafoglio?
Young woman:	Non lo so esattamente ... me l'hanno regalato ... venti, forse trentamila lire.
Male employee:	Ho capito. Scrivo trentamila. C'erano il Suo nome e indirizzo?
Young woman:	Sì. Li avevo scritti su di una cartolina che tenevo all'interno. Va bene?
Male employee:	Certo. Allora, mi può dire il Suo nome e cognome per favore?
Young woman:	Bettini, Daniela.
Male employee:	Professione?
Young woman:	Sono studentessa.
Male employee:	E dove abita, signorina?
Young woman:	Abito in Viale Galileo, 46B, 50125 ...
Male employee:	Un momento ... piano ... ha detto Viale Galileo 46B, e poi ...
Young woman:	50125 Firenze.
Male employee:	Ho capito, benissimo. Ha un numero di telefono per favore?
Young woman:	Sì, certo, è il 382723.
Male employee:	Ha forse un indirizzo locale ... per Arezzo?
Young woman:	Sì, fino a domani sera, può trovarmi all'Albergo Moderno, Via Roma.
Male employee:	Lo conosco. Va bene signorina. Se viene ritrovato il Suo portafoglio Le telefonerò.
Young woman:	Grazie.
Male employee:	Prego signorina.

B Using the form in the Students' Book as a guide, the students recreate the conversation in the lost property office, in pairs. If possible, record some of these. Play the recordings to the class. The students spot, and comment on, any differences between what various pairs have recorded.

C Continue work on *Scoprite qualcosa di più* (pages 165-167).

Gli annunci gratuiti (page 70)

Main aim: **To develop reading and writing skills**

A Give the students a few minutes to read this item. Ask some to explain what it is about. As a class, agree on a strategy for going about this, e.g. study the printed advertisements carefully and use these as a basis for writing the other advertisements.

B When you give back the corrected advertisements you could practise scan reading with the class. You could get the students to race to find the information you ask for, e.g.

- Who is offering a million lire and why?
- How many people have lost spectacles?
- Why would you ring 0541-25348?
- Describe the missing Vespa.

C Continue work on *Scoprite qualcosa di più* (pages 165-167).

Spettabile Direzione (page 71)

Main aim: To develop the ability to read and write a letter

A Give the students just two minutes to skim read this item and then to tell you what it is about.

B Give practice in finding specific details as quickly as possible, e.g.

- Who wrote this and when?
- Who is the letter to?
- Why is she writing?
- How long did she stay there?
- When did she stay?
- Describe what she has left behind.
- What does Lucy send?
- Why?

C Get the class to adapt the model letter orally to fit other needs, e.g.

- a gold watch left in a hotel after a two week holiday there in July
- a brand new camera left in a restaurant in Arezzo on 5th August
- a pair of glasses left in a museum on 20th May.

The students then write the letter outlined.

D Complete work on *Scoprite qualcosa di più* (pages 165-167).

E Extension tasks for more able students could include the following:

- Write a letter to the lost property office in Arezzo station (Ferrovie dello Stato, Piazza della Repubblica, 52100 Arezzo) saying you left a silver Omega watch on the train from Florence to Arezzo on 23rd March. Say that the train arrived at Arezzo at 8 p.m. Ask them to send it to you and say you are enclosing a Eurocheque for 3.000 lire.
- Write a letter to the restaurant La Tavernetta, Via Madonna del Prato, 52100 Arezzo, saying that your friend left a Pentax camera there at lunchtime on 10th August. Ask them to send it to you and say you are enclosing a Eurocheque for 10.000 lire.

Adesso, tocca a te! (page 72)

Main aim: To demonstrate that the language of this unit has been mastered

Exercise 1

Language area: Saying when and where something was lost
Skill area: Listening

Ask students to write three headings in their exercise books: item lost; where lost; when lost; and to number down the left-hand side of the page 1–5. Do the example together first, for practice. See how many of the details for each one they can get after only one hearing. Then play the recording again for them to check and to fill in any gaps.

🔊 Adesso tocca a te!

Esempio

Girl: Ho perduto la mia macchina fotografica. L'ho perduta oggi quando siamo andati a Londra. L'ho lasciata in autobus. È una bella macchina fotografica gialla.

Numero 1

Boy: Ho perduto il mio zaino, sai, uno di quegli zaini verdi della scuola. L'ho lasciato forse in un negozio, ma non so ... sì, forse in quel negozio di souvenir vicino alla chiesa, dove sono stato stamattina.

Numero 2

Girl: Ho perduto il mio orologio. Forse l'ho perduto quando siamo andati in piscina oggi pomeriggio. È un bell'orologio digitale. È rosso.

Numero 3

Boy: Ho perduto i miei occhiali da sole ... quel paio nuovo che ho comprato qui. Sono neri. Non so dove sono.
Girl: Ma forse nel museo dove siamo stati martedì.
Boy: Sì, è vero. Ho comprato quel paio di occhiali martedì e poi siamo andati nel museo.

Numero 4

Girl 1: Ho perduto un orecchino. È bianco come questo. Non so dove sia.
Girl 2: Quando l'hai perduto?
Girl 1: Adesso, due minuti fa.
Girl 2: Dove sei stata? Sei andata in salotto a guardare la televisione? Hai cercato in salotto?
Girl 1: Buon'idea. Mi aiuti a cercare in salotto?

Numero 5

Boy 1: Ho perduto la mia maglia blu, quella che avevo per giocare a tennis ieri.

Boy 2: Ma non l'hai messa vicino alle docce?

Boy 1: Sì, è vero, l'ho lasciata lì quando sono andato a fare la doccia ieri dopo la partita.

Exercises 2 and 3

Language area: Finding a lost property office and describing lost property

Skill area: Speaking

Each student prepares these roles. In pairs, they then perform them, playing each role in turn. They then help each other to improve, practise together, and perform the roles again, recording them if possible for you to assess.

Exercise 4

Language area: Finding lost property
Skill area: Writing

Each student produces an appropriate advertisement.

Exercise 5

Language area: Finding lost property
Skill area: Reading and writing

Each student writes an appropriate letter, based on the model.

Ora sai (page 73)

Main aim: **To act as a summary and reference point for the main language of this unit**

The students use this item to learn and revise the main parts of this unit, and to develop their study skills, e.g.

- In pairs, student A covers the English and student B reads an English expression from the list: student A gives the matching Italian phrase.

- Do the same thing in reverse, covering the Italian.

- The students race to find and copy every Italian sentence which contains a verb in the perfect tense.

- The students race to find and copy all the Italian words which appear more than once on this page.

Revision

1 Travelling by bus (Book 1, Unit 5)

A Give each student a copy of Copymaster 42. They first copy all the words which refer to things they can see in the picture. Ask students to read out their lists while the others listen and try to spot any which are omitted and any which should not be there.

B Ask each student to close their eyes and imagine where they would most like to go in Italy. They open their eyes and write a dialogue in which they find out which bus will take them there, buy their tickets and confirm they're getting on the right bus.

2 School (Book 2, Unit 8)

A Present the following on the board or OHP. Make sure that everyone knows what to do. The students then write their answers. Ask them to explain their answers.

Scegli la parola adatta				
Esempio				
hello	: inglese	ciao	?	francese, scienze, italiano, ginnastica
La risposta, ovviamente, è: 'italiano'. (Si dice 'hello' in inglese e si dice ciao in italiano.)				
1 20 minuti	: intervallo	60 minuti	?	pasto, pizzeria, lezione, matita
2 piano	: musica	computer	?	ginnastica, liceo, scuola, informatica
3 sto	: stai	faccio	?	facciamo, fate, fanno, fai
4 prima	: I	quinta	?	7, 9, 5, 15
5 piccolo	: grande	facile	?	freddo, difficile, presto, pronto
6 nuovo	: vecchio	interessante	?	noioso, grande, naturale, sporco
7 finisco	: finiamo	sono	?	sei, siete, siamo, è
8 frutta	: mela	materia	?	casa, storia, cotone, pelle
9 ufficio	: impiegato	liceo	?	professore, gestore, autista, poliziotto
10 italiano	: parlare	musica	?	correre, giocare, andare, studiare

B Present the following questions on the board or OHP. The students work in pairs to produce and practise their answers. Move around as they do so, listening and helping.

I Quanti ragazzi ci sono nella tua scuola?
2 Com'è la tua scuola?
3 Quali materie ti piacciono?
4 C'è qualcosa che non ti piace a scuola?
5 Sei già stato(a) in una scuola italiana?

3 Fare: present tense (Book 2, Unit 8)

A Base a few minutes of verb circle practice on the following:

– Il lunedì faccio inglese.
– Dove fai i compiti?
– Non facciamo del windsurf oggi.
– Claudio fa il meccanico.
– Non faccio un'escursione domani.

B Present the following questions on the board or OHP. The students should appreciate that they are all questions which they may want to ask or which may be put to them. Practise asking and answering them with the class and then in pairs.

– Che classe fai?
– Fai molti compiti?
– Dove fai i compiti?
– Quali compiti fai?
– Fai francese a scuola?
– Quali materie fate alla vostra scuola?
– Fai il pattinaggio (del windsurf) qualche volta?
– Che cosa fai stasera?
– Che lavoro fa tuo fratello (tua sorella, tuo padre, tua madre)?

4 Hotels (Book 3, Unit 4)

A Play a few games of 'Categorie'. The class races to categorise as quickly as possible the following words, saying into which category each goes. Write the categories on the board:
'Autobus', 'Scuola', 'Albergo'.
Play the game a few times with the same words, changing the order each time.

biglietto, liceo, classe, istituto, blocchetto, professore, sapone, ginnastica, camera, quinta, notti, in centro, ascensore, stazione, zainetto, tabaccheria, matematica, singola, compiti, comincia, vorrei, orario, banconota, capolinea, materia, latino, fermata, libera, uscita, doppia, scendere, informatica, insegnante, doccia, asciugamano, edicola, parcheggio, il prossimo, bagno, finisce, lampadina.

B Give each student a copy of Copymaster 43. Give them time to work out what they have to do, and make sure they know that the order of room numbers in the instructions is the same as that on the cassette.
When everyone knows what to do, play the recording twice. Check the answers at once, clear up any problems and play the tape again to ensure that everyone hears it at least once with good understanding.
The correct room allocation is:
Mackenzie - 309
Aumonier - 106
Crompton - 717
Wovenden - 701
Lejeune - 105
Jardine - 123
Ginsberg - 517

🚌 I canadesi arrivano ad Arezzo

Esempio

Receptionist: Allora vediamo quali camere sono libere. C'è la camera numero 309. È una doppia, con letto matrimoniale e doccia. C'è anche un bel balcone. La 309, è una bella camera.

Receptionist: Poi c'è la camera 517, è una stanza singola con bagno, e la camera 517 ha anche il balcone e una bella vista sulla città.

Poi c'è la stanza 106, una stanza grande con un letto matrimoniale e uno singolo, con il bagno. Questa stanza, la 106, è situata vicino alla sala da pranzo e alla sala giochi.

Poi abbiamo la stanza 717, è una stanza singola, è piccolissima, non c'è il bagno, però per la stanza 717 c'è una riduzione del venti percento sul prezzo normale.

Quindi abbiamo la stanza 123, è una stanza grande al pianterreno. Ci sono due letti singoli e uno matrimoniale. Naturalmente c'è il bagno. Questa stanza la 123, è situata nella parte posteriore dell'albergo ed è tranquillissima.

La stanza 701 è una stanza bellissima, molto tranquilla con una vista fantastica. È una stanza con un letto matrimoniale e c'è anche il bagno.

Per finire la stanza 105, con due letti singoli, la doccia, e la stanza 105 è situata al pianterreno.

5 Direct object pronouns after 'ecco' (Book 3, Unit 4)

A Write the following on the board or OHP:

Eccolo   Eccola   Eccoli   Eccole

Divide the class into two teams. Give them four minutes to prepare: you will say one of the words on the board and the first to point to something in the room that it could refer to and name it wins a point. Practise a few times to ensure that everyone understands, e.g.

– Eccola.
– La tavola.

B Play a game of 'Pass the parcel'. You give a picture to a student and say, e.g.

– Ho un regalo per te. È un orologio. Eccolo.

This student takes the picture, and passes it on to another student, repeating exactly what you said. If he/she does this, the other student has to take the picture and tries to pass it on in the same way. A student who does not repeat exactly what you said pays a forfeit, e.g. counts from 40 to 50, spells a word on the board or answers a question. You then start again with another picture.

6 Camping (Book 3, Unit 7)

A Present the following sentences on the board or OHP. Give the class two minutes to read them and to decide individually where each one would be said. They compare their ideas in pairs and then several report to the class, e.g.

– Secondo te, dove si può dire (no. 1)?
– Secondo me, si può dire questo al campeggio.
– Sei d'accordo, Tom?
– Sì, sono d'accordo.

  1 Avete ancora posto per una piccola tenda?
  2 È questa la fermata per la stazione?
  3 Scusi, cerco il locale ritrovo.
  4 Dove possiamo sistemarci?
  5 L'ascensore non funziona.
  6 C'è un posto all'ombra?
  7 Mi dia un blocchetto per favore.
  8 Quanto costa al giorno per una roulotte?
  9 Avete una camera libera?
 10 Ho dimenticato il sacco a pelo.

B Repeat the above procedure with the following sentences: this time, the students have to decide to whom they would say each one.

  1 Mi sa dire dov'è lo spaccio?
  2 Quando si deve pagare?
  3 Mi dà la chiave, per favore.
  4 Quanto costa al giorno, per una macchina?
  5 Frequento la scuola media.
  6 Ho prenotato un posto per sette giorni.
  7 È questo l'autobus per il castello?
  8 C'è una lavanderia qui?
  9 Scusi, il telefono è guasto.
 10 Cosa vuol dire 'acqua potabile'?

7 Potere + infinitive (Book 3, Unit 7)

A Organise some verb circle practice, starting with, e.g.

– Posso andare in bagno, per favore?
– Possiamo giocare a tennis qui?
– Gli adulti possono andare nel bar.
– Potete venire al cinema stasera.

B Present this table on the board. Give the class just five minutes to make up as many sensible and correct sentences as they can, using the table.

In campeggio Hai esattamente cinque minuti. Quante frasi giuste puoi fare?	
In campeggio si può	parlare italiano. scrivere una lettera. fare la quinta classe. fare una vacanza. andare in chiesa. andare a pescare. fare una vacanza tranquilla. lasciare un documento. bere l'acqua non potabile. dormire in una camera. fare i compiti. vedere una roulotte. comprare un blocchetto. far rumore a mezzanotte.

9ª Unità
IN FAMIGLIA

Main aim

~ To fit in and feel at home when staying with an Italian family

Materials

~ Tape

Ciao o buonasera? (Teacher's Book page 107)
Hai fatto buon viaggio? (Teacher's Book page 107)
Ti presto un golf? (Teacher's Book page 109)
L'arrivo in famiglia (Teacher's Book page 109)
Questo è per te (Teacher's Book page 110)
La tua camera in Italia (Teacher's Book page 111)
Dove posso mettere ...? (Teacher's Book page 111)
Adesso, tocca a te! (Teacher's Book page 114)

~ Copymasters 44–47

Grammar in *Scoprite qualcosa di più*

~ Pronouns following prepositions: me, te, lui, lei, etc

Revision

~ Buying postcards and stamps (Book 1, Unit 6)
~ Plural of nouns (Book 1, Unit 6)
~ Daily routine (Book 2, Unit 9)
~ Reflexive verbs: present tense (Book 2, Unit 9)
~ Talking about a recent holiday (Book 3, Unit 5)
~ Perfect tense with 'essere' (Book 3, Unit 5)
~ Lost property (Book 3, Unit 8)
~ Perfect tense with 'avere' (Book 3, Unit 8)

Vocabulary

A: Productive

l'aeroporto	nel, nella, nell'
avere caldo	il pigiama
avere fame	prestare
avere freddo	un ritardo
avere sete	una scarpa
avere sonno	uno sciopero
il dentifricio	lo shampoo
un fon	sopra
una giacca	sotto
un incidente	lo spazzolino da denti
Lei	stanco
lei	su, sul, sulla
lui	la valigia
loro	i vestiti
la macchina	il viaggio
me	

B: Receptive

l'armadio	gentile	salutare
avere bisogno di	la giornata	una sedia
un cassetto	giù	le tapparelle
dei cioccolatini	la lampada	tipico
divertirsi	un maglione	una tradizione
fermarsi	maleducato	veloce
la finestra	un(') ospite	vuoto

In famiglia (page 74)

Main aim: To ensure that the students understand and accept the objectives of this unit

A Ask the students to read the introduction. Use their questions and comments to arouse their interest in, and enthusiasm for, this unit, e.g.

- talk about your own Italian contacts and friends
- describe some pleasant visits to, and from, Italian friends
- ask the students about any Italian contacts or friends of theirs.

B Give the students just five minutes to scan read the rest of the unit and to write a list of what they expect to learn to do in Italian during the unit. As students report back, ask them to say when each point they mention would be useful or interesting: involve as many students as possible in this.

Permesso (page 74)

Main aim: To introduce an important cultural point

A Give the students just two minutes to read and to try to remember as much as they can about this text. They close their books and write their answers to these questions (presented on the OHP or board):

1 What should you say as you go into someone's home in Italy?
2 Do you have to say this every time you go into their home?
3 What is the equivalent expression in English?
4 Write two expressions that Italians say to invite you into their home.
5 At what other times do you use this important word?

When the students have written their answers, give them one more minute to read the text again and to check their answers. Then go over their answers with them and use this to clear up any misunderstandings and to increase their insights, e.g.

- ask if there is anything similar in their culture

– point out other situations where 'Permesso' is used, e.g. to get off a crowded bus

– 'Permesso' is used on a first visit and when you re-visit a home after a time away: so, a mother would say 'Permesso' on entering her married son's home to indicate that she does not live there.

B Encourage the students to say 'Permesso' from now on when they enter your classroom.

Ciao o buonasera? (pages 74-75)

Main aim: To learn how to make appropriate greetings

A First make sure that everyone understands the purpose of this item. Students then read the three short dialogues, listen to them and try to work out the answers to the two questions. When everyone is clear about these answers, they hear and read them again and then act them out in pairs.

🔊 Ciao o buonasera?

Dialogo 1

Monica:	Ciao Giulio!
Giulio:	Ciao Monica!
Monica:	Come stai?
Giulio:	Sto bene. E tu?
Monica:	Benissimo grazie.

Dialogo 2

Woman:	Ciao Marco!
Marco:	Buonasera, signora.
Woman:	Come stai?
Marco:	Sto bene, grazie. E Lei, come sta?
Woman:	Bene, grazie.

Dialogo 3

Man:	Buongiorno Anna.
Anna:	Buongiorno signore.
Man:	Come stai stamattina?
Anna:	Bene grazie. E Lei?

B The students copy and complete the table. Allow them to consult and to help each other.

C The students look at the four pictures. You say one of the times illustrated and the students point to the picture it goes with and say the number. You then say an appropriate greeting for one of the pictures: the students point to the picture and say the number. After this input, the students make up a dialogue for each picture: they act these out and the others say at what time each dialogue takes place.

Hai fatto buon viaggio? (page 76)

Main aim: To talk about journeys

A Work on the list using previously successful techniques. You could also introduce some new activities, e.g.

● Flash a phrase from the list very briefly on the OHP. The students try to copy it exactly.

● The students copy a phrase from the list and keep on saying it quietly to themselves while they copy it. This is not as easy as it sounds!

● When the students are fairly familiar with the list, give them two more minutes to study it. Then dictate some short sentences on the topic of a journey. Some of your sentences should be straight from the list and others should be similar but different. The students write all the sentences you dictate and add a tick to those which they think are taken unchanged from the list. They then check with the list.

B Before playing the tape, ask the students to study the pictures and to try to guess what the people in the pictures would say in answer to the question 'Hai fatto buon viaggio?'. For each picture each student could copy, and adapt, expressions from the list. You could point out that this ability to predict much of what people will say in given situations helps us to understand more easily what they do say, in life and in exams!

C Play the recording. The first time they hear it, the students tick the expressions in their lists as they hear them. At the end, ask if they heard what they expected to hear and if anything surprised them.

🔊 Hai fatto buon viaggio?

Numero 1

– Tutto è andato bene quando abbiamo attraversato la Francia, ma poi nelle Alpi abbiamo avuto un problema con la macchina. Accidenti! Il motore si è surriscaldato e abbiamo dovuto fermarci. Fortunatamente avevo dell'acqua che abbiamo messo nel radiatore, e poi abbiamo continuato.

Numero 2

– Sì, sono stanca perché, sa, il viaggio in pullman dall'Inghilterra è sempre lungo e poi c'è stato moltissimo traffico. Siamo stati quasi fermi sull'autostrada per due ore. Sì, in due ore abbiamo fatto appena tre chilometri.

Numero 3

– Abbiamo passato delle bellissime vacanze al mare, ma poi il viaggio di ritorno è stato un disastro. Siamo stati alla stazione per tre ore e mezza perché c'era uno sciopero. Era noioso e non c'era niente da fare alla stazione.

Numero 4

– Siamo stati in Sicilia per Natale. E poi al ritorno, siamo stati quattro ore all'aeroporto perché c'è stato un ritardo a causa del tempo.

Numero 5

– Il viaggio è andato bene, solo che abbiamo visto un incidente. Ecco, c'è stato un incidente con un grosso camion. Un'ambulanza è arrivata e anche la polizia, ma il traffico è stato un po' bloccato lo stesso.

D The students listen to the recordings again. After each one, stop the tape and ask the students to say which picture it goes with. Then ask them to say what the key expressions were which gave the answer away: play the recording again to help them do this.

E In pairs, the students make up a dialogue for three of the pictures. They act one out and the others guess which picture it is based on.

Il viaggio di ritorno (page 77)

Main aim: Reading and writing a letter about a journey

A The students read the letter and answer your questions, e.g.
– What was this person's journey like?
– Why?
– What happened at Gatwick?
– What was the result?

B The students study the letter again and pick out eight to ten key words, the words which convey the key points. Discuss these and try to agree on the key words. Write these on the board.
Without looking back at the letter, the students try to re-create it from the key words. They do this orally and you write what they say on the board or OHP. They then compare this with the original and discuss the differences: are any differences just different ways of saying the same thing or is any information incorrect, omitted or added in their letter?

C Write on the board or OHP the key words for another, similar, letter. Orally, the students expand on this and produce a letter which you, with help from them, write on the board.

D As a class exercise, jointly agree on eight to ten key words for another letter about a journey. Each student then writes a letter around these key words. They compare the results and may be surprised!

E They each choose one of the pictures on page 76 and write a paragraph of a letter. You could advise them to make a list of eight to ten key expressions to use before they start to

write. This is a useful exam technique: it helps the students to use good expressions which they feel confident about.

F As students finish the above task, you could ask them to work on the task below, which can be presented on the board or OHP:

– Lavora con un(a) partner. Scegli segretamente una figura a pagina 76. Il tuo/la tua partner deve fare delle domande per scoprire la figura giusta. Tu devi rispondere alle sue domande usando soltanto le parole 'Sì' e 'No'.

Esempio:

Partner: C'è stato un incidente?
Tu: No.
Partner: C'è stato uno sciopero?
Tu: Sì.
Partner: Allora, è la figura A.

Hai fame? (page 77)

Main aim: To introduce ways of asking and answering questions about whether people are hungry, hot, etc

A Work on the list using previously successful techniques. You could also use some new activities, e.g.

• Display several sentences based on the list, some complete and others incomplete. Instruct the students to copy only the complete sentences. Alternatively, they can be told to ignore the complete sentences and to copy and complete the others.

• Each student in turn chooses a phrase or word in the list and mimes it: the others guess what she/he is miming. Once a phrase has been mimed, it cannot be done again. You can tell students that it is, therefore, best to volunteer early to get an easy word or phrase.

B Students now make up dialogues based on pictures 1 to 5.

C As students finish their dialogues they could begin on the following exercise which can be presented on the board or OHP:

– Gli studenti lavorano a due. Uno studente fa la parte di un ospite italiano. L'altro cerca di scoprire esattamente come si sente il suo ospite. Decidi se hai fame o sete o altra cosa. Il tuo/la tua partner deve scoprire che cos'hai.

Esempio:

Partner: Come stai? Hai caldo?
Tu: No, non ho caldo.
Partner: Hai sete?
Tu: Sì, ho sete.

Ti presto un golf? (page 78)

Main aim: **To practise some key expressions and to develop communication strategies for understanding**

A Ensure that the students realise that the task is to find, and to work out the meaning of, the sentences in the box. Work on one at a time: the students find the sentence in one of the dialogues, read the dialogue and then report back on the meaning of the sentence and the rest of the dialogue. Encourage them to say how they worked out the meanings: try to find as many different techniques as possible from the class.

B The students read again, listen to and act in pairs the five dialogues.

🔊 Ti presto un golf?

Dialogo 1

Girl 1:	Come stai?
Girl 2:	Sono un po' stanca.
Girl 1:	Vuoi andare a dormire?
Girl 2:	Sì, grazie.

Dialogo 2

Man:	Hai sete?
Girl:	Un po', sì.
Man:	Vuoi bere qualcosa?
Girl:	Sì, grazie.

Dialogo 3

Woman:	Come stai?
Girl:	Ho un po' caldo.
Woman:	Apriamo una finestra?
Girl:	Va bene. Grazie.

Dialogo 4

Girl 1:	Hai fame?
Girl 2:	No, ma ho freddo.
Girl 1:	Hai freddo? Ti presto un golf?
Girl 2:	Oh, grazie.

Dialogo 5

Boy 1:	Come stai? Hai fame?
Boy 2:	No, sto bene, grazie.
Boy 1:	Sei sicuro? Vuoi mangiare qualcosa?
Boy 2:	Va bene. Un panino.

C As a homework task, each student could make up new dialogues containing the five key expressions. In class, they could show these to their partners and help each other to correct their dialogues.

D The students cover up the dialogues on this page and make up, in pairs, a brief dialogue based on each picture. They could either try to make their dialogues as close as possible to those in the book or aim to make them completely different, but still based on the pictures.

L'arrivo in famiglia (page 79)

Main aim: **To practise expressing needs**

A The students could read this as a homework task and then ask about anything which is not clear. You could ask them to comment on the hosts and the guest, e.g.

– What does Signora Cosenza think of Paul?
– What does he think of her?
– Would you like to stay with the Cosenza family? Why (not)?

B Play the recording as the students follow the text. Stop the tape from time to time, using the pause button, and ask someone to continue immediately, without a gap.

🔊 L'arrivo in famiglia

Francesco:	Ciao Mamma! Questo è Paul.
Signora Cosenza:	Ciao Paul! Come stai?
Paul:	Bene grazie. E Lei, signora?
Signora Cosenza:	Bene, bene. Mi capisci quando parlo italiano?
Paul:	Sì, capisco un po'.
Signora Cosenza:	È meglio parlare piano però?
Paul:	Sì, piano per favore.
Signora Cosenza:	Hai fatto buon viaggio? Un po' lungo forse?
Paul:	Sì, un po' lungo.
Signora Cosenza:	Sei un po' stanco?
Paul:	Sì, sono stanco.
Signora Cosenza:	Hai sete? Vuoi qualcosa da bere? Un tè, per esempio, o c'è della limonata, del succo di arancia o dell'acqua minerale.
Paul:	Sì, potrei avere un bicchiere di acqua minerale, per favore?
Signora Cosenza:	Certo ... Eccoti.
Paul:	Grazie.

C You read the conversation aloud as the students follow the text. From time to time, change a word or a phrase, concentrating on those which are underlined. Students race to stop and correct you. This could be done as a team competition.
You could repeat this activity with the Students' Book closed.

D In pairs, the students adapt the conversation orally, changing the words which are underlined.

E As students finish **D** above, they could be told to write the conversations which they have made up.

Questo è per te (page 79)

Main aim: Learning how to give, and to receive, gifts

A Read the introduction with the class and make sure that everyone understands it. Ask for ideas for gifts and start to write a list on the board or OHP: you could introduce words from Book 2, Unit 6 e.g. 'sciarpa', 'ombrello', 'cintura', 'profumo', etc. Give the students four minutes to write their own lists, looking for ideas in the Students' Book or in a dictionary. Then ask for more ideas to add to your list: accept all which are correct and add them to your list.
You could base a 'Kim's game' (see Teacher's Book page 6) on your list.

B The students read, listen to and act in pairs the three dialogues.

Questo è per te

Dialogo 1

| Boy: | Questo è per Lei. |
| Woman: | Grazie, ma non dovevi. |

Dialogo 2

| Girl 1: | Questo è per te. |
| Girl 2: | Grazie, come sei gentile. |

Dialogo 3

Girl:	Questo è per voi.
Woman:	Oh, che bello!
Man:	Grazie. Ma che cos'è?
Girl:	Sono biscottini.

C They could extend the first two dialogues, following the model of the third, to say what the present is. There is, of course, no one right answer and the students may enjoy hearing what others say it is.

D This would be a good time to start work on *Scoprite qualcosa di più* (pages 167-170).

E Look again at the three dialogues on page 79. Ask the students to explain the use of: 'Lei', 'te', 'voi'.
You could explain that Italians are usually very generous with gifts. Try to draw up a list of suitable presents to take from where you live to a family in Italy. These need not be

expensive (e.g. a tea cosy, table mats, tea, biscuits, jam, fudge, bubble bath).
Try to have available some suitable items. You could offer a gift to a pair of students. If you say, e.g.

– Questo è per voi.

both should thank you.
If you say, e.g.

– Questo è per te.

only one of them should thank you, the one in front of whom you put it.

F You and the students should, from now on, use this language regularly in class when giving back exercise books, borrowing pencils, etc.

Ma non dovevi, Matilde! (page 80)

Main aim: To practise saying the right thing when giving, and receiving, presents

A Ask the students to identify all the presents illustrated. Write these on the board and then rub off a few letters from each word. The students copy them all in full. When they have finished, fill in the missing letters to allow the students to check their lists.

B The students tell you what they would say when giving a gift to each of the people illustrated. Write these on the board. Use a 'snowballing' technique to involve as many students as possible, e.g.

Teacher:	Che cosa si dice ai nonni?
Student:	Si dice 'Questo è per voi'.
Teacher:	E che cosa si dice a Luigi?
Student:	Si dice 'Questo è per te'.
Teacher:	Che cosa si dice ai nonni e poi a Luigi?
Student:	Si dicete 'Questo è per voi' e poi 'questo è per te'.

C Work on the 'Warning' box and ensure that everyone understands.

D As a class, start to make up dialogues based on the maze and the model.

After doing this orally, the students each write four or five dialogues which they could then act in pairs.

E You could ask some questions based on the maze, e.g.

– Che cos'ha comprato per X?
– Che cos'ha offerto a Y?
– Che cos'ha dato a Z?
– Che cos'ha ricevuto A?
– Che cos'hanno ricevuto B e C?

F Return to the *Scoprite qualcosa di più* section and continue to work on it with the class.

La tua camera in Italia (page 81)

Main aim: To learn the key words needed to show a bedroom to a visitor, and to be shown a bedroom

A The students should first list in their exercise books all the words which are used as labels in the picture. Then they try to work out what they all mean: when everyone is sure what they all mean, they could write the English equivalents in their exercise books.

B You describe orally the differences between this room and your bedroom, following the model. The students listen and then try to summarise the differences. Each student now writes a list of the differences between this room and his/her bedroom.

C Encourage the students to ask you how to say in Italian the names of other items of furniture, etc. which they have in their rooms. When you give a word, say it several times as you go to the board and write it. Say it several times more and encourage the student to say it as he/she writes it in his/her book.
Ask the students to suggest an activity to help them to learn these words. Use the activities they suggest. You could also use one of the following ideas:

• Get the students to list all the words in order of importance for a holiday bedroom and then to compare their lists.

• Ask them to say, in one minute only, as many as possible of these things that they would find in 'un'aula', 'una camera d'albergo', 'una sala d'attesa alla stazione', 'una tenda'.

D Play the following recording. The students listen and try to list all the items of furniture which are mentioned.
Check the students' lists and play the recording again to allow them to check.
Ask what 'le zanzare' are and ask how the students understood. You could discuss the problem of mosquitoes and what to do about them.

🔊 La tua camera in Italia

Friend: Ecco. Qui c'è la tua camera.
Guest: È proprio bella.
Friend: C'è posto in questo armadio vicino al letto per mettere i tuoi vestiti. Va bene?
Guest: Sì, va benissimo.

Friend: E poi c'è anche questo cassetto vuoto che puoi usare.
Guest: C'è molto posto. Grazie.
Friend: Ecco le tapparelle. Non le avete da voi, è vero? Come si dice tapparelle in inglese?
Guest: Si dice 'blinds'.
Friend: 'Blinds'. Allora in italiano le tapparelle. Ecco. Si tirano su così ... e poi si tirano giù così. Va bene?
Guest: Sì, benissimo.
Friend: Un'altra cosa. Non accendere la luce a quest'ora. Altrimenti entrano le zanzare, zzzz le zanzare, capisci?
Guest: Sì.

E At home, each student draws a picture of his/her bedroom and labels it. In class, they use their pictures to make up dialogues in pairs as if they were showing their rooms to an Italian visitor.

Dove posso mettere ...? (page 81)

Main aim: To learn how to ask, and to say, where things go

A The students work on this item along the lines suggested in the Students' Book.

🔊 Dove posso mettere ...?

Esempio

Girl 1: Ecco la tua camera. C'è posto qui nell'armadio per i tuoi vestiti e c'è anche un cassetto vuoto qui.
Girl 2: Perfetto. Senti, dove posso mettere la mia giacca?
Girl 1: La tua giacca ... vediamo ... sì, mettila nell'ingresso con tutte le altre giacche. Va bene?
Girl 2: Sì, grazie.

Dialogo 1

Girl 2: Ho quasi finito di mettere tutto a posto.
Girl 1: Brava. Vuoi che ti dia una mano?
Girl 2: Beh ... dimmi, dove posso mettere il mio spazzolino da denti?
Girl 1: Mettilo in bagno. C'è un bicchierino sul lavandino, lo puoi mettere lì dentro.
Girl 2: Nel bicchiere in bagno?
Girl 1: Esatto.

Dialogo 2

Boy 1: Senti, ho già messo via l'altra roba ma non so dove mettere le mie scarpe. Ho queste scarpe da ginnastica e quest'altro paio di scarpe.
Boy 2: Beh, io le metterei qui, sotto il letto.
Boy 1: Sotto il letto? Va bene.

Dialogo 3

Boy: Hai finito? Vuoi bere qualcosa?

Girl: Non ancora, un momento. Devo mettere via la valigia. Dove posso metterla, secondo te?

Boy: Vediamo ... mettila lì accanto alla sedia, vicino alla finestra.

Girl: Così, va bene?

Boy: Perfetto.

Dialogo 4

Woman: Tutto bene? C'è abbastanza posto?

Girl: Sì, sì. Ho messo i miei vestiti qui nell'armadio e le maglie qui nel cassetto.

Woman: Brava!

Girl: Senta, dove posso mettere il mio pigiama?

Woman: Mettilo in bagno, dietro la porta. Ci sono dei ganci in bagno dove lo puoi appendere.

Girl: Va bene, grazie.

Dialogo 5

Girl: Allora, Sandro, hai finito di mettere via tutta la tua roba?

Boy: Più o meno, sì. Rimangono soltanto questi vestiti.

Girl: Soltanto i vestiti?

Boy: Eh, sì. Ho messo via tutte le altre cose. Dimmi, dove li metto questi vestiti?

Girl: Che sono? Sono maglie e T-shirt ... . Mettili qui nel cassetto vuoto.

Boy: OK. Mi apri il cassetto, per favore?

B When correcting the answers to the listening exercise, you could ask, e.g.

- Nell'esempio, dove ha messo la sua giacca?
- Ha messo la giacca nell'ingresso.

C You could base an oral drill on the table, e.g.

Teacher: Il pigiama.

Student A: Mettilo qui.

Student B: Lo puoi mettere qui.

D Play a memory game: the students close their eyes and tell you where things are in the room. A variation of this is to put some objects in unusual places before the students arrive. The students try to spot these. When they do, ask them where you should put them.

E Give each student a copy of Copymaster 44. Make sure that everyone knows what to do. They could then do the exercise at home and check their answers in pairs in the next lesson.

F Give each student a copy of Copymaster 45. Also make a copy to show on the OHP and a copy of the mosquitoes to use later.

Explain that twelve mosquitoes are hidden in the room. These are represented by dots in the picture.

Using the table, the students locate the mosquitoes. As they describe the location, if correct, the teacher gives a student a mosquito cartoon to place over the appropriate dot on the picture, e.g.

Student: C'è una zanzara sotto il letto.

Teacher: Bravo(a). Ecco una zanzara. Mettila sotto il letto.

The student puts the mosquito cartoon in position and the teacher does the same on the OHP.

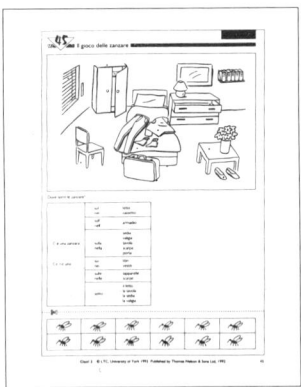

G The students can then play 'Secret choice' in pairs or groups. Student A secretly decides on the position of a mosquito. This could be in the same position as on the Copymaster, or in a different place. They write down the place. Student B has to guess where it is, e.g.

- È sul letto?
- È sotto l'armadio?

They then change roles.

The winner is the person who guesses the location by asking the fewest questions.

You could cover the table at this stage.

You could use a variation on this game to revise:

vicino a   accanto a   davanti a.

The mosquitoes are not on any particular piece of furniture but buzzing round, hovering.

Mi puoi prestare un asciugamano? (page 82)

Main aim: To practise borrowing and lending useful items

A Work on this item along the lines suggested in the Students' Book.

B Draw on the board the grid to play 'Noughts and crosses'.

Divide the class into two teams. They indicate where you should put their nought or cross by asking to borrow the item in the corresponding box.
The students could continue to play this in pairs.

C Outline a problem and ask the class to suggest what you should ask to borrow, e.g.

– Usciamo stasera e non voglio prendere freddo.
– Devo scrivere ai miei genitori. Ho della carta e una busta.

D The students listen as you ask to borrow a number of items. From the language you use, they try to guess who you are talking to (e.g. your spouse, headteacher, brother, friend, Italian host, police officer, a complete stranger).
You could then give them a list and ask them to practise how to ask everyone on it if they could borrow a pencil, e.g.

il professore/la professoressa
un(a) partner
il padre di un(a) amico(a)
un poliziotto
un(a) amico(a)

E You and the students should, from now on, use this language regularly in class.

F Give each student a copy of either Copymaster 46A or Copymaster 46B. Make sure that they know what to do in pairs: you and your assistant (or a student) could start work together as a model.
As the students work on this, move around, listening and helping.

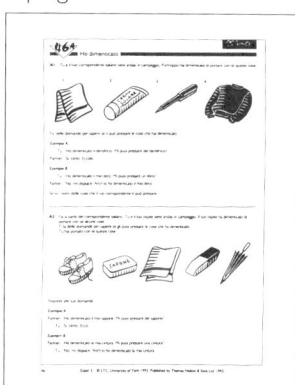 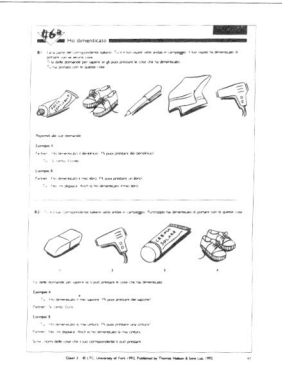

Che giornata! (page 83)

Main aim: To practise using 'noi/voi' + verb phrase in perfect tense

A The students read, listen to, play-read and adapt this dialogue.

B The students listen and say which picture what you say refers to, e.g.

– Abbiamo fatto un po' di shopping.
– Abbiamo giocato a calcio.
– Abbiamo comprato delle cartoline.
– Siamo andati al cinema.

C In pairs, each student makes up two sentences based on the table. You ask questions to try to find out what sentences they have made up, e.g.

Teacher: Avete comprato qualcosa?
Student: Sì.
Teacher: Avete comprato un gelato?
Student: No.
Teacher: Avete comprato una pizza?
Student: Sì, abbiamo comprato una pizza.

Write a model like this one on the board and leave it there for the students to refer to as they continue this activity in pairs.

D Ask the students to suggest as many sentences as they can for each picture, e.g.

– Abbiamo fatto dello shopping.
– Abbiamo comprato dei regali.
– Siamo andati nei negozi.

Write their suggestions on the board, correcting tactfully where necessary as you do so. Give the class three minutes to study the sentences and then rub off parts of them and invite students to come to the board and complete them.
Each student now writes a sentence for each picture. They use these as a basis for role-playing in pairs, each taking a turn to be someone in the Italian family asking what the visitor has done today.

Adesso, tocca a te! (page 84)

Main aim: To demonstrate that the language of the unit has been mastered

Exercise 1
Language area: Asking to borrow things
Skill area: Listening

Play the recording twice. The students write notes in English.

▭ Adesso, tocca a te!

Numero 1

– Ho dimenticato la mia penna. Mi può prestare una penna?

Numero 2

– Ho freddo. Non so dove ho messo la giacca. Mi può prestare una giacca o un maglione?

Numero 3

– Ho fame. C'è qualcosa da mangiare?

Numero 4

– Ho tanta sete. Posso avere un bicchiere d'acqua?

Numero 5

– Voglio lavarmi i capelli. Ha un fon da prestarmi?

Exercise 2

Language area: Staying with a family
Skill area: Speaking

Make the students responsible for their own and their partners' performance: they should help each other to do this well. Encourage independence, especially in answering open-ended questions. Help them to avoid replying with simply 'Sì' or 'No'.

Exercise 3

Language area: Staying with a family
Skill area: Speaking

Students work on this in pairs along the lines recommended for exercise 2.

Exercise 4

Language area: Describing a day out
Skill area: Writing

Each student works alone to do this: they can base what they write on the model or feel free to move away from it. When this work has been corrected, encourage them to compare what they have written.

Ora sai (page 85)

Main aim: **To act as a summary and reference point for the main language of this unit**

To help the students to master and to revise this key language, they could use, discuss and assess the following techniques:

● Pick out, write and say the expressions here which are generally true for them, and compare with others. They could repeat this for expressions which are true for them today and again for what is true for them now.

● They could race to find and say phrases which they could say when, e.g.

– entering an Italian home
– they feel hungry (thirsty, etc.)
– they have had a good journey.

After some classwork on this, they could continue in pairs, asking each other what to say when ...
This could be varied by finding what to say if, e.g.

– they forgot their pen
– someone needed an umbrella
– they wanted to know where to put their jacket.

● Each student makes up two Italian examples for each English description in the left-hand column, different from those on the right. They compare with each other what they have written.

Revision

1   Buying postcards and stamps (Book 1, Unit 6)

A To revise some of the key words, play a game of 'Categorie'. See how many words the class can categorise correctly in 60 seconds, e.g.

● Bisogna dire se ogni parola è un numero o un paese: venti, la Gran Bretagna, sessanta, novanta, settanta, l'Italia, la Francia, ottanta, cinquanta, quaranta, l'Irlanda, la Spagna, l'Australia, trenta, due, cinque.

● Bisogna dire se ogni parola è singolare o plurale: cartolina, francobolli, lettera, scarpe, macchina, pigiama, denti, valigie, vestiti, viaggio, cioccolatini, cassetto, finestra, lampade, sedia, armadio, tapparelle, cartoline, francobollo, lettere, amiche, parchi, laghi.

B Give each student a copy of Copymaster 47. They work on this along the lines suggested. Move around, listening and helping.

2   Daily routine (Book 2, Unit 9)

A   To remind the students of the key words, you could write the following on the board:

alzarsi, andare a letto, cenare, fare colazione, lavarsi, pranzare, svegliarsi, arrivare a scuola, lavarsi i denti, indossare il pigiama, divertirsi.

Then draw three columns on the board and head them with: 'la mattina', 'il pomeriggio', 'la sera'.

The students draw the same columns in their exercise books and then copy the words from the board in the appropriate columns: tell them that some words may appear in two or three columns.
When they have finished, they compare their lists and discuss any differences.

B   Organise some brief verb circle practice, starting with, e.g.

– Mi alzo alle sette.
– Mi diverto in Italia.

C   Ask the students to describe the most boring possible day of a holiday, e.g.

– Mi alzo, mi lavo in bagno, mi vesto, faccio colazione, vado in spiaggia, etc.

After some class practice, everyone writes an account of the most boring day possible and illustrates it. Make a display of the results.

3   Talking about a recent holiday (Book 3, Unit 5)

A   The students revise the *Ora sai* section for Unit 5 on page 47 of the Students' Book. Ask them to say what techniques they are planning to use: this will give some ideas to those who may not know what to do.

B   Organise some verb circle practice with, e.g.

– Sono andata all'aeroporto.
– Sono venuto in macchina.
– Sono arrivato in ritardo.

C   You, an Italian assistant or a student on teaching practice, could tell the class about a recent holiday. The class could ask questions to find out more. They could then summarise what they have found out.

4   Lost property (Book 3, Unit 8)

A   The students look back at the *Ora sai* section for Unit 8 on page 73 of the Students' Book. Students list the words or phrases which they have forgotten or found hard to learn. They give these to their partners who try to find a way of helping them to learn them.

B   Organise some verb circle practice, e.g.

– Ho perso la valigia.
– Ho lasciato il fon a casa.
– Non ho comprato il dentifricio.

C   Make some flashcards, on thin card or paper, folded in two. On the outside, draw a 'container' (e.g. a case, wallet, purse, bag) and on the inside draw something that could go into that 'container'. You could use pictures from magazines, e.g.

Show the 'container' to the class and ask, e.g.

– Che cos'è questo?
– E che cosa c'è dentro?

When a student guesses correctly, open the card to confirm it, e.g.

– Giusto! Apro così e dentro troviamo un orologio. Riesci a descrivere l'orologio?

D   The students should make more cards of their own like these to present to the class. You collect these in and show them one at a time, asking, e.g.

– Chi ha perduto questa borsa?

Ask the student who claims it what is inside and to describe it. If this is done successfully, return the card to him/her.

10ª Unità

A TAVOLA

Main aims

~ To ask and tell people about arrangements for meals
~ To react to offers of food and pay compliments
~ To ask for things at table
~ To offer to help

Materials

~ Tape

A che ora si mangia? (Teacher's Book page 117)
Sì, grazie, mi piace (Teacher's Book page 118)
Sono cortesi? (Teacher's Book page 119)
Buon appetito (Teacher's Book page 120)
Grazie del tuo aiuto (Teacher's Book page 122)
Adesso, tocca a te! Teacher's Book page 122)
Il listino prezzi (Teacher's Book page 123)

~ Copymasters 48–52

Grammar in *Scoprite qualcosa di più*

~ Impersonal 'si'

Revision

~ Buying drinks in a bar or café (Book 1, Unit 7)
~ Indefinite article: un' (Book 1, Unit 7)
~ Free time, leisure activities (Book 2, Unit 10)
~ Present tense: 'io' and 'tu' forms (Book 2, Unit 10)
~ Indirect object pronouns (Book 3, Unit 6)
~ Staying with an Italian family (Book 3, Unit 9)
~ 'Noi' and 'voi': present and perfect tenses (Book 3, Units 1, 5, 9)
~ Pronouns following prepositions (Book 3, Unit 9)

A: Productive

altrettanto	delizioso	un pollo
apparecchiare	i fagioli	un po' di
asciugare	fare male	provare
una bistecca	una forchetta	il sale
buon appetito	un frigorifero	salute
cin-cin	frutti di mare	una scodella
un coltello	il pepe	sparecchiare
un cucchiaino	un piatto	vegetariano(a)
un cucchiaio	i piselli	volentieri

B: Receptive

l'armadietto	melone	tagliatelle
il cibo	mozzarella	una tovaglia
gnocchi	però	un tovagliolo
una lavastoviglie	pochino	
maccheroni	risotto	

A tavola (page 86)

Main aim: To introduce the aims of this unit and to interest the students in them

A Give the students just three minutes to read this information, to find the main points in it and to try to remember them. They then close the Students' Book and try to answer these questions:

1 Name two things to eat which are typical of Italy.
2 Which is the most important meal of the day in Italy?
3 Where do most Italians eat lunch?
4 Which of the following will you learn to do in this unit?
   a Cook risotto alla milanese.
   b Say what you like to eat.
   c Ask for something at table.
   d Enjoy Italian seafood.
   e Offer to help in the kitchen.
5 What else would you like to learn to say and do when eating in Italy?

When the students have written their answers, give them one more minute to read the text again and to check their answers.

B Discuss their answers with them. Help them to understand how important it is to know what to say and do when eating with an Italian family.
During the discussion, you could introduce more information about meals in Italy, e.g.

● Italians don't eat much for breakfast – 'caffelatte' or 'cappuccino' – perhaps 'pane' and 'marmellata'. Some people have coffee and a pastry or croissant in a café or bar near where they work.

● Many people still get a two-hour lunch break (sometimes more!) and eat a three-course meal for both 'pranzo' and 'cena'. In the cities many large companies now have 'l'orario continuato', so called because they only have one hour for lunch. Most of those who have a long lunch break tend to go home as they often live near their place of work. Commuting over long distances is not popular.

● Meal times depend on the region. 'Un milanese' may have 'il pranzo' at 12.30 or 1p.m. while 'un romano' will eat an hour or so later. 'La cena' is also eaten earlier (from 7 p.m.) in the north than in the south.

C If you have pictures, such as magazine cuttings, of different Italian dishes, you could use them to ask, e.g.

– Avete già mangiato un pasto all'italiana?
– Dove?

- Avete già mangiato frutti di mare?
- Che cosa hai mangiato?
- È stato buono?
- Avete mai mangiato gli gnocchi?
- Capite che cose sono?
- Puoi spiegarmi che cose sono?

A che ora si mangia? (page 86)

Main aim: Finding out, and talking about, meal times

A Give the students just ninety seconds to skim this and to find out the gist, or what it is about. When they have told you, ask them how they found out, e.g. the title, the illustrations, the key words and sentences. This can help those who have still not mastered the techniques for quickly finding the gist of a text to do so.

B Give practice in scan reading by asking the students to find specific, important details in the text as quickly as possible, e.g.

- Where does this family have breakfast?
- When does this family have lunch?
- Where does this family eat in the evening?

C The students play-read the questions and answers, in pairs. Still in pairs, they then adapt the text to ask each other about when and where they eat, and to answer the questions. They write notes about their partners' answers and then compare this information with that in the Students' Book. Discuss with them the similarities and differences, e.g.

- Si fa colazione in cucina in casa tua?
- Mangiamo verso le dodici e mezza.

Help them to draw appropriate conclusions.

D Before the students listen to *A che ora si mangia?*, encourage them to predict what the young Italians will say. They could do this orally first and then write what they expect to hear.
As they listen, they should note what differences the Italians mention. Play the recording twice to allow time for this. They then discuss the recording, e.g.

- Did the Italians say what they were expected to say?
- Do your students agree with what the Italians said?
- Did the Italians sound happy?
- What other words could be used to describe the Italians (surprised, amazed, horrified, disappointed, pleased)?

A che ora si mangia?

Boy: Ti ricordi che bello in Inghilterra facevamo colazione alle otto?

Girl: Sì, certo che mi ricordo, però io preferisco fare colazione alle sette. E poi, la cena in Inghilterra è così presto!
Boy: Sì, mi ricordo, cenare alle sei. Preferisco qui in Italia, alle otto.
Girl: Io non avevo mai fame alle sei.
Boy: Neanche io. Il pranzo, a che ora era in Inghilterra?
Girl: Il pranzo, verso le docici e mezzo.
Boy: Non alle una e mezzo come qui in Italia?
Girl: No, molto prima.

E This would be a good time to start work with the class on *Scoprite qualcosa di più* (pages 170-172).

Che cosa ti piace mangiare? (page 87)

Main aims: Talking about food
Expressing likes and dislikes

A The students use the visuals and the captions to identify all the food on this page. To help them, you could ask, e.g.

- What number is the mixed salad (the roast chicken, etc.)?
- What is the Italian for macaroni in tomato sauce (beans, etc.)?

B To help the students to start to learn these words, you could ask them to categorise them, orally first and then in writing, e.g.

frutta, verdura, carne, pesce, formaggio.

You could repeat this activity with more sophisticated categories, e.g.

Qualcosa di salato che non mi piace.
Qualcosa di dolce che non mi piace.
Qualcosa di caldo che non mi piace.
Qualcosa di freddo che non mi piace.

C Give the students three minutes to study and discuss Matteo's likes and dislikes. They then cover up the table and, looking only at the pictures and captions, answer your questions, e.g.

- A Matteo piacciono prosciutto e melone?
- Gli piace qualcos' altro?
- Che cosa non gli piace?

They then look again at the table and say whether or not they agree with Matteo. Do this first as a class and then in pairs. Each student now writes a similar list, putting the foods on this page (and any others they wish to mention) into four columns to show what they like and dislike. In pairs, they compare their lists and discuss differences and similarities.

D Each student writes the names of two of the dishes on this page which they are finding it difficult to learn. They show these to their partners and ask them to help. They repeat this with two or three other students.

E By now the students should know all about what their partners like, and do not like, to eat. Invite a pair of volunteers. One leaves the room. The other students put five questions to the one remaining about what he/she likes, and does not like, to eat. This student replies as he/she thinks his/her partner would reply, e.g.

– Ti piacciono i fagioli?

– No, non mi piacciono i fagioli.

The partner then comes in and answers the same questions. You could add an element of competition with the pair who answer most questions correctly receiving a prize.

F Give more able students a copy of one of the role-play sheets: either Copymaster 48A or B. They use these, working in pairs, to practise explaining various dishes to an Italian visitor.

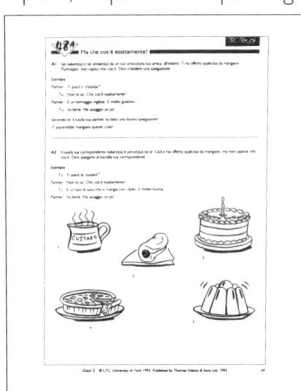
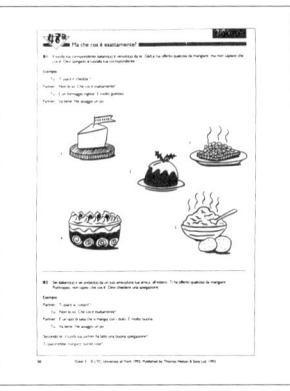

Sì, grazie, mi piace (page 88)

Main aim: To present some of the key language for talking at table

A Work on this list using previously successful techniques. Practise the expressions in the second part of the list:

• Go back to the previous section and offer the dishes displayed to individual students, e.g.

– Vuoi dei fagioli?

The students adapt the answers in the list to answer your questions. The students could continue to do this in pairs.

• A student reads any word from the list. Another student says any word which the first word suggests to him/her. After five, ask someone to remind the class how they got from the first to the fifth word.

B To prepare themselves to listen to the tape the students could look at the pictures and discuss what each person is likely to say. They could write two sentences which they expect to hear in each dialogue.

They listen and see how close they came to anticipating what would be said. They listen again and summarise the content of each dialogue and report on the attitude of each speaker.

🔊 Sì, grazie, mi piace

Numero 1

Woman:	Buon appetito.
Family:	Grazie, altrettanto.
Woman:	Paolo, ti piacciono i frutti di mare?
Boy:	No, non mi piacciono, e mi fanno male ...

Numero 2

Man:	Vuoi un altro po' di spaghetti?
Boy:	Sì, grazie. Questi spaghetti sono buonissimi!

Numero 3

Man:	Che cosa ti posso offrire?
Girl:	Posso prendere qualcosa di dolce?
Man:	Ti posso offrire un gelato. Ti piace il gelato italiano?
Girl:	Mm, questo gelato è molto buono.

Numero 4

Woman:	Tutti a tavola!
Girl:	Buon appetito.
Family:	Grazie, altrettanto.
Woman:	Anna, vuoi una bistecca?
Girl:	No, grazie. Non mangio carne, sono vegetariana.

C The students make up questions for each picture, based on the list, and put these to each other.

Prendo un espresso (page 88)

Main aim: To develop reading and writing skills on the topic of meals

A Give the students one minute to skim this and to get the gist of it.

When everyone understands the gist, ask them to read it again to find out what they expect to like, and to dislike, when they visit Luca. Discuss their responses.

B Each student writes two lists. In the first, they write fifteen to twenty key words about food and meal times at Luca's house. In the other, they write fifteen to twenty key words about food and meal times in their house.

C Practise adapting the key parts of the letter orally to describe meals in your homes. Use a 'snowballing' technique. You could write key expressions on the board or OHP. Each student then adapts this letter to describe meals in his/her home to an Italian penfriend who is coming to stay with them.

D After you have handed back the corrected letters and gone over any points which need more explanation or practice, you could base a memory game on the visuals. Give the students ninety seconds to study them. They then close the Students' Books and answer your questions, e.g.

- Ci sono delle uova nel disegno (della carne, ecc.)?
- In quale pasto si mangia il minestrone?
- Gli piace l'insalata (la carne, ecc.)?
- Che cosa si mangia per colazione?

After a while, the students could continue this in pairs: the one asking the questions can look at this page, the other cannot.

E Play a game of 'Odd-one-out' to practise some of the key words, e.g.

formaggio, insalata, melone, <u>minestra</u>
spaghetti, risotto, <u>bistecca</u>, tagliatelle
<u>bistecca</u>, piselli, fagioli, pomodori
uovo, <u>vino</u>, biscottini, panini
prosciutto, bistecca, <u>piselli</u>, carne
piselli, pomodori, fagioli, <u>pere</u>
bistecca, pollo, <u>pesce</u>, prosciutto
<u>pollo</u>, melone, pere, mele
prosciutto, insalata, mozzarella, <u>spaghetti</u>
maccheroni, minestra, fagioli, <u>melone</u>

The students listen and say which is the odd-one-out and why, e.g.

- Minestra: Si mangia la minestra con il cucchiaio e si mangiano gli altri cibi con la forchetta.
- Bistecca: La bistecca è un tipo di carne; le altre cose non lo sono.

You could present this on the board or OHP and leave it there as a model.

A tavola (page 89)

Main aim: To practise offering, accepting and refusing food

A Work on the list using a combination of techniques which have already proved successful and other techniques, e.g.

• Give each student a piece of paper with a two-word sentence on it, taken from the list. They keep their sentences a secret. You say:

- Tre, due, uno, zero!

In pairs, they say their sentence at the same time. They then try to say what the other sentence was.
Students can exchange sentences and do this again.

• Each pair agrees on a two-word sentence in the list and each chooses one word in it. On your signal, they each say their word. The rest of the class listen and try to say what the sentence is. You could repeat this with three-word sentences and groups of three.

• Write on the board ten words from the list. The students copy them. You then begin to rub them off the board, one at a time, and the students try to guess which one you will rub off next and tick it on their lists. To maintain attention and fun, pretend to go to rub off one word and then move quickly to another. After rubbing off a word, ask five or six students, in quick succession, to read out the word they chose.

B The students practise offering each other the food in the pictures. After some class practice with the first three or four to ensure that everyone can do it, this can be done in pairs.

C The students adapt what they said in **B** above to introduce typical dishes in their own country. They work out what they would say and imagine how Italian visitors would respond: they develop this in pairs.

D The class could continue work on *Scoprite qualcosa di più* (pages 170-172).

Sono cortesi? (page 89)

Main aims: To develop the ability to respond politely
To develop listening skills

A The students read these dialogues quietly to themselves and then listen to them. In pairs, they work on the dialogues and try to improve them.
Each pair then chooses one and prepares to act it out in two versions: one as it is and the second after their charm school treatment. If possible, video these and then watch and discuss the recordings.

📼 Sono cortesi?

Dialogo 1
Signora Cosenza: Vuoi un caffelatte, Paul?
Paul: No. Mi dia un tè.

Dialogo 2
Signor Bianchi: Vuoi un bicchiere d'acqua minerale?
Susan: No. Detesto l'acqua minerale. Mi dà una coca cola?

Dialogo 3

Signora Berti:	Vuoi un altro po' di pollo, Mark?
Mark:	Sì, grazie, ma pochino, però. È buonissimo.

Dialogo 4

Signor Bruni:	Vuoi un altro po' di dolce?
Sarah:	Sì, grazie, volentieri. È delizioso!

Dialogo 5

Signora Ferri:	Ti piace la bistecca?
Andrew:	No. Preferisco il pollo arrosto.

Dialogo 6

Signor Maldini:	Vuoi un altro po' di minestra?
Deborah:	No, non mi piace la minestra. Vorrei qualcos'altro!

B Continue work on *Scoprite qualcosa di più* (pages 170-172).

Buon appetito (page 90)

Main aim: **To practise reacting to offers of food and paying compliments**

A The students read this silently, ask any questions they may have and then listen to it once or twice. Before they listen to the recording, you could ask them to say what they think about the personality of each speaker; ask later if hearing it has changed their minds and, if so, how and why.

🔊 Buon appetito

Uncle:	Paul, vuoi un po' di vino italiano?
Paul:	Sì, pochino però.
Francesco:	Cin-cin. Salute, e buon soggiorno in Italia, Paul.
Adults:	Cin-cin.
Paul:	Cin-cin.
Aunt:	Tutti a tavola. Avete fame, spero!
Francesco:	Sì, ho fame.
Aunt:	Per primo abbiamo delle tagliatelle alla panna. Ti piacciono?
Paul:	Non so come siano, ne assaggio un po'.
Aunt:	Ne vuoi ancora un po'?
Paul:	Basta così, per cominciare, grazie.
Uncle:	Buon appetito.
Francesco:	Grazie, altrettanto.
Aunt:	E il pollo arrosto, ti piace?
Paul:	Sì, è molto buono.
Francesco:	Vuoi delle patate?
Paul:	Sì, grazie, volentieri!
Uncle:	C'è anche dell'insalata, del formaggio e per finire della frutta.
Aunt:	Vuoi altro?
Paul:	No, grazie. Ho mangiato molto bene.
Francesco:	Davvero, non ne posso più.

B In groups of four, the students act out the conversation, changing the words which are underlined in the Students' Book. Alternatively, this could be done in pairs, with each student playing two roles. This should be done twice, with the students changing roles.

C In groups of four, the students play a variation of 'My mother went to market'. They could begin with 'Si mangiano ...' and each add a word. They keep going as long as possible, reminding each other whenever necessary, e.g.

– Si mangiano del formaggio, delle tagliatelle, dell'insalata, un pollo e anche della frutta.

If this is popular, you could play it again with a different start to the sentence, e.g.

– Vuoi ...
– Posso prendere ...
– Ho mangiato ...

Mi può passare un coltello, per favore? (pages 90-91)

Main aim: **To practise asking for things at table**

A The students read this item with the aim of finding out what their learning task is. Discuss this with them and, when everyone is sure what it is, help them to achieve it, e.g.

• Give the students five minutes to teach each other, in pairs, the nine key words in the pictures.

• Use the pictures to play 'Noughts and crosses' (see Teacher's Book page 6), in class and then in pairs.

• Play at 'È vietata la lettera **h**'. You say a sentence. If a word in it contains the letter **h** the students should put up their hands and then say the word, e.g.

Teacher:	Mi può passare un cucchiaio, per favore?
Student:	Cucchiaio.
Teacher:	Bene.

Other sentences could include:
– Mi può passare una forchetta?
– Mi può passare un cucchiaino?
– Mi può passare una scodella?
– Ho bisogno del sale.
– Che cosa manca?
– Non hai un piatto?
– Vuoi un altro po' di maccheroni?
– Devi chiedere una scodella.
– Mi puoi passare il pepe, per favore?

• You could base 'Kim's game' on the nine pictures: you say a number and the students write the name of the object. You could reverse this, with the students naming the object and you having to give the number from memory.

B Form groups of three or four students. For each group, make four copies of Copymaster 49. These need to be cut up to make 64 cards.

Object of the game: to collect sets of four of an item.

How to play:

Four cards are dealt to each player and the rest are kept face down 'in cucina'.

Player One asks any other player for a card, saying, e.g. 'Mi può passare una forchetta, per favore?'

Players can only ask for an item of which they already have one. If the player asked has the card, he/she says 'Sì, certo' and hands over the card.

Player One can then continue, by asking anyone for a card until someone asked has not got the correct card and replies, e.g. 'No, mi dispiace. Devi cercare in cucina' (or a more complicated version, 'No, mi dispiace. Non ne ho. Devi cercare in cucina.').

Then Player One 'va a cercare in cucina', i.e. picks up a card from the pile.

It is then the turn of the player who said, 'No, mi dispiace ...'

If a player has more than one of an item, he/she must hand them all over.

When a player has collected a set of four, he/she puts them face down on the table, taking care to keep them separate from anyone else's sets.

The game continues until all the cards have been made into sets. The player with the most sets wins.

Write a model exchange on the board and leave it there throughout the game for students to consult if they need to, e.g.

- Mi può passare una forchetta, per favore?
- Sì, certo.
- Grazie. Mi può passare anche il sale?
- No, mi dispiace. Devi cercare in cucina.
- Che noia!

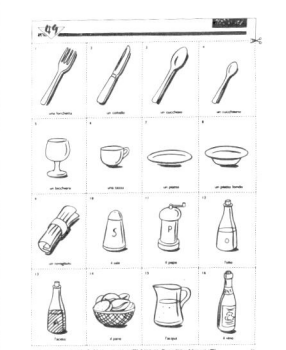

C In pairs, the students play the game on page 91. They spot what is missing in each picture and ask for it.

Posso aiutare? (page 91)

Main aim: To present some of the key language needed when offering to help

A Work on the list using a combination of familiar and new activities, e.g.

• After some work on the list, write on the board the first letters only of some sentences in the list, e.g.

D s m i s ?

The students race to find and to read to you the full sentence. After a few examples with the class, they could continue in pairs.

• Base a game of 'Il gioco degli spazi' on the list, e.g.

- La tovaglia si trova nel _____ .
- Dove si mettono i _____ ?
- Dove si mette il _____ ?
- Posso lavare i _____ ?
- Posso _____ ?

B The students make up a dialogue on each of the pictures. After they have been doing this for a while, give them two minutes to perform a dialogue on all six pictures.

C Each student writes a list of his/her favourite jobs. In pairs, they then try to discover their partners' rank order by asking questions, e.g.

A: Preferisci lavare i piatti?
B: Sì.
A: E ti piace asciugare?
B: No. Tocca a me ...

They could repeat this activity with their least favourite jobs. For each, present a model dialogue on the board and leave it there throughout the activity.

L'ospite perfetto (page 92)

Main aim: To practise role-play on the topic of this unit

A Give the students a few minutes to re-read everything they have done in this unit and to revise it.

B Each student prepares the responses in this role-play and they practise it in pairs, each performing each role.

C The students write the conversation in full: this could be done as homework.

D In class, and then in pairs, the students practise adapting the key expressions, e.g.

How would you say:
- The forks (knives, etc.) are in the drawer.
- The tablecloth is in the cupboard.
- The cups (plates, etc.) are in the dishwasher.
- Can I lay the table (wash up, etc.)?

Grazie del tuo aiuto (page 92)

Main aim: **To practise offering, and responding to offers, to help in the kitchen**

A Complete the work on the impersonal use of 'si' in *Scoprite qualcosa di più* (pages 170-172) before starting on this item.

B Work on this item along the lines suggested in the Students' Book.

C To give more practice, you could:

- See how many appropriate items the students can suggest to put into a fridge, then a drawer and then a cupboard, each in one minute. Then do it again and try to improve on the first score.

- Play a game of 'Battleships' ('La battaglia navale'). Draw a grid with twelve squares, on the board, with each square numbered. The students copy this and then write the name of the objects on this page, one to a square, in their grids. They then try to find where their partners' objects are, e.g.

- Le forchette si mettono nel primo cassetto?
- Sì.

If the answer is 'No', it is the other player's turn to guess.

D Students then listen to the recording of the Italians and, using a different colour pen, write where they put each item.

🔊 Grazie del tuo aiuto

Laura: Grazie del tuo aiuto. Allora i fagioli si mettono in frigorifero.
Padre: Sì, e il pane si mette nell'armadietto.
Laura: I bicchieri invece si mettono in quell'altro armadietto.
Padre: Vediamo un po' i piatti. Questi piatti si mettono nell'armadietto, quell'armadietto lì.
Laura: E anche le scodelle, nello stesso armadietto.
Padre: I coltelli invece vanno messi nel cassetto.
Laura: Ecco un'altra forchetta ... Sì, certo, si mettono anche le forchette in quel cassetto.
Padre: E i cucchiaini si mettono nello stesso cassetto.
Laura: Il formaggio? Mettilo in frigo.

Padre: E lo zucchero si mette con il pane nell'armadietto.
Laura: Sì, certo, l'acqua minerale si mette in frigo.
Padre: E il sale si mette con il pane nell'armadietto. Grazie del tuo aiuto!

E Make five copies of Copymaster 50.
Cut each one up so that you have five sets of questions and answers.
Divide the class into five groups and give each group a set of questions and answers.
They have to match up each question with a suitable answer.
The first group to complete this wins.
Then they can prepare a role play putting the questions and answers into a sensible sequence and acting it out.

Adesso, tocca a te! (page 93)

Main aim: To demonstrate mastery of the main points of the unit

Exercise 1
Language area: Food
Skill area: Listening

The students listen to the unscripted recording and look out for the points mentioned. Discuss their answers, and especially their answers to question 4.

🔊 Adesso, tocca a te!

Boy 1: Senti se c'era una cosa che non potevo sopportare la mattina, era mangiare il 'peanut butter' e la 'marmite'.
Boy 2: Ah, io avevo le odiate 'sausages', che schifo!
Girl 1: Io invece all'ora del tè adoravo quei biscotti come sì chiamano, 'butter cookies'.
Boy 2: O che buono il 'jelly'.
Girl 1: Quale, quello di arancio o quello di lampone?
Boy 2: Quello di lampone, per il colore.

Girl 2:   Nella mia famiglia varie volte la settimana per cena ci davano i 'baked beans'. A me non piacevano proprio per niente. Però, poi il lunedì, il martedì e il mercoledì c'era anche un dolce con il 'custard'. Buonissimo.

Boy 2:   Ma che cos'è il 'custard'?

Girl 2:   Praticamente è una crema vanigliata.

Boy 1:   Beh, insomma, speriamo che l'anno prossimo ci diano un po' di pizza e di pasta.

Boy 2:   Sì, sì, vero.

Girls: Hai proprio ragione.

Exercise 2

Language area: Food
Skill areas: Reading and writing

The students adapt the model to write a postcard of their own.

Exercise 3

Language area: Kitchen utensils
Skill area: Reading

The students translate the list into English.

Exercise 4

Language area: Helping with chores
Skill area: Reading

The students find the appropriate chores and make a list of them in English.

Exercise 5

Language area: Talking at table
Skill area: Speaking

In pairs, the students help each other to act out both roles as well as possible.

Ora sai (page 94)

Main aim: **To act as a summary and reference point for the main language of this unit**

The students use this page as an aid to learning and revision. They should be encouraged to use techniques which they have already found enjoyable and useful. You could introduce others for them to try, discuss and add to their repertoire, e.g.

● Give each student a copy of Copymaster 50. They decide which category of *Ora sai* each sentence should go with. They could write out sentences taken, and adapted, from the unit and ask their partners to group these, e.g.

– Ti piacciono i dolci italiani?
– Sì, volentieri.
– Grazie del tuo aiuto.
– Qui si fa colazione alle sette e mezza.

– Posso prendere un altro po' di dolce?
– Questa pizza è molto buona.
– Mi può passare l'acqua?
– Ti piace il pesce?
– I coltelli si mettono nel cassetto.
– No, grazie, abbiamo la lavastoviglie.
– Mi dispiace, non mi piace il prosciutto.
– A che ora si pranza da voi?
– Vuoi un altro po' di formaggio?
– Posso sparecchiare?
– Non so com'è, ne provo un po'!
– Queste tagliatelle sono deliziose.
– Ho bisogno di un cucchiaio.
– Dove si mette il sale?
– Mi dispiace, i frutti di mare mi fanno male.
– Mi puoi passare il sale?
– A casa mia si cena alle sette e mezza.
– Manca il pepe.
– Posso mettere via la roba?
– Vuoi dell'insalata?
– Di solito prendo un tè.
– Dove si mettono le forchette?

● Each student makes up a test for his/her partner to make sure that he/she understands and can use everything on this page.

Revision

1 Buying drinks in a bar or café (Book 1, Unit 7)

A Explain that many cafés have a blackboard with suggestions for things to eat, drinks, and their prices. The students listen to the recording of a café owner telling the waiter what to write on the board. The students try to write all this in their books: they can then compare their results.

Il listino prezzi

Waiter: Allora, che cosa scrivo sulla lavagna? Bibite? Bevande?

Owner: Aspetta. Fa caldo oggi, allora scrivi 'Bevande fredde'.

Waiter: Va bene. 'Bevande fredde'. Ecco.

Owner: Vediamo. Succo di arancia, 3.800 lire.

Waiter: Ho capito. Succo di arancia 3.800 lire e poi?

Owner: Poi, birra, 4.500 lire.

Waiter: Birra, 4.500 lire. Basta così?

Owner: No, scrivi anche acqua minerale, 2.800 lire.

Waiter: Va bene, acqua minerale, 2.800 lire.

Owner: E per finire scrivi panini al prosciutto, al formaggio, 3.300 lire.

Waiter: D'accordo, scrivo panini, al prosciutto, al formaggio, 3.300 lire. Va bene così?

Owner: Perfetto, grazie, Mauro.

B Divide the class into two teams. They are rival cafés and should pick appropriate names.

A student from team 1 says:

– Qui si vende vino rosso.

A student from team 2 then says:

– Qui si vendono panini.

The teams take it in turns. They mention a different item each time until one team can think of nothing new and then the other team has won.

2 Indefinite article: un' (Book 1, Unit 7)

A Present these gapped sentences on the board. The students complete them orally and then write the missing words.

1 ＿＿＿ tè al limone, per favore.
2 ＿＿＿ espresso e ＿＿＿ birra, per favore.
3 ＿＿＿ aranciata e ＿＿＿ coca cola. Subito, signorina.
4 ＿＿＿ tazza di tè al latte, per favore.
5 ＿＿＿ cappuccino e ＿＿＿ cornetto, per favore.
6 Allora ＿＿＿ pasta e ＿＿＿ cioccolata, per favore.
7 Per me, ＿＿＿ caffè freddo e ＿＿＿ toast al formaggio.
8 Va bene, ＿＿＿ succo di pompelmo e ＿＿＿ panino al salame.

B Give the class five minutes to find and copy as many sentences as they can in Students' Book 3 which contain 'un''.

They then compare their sentences.

C Draw on the board or OHP four frames like this.

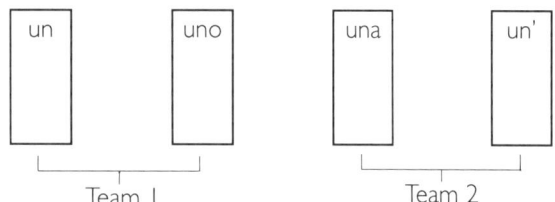

Divide the class into two teams. Someone in each team in turn calls out any word they know which can have 'un', 'uno' or 'un'', 'una' in front of it, e.g. 'aranciata', 'casa', 'autobus', 'studente'. Then someone from the same team goes to the team's frames and draws the object or person in the right box. The first to do this correctly wins a point for their team. This game can be re-used often to revise 'un', 'uno', 'un'', 'una'. The game can also be adapted to revise 'il', 'lo', 'la', 'l''. You can also add columns for plurals. Instead of drawing, the students could, where appropriate, write the words.

3 Free time and leisure activities (Book 2, Unit 10)

A Give each student a copy of Copymaster 51. Do some oral work on this with the class, e.g.

– Ti piace fare lo sport?
– Come si dice 'football' in italiano?
– Ti piace ascoltare la musica?
– Preferisci guardare la televisione o andare al cinema?
– Che cosa ti piace fare?

The students then work to complete the puzzle and to find the mystery word.

Solution:

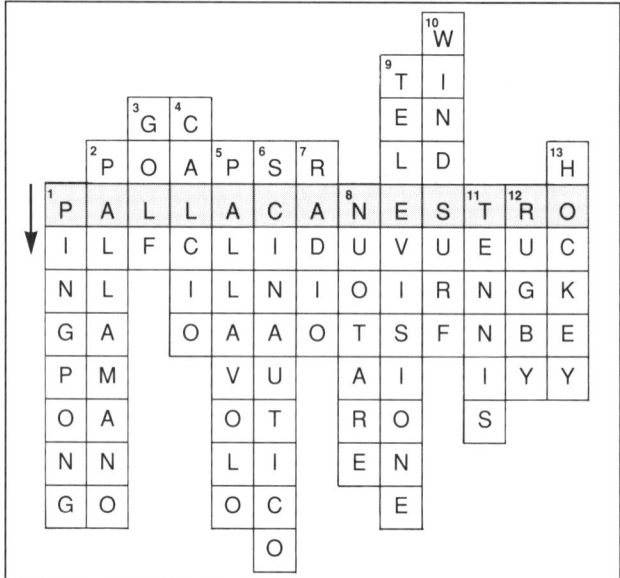

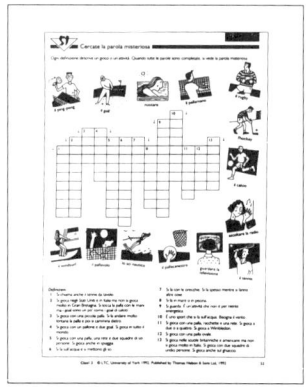

B Each student prepares a full answer to the question:

— Qual è il tuo passatempo preferito? Perché?

Help everyone to write out a full and interesting answer. They then practise asking and answering the question with several others.

4 Present tense: 'io' and 'tu' forms (Book 2, Unit 10)

A Organise a race: see who can find and copy correctly in five minutes the most examples in Students' Book 3 of present tense verbs in the 'io' and 'tu' forms.

B Organise some verb circle practice, e.g.

— Non asciugo i piatti.
— Ma io lavo i piatti.
— Metti via la roba?

C Tell students what you like doing: e.g.

— Mi piace fare lo sport.
— Gioco a tennis.
— Faccio del windsurf.
— Suono la chitarra.

Then do the same for what you do not like to do: e.g.

— Non ascolto la radio.
— Non leggo i fumetti.
— Non gioco a scacchi.

After that mix what you do and do not do: e.g.

— Non gioco a ping-pong.
— Guardo la televisione.
— Leggo le riviste.
— Non suono il pianoforte.

Now test your students' observation and memory. This time ask if you like doing activities, e.g.

Teacher: Gioco a ping-pong?
Students: No.
Teacher: Leggo le riviste?
Students: Sì.
Teacher: Avete ragione. Leggo le riviste.

5 Indirect object pronouns (Book 3, Unit 6)

A Present these incomplete sentences on the board for the students to complete:

1 M_ p_ò l_var_ il pa_ab_ez_a?
2 Mi f_ il p__no d_ sup_r_ _er _ore?
3 Sc_si, m_ può _ontr_l_are l'_l_o, per favore?
4 Qua_to L_ de_o?
5 _e s_rvo a_tro?
6 C_ sa d_re se c'è u_a t_il_ette?
7 C_ s_ di_e qu_nto è l_nt_na Arezzo?
8 S_u_i, av_te d_lle c_r_melle?

B Organise a short oral drill along the following lines:

Teacher: Mi può dare il quaderno?
Student: Sì, Le posso dare il quaderno.
Teacher: Mi può presentare il Suo amico?

— Mi può dire il Suo nome?
— Mi può telefonare?
— Mi può lavare il parabrezza?
— Mi può dire il Suo indirizzo?
— Mi può comprare un regalo?
— Mi può scrivere una lettera?
— Mi può controllare l'olio?
— Mi può dare una carta?
— Mi può parlare della Sua famiglia?

C You could present this exercise orally or on the board.

Domanda: Allora, mi dai un piatto?
Risposta: Sì, certo, ti do un piatto.

1 Allora, mi scrivi una lettera?
2 Allora, mi leggi questa lettera?
3 Allora, mi parli delle tue vacanze?
4 Allora, mi puoi dare una forchetta?
5 Allora, mi spieghi quello che è successo?
6 Allora, mi mandi una cartolina?
7 Allora, mi rispondi?
8 Allora, mi fai delle domande?

6 Staying with an Italian family (Book 3, Unit 9)

Give each student a copy of Copymaster 52A or B.
They work in pairs to find the picture that matches. First, introduce any new vocabulary students may need, e.g. 'il cassettone' (chest of drawers) and 'la scrivania' (desk).
Work with one or two students in class first and write the examples on the board or OHP for guidance, e.g.

Teacher: Sul disegno uno, c'è una lampada sul cassettone.
Student: Sì, c'è una lampada sul cassettone.
Teacher: C'è una sedia.
Student: No, non c'è una sedia.

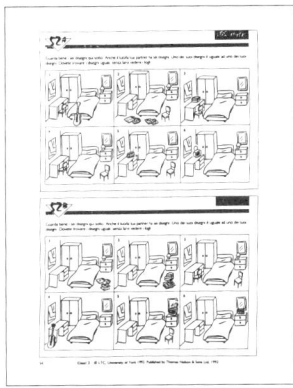

7 'Noi' and 'voi': present and perfect tenses (Book 3, Units 1, 5, 9)

A Organise some verb circle practice, e.g.

– Suonate il flauto?
– No, suoniamo la chitarra.
– Guardate la televisione?
– Guardiamo un video.
– Ascoltate la radio?

B The students practise making suggestions and responding to invitations, e.g.

Teacher: Ti piacerebbe andare in pizzeria?
Student: Buona idea. Andiamo in pizzeria.

– Ti piacerebbe ascoltare la radio?
– Ti piacerebbe guardare il film?
– Ti piacerebbe andare a pattinare?
– Ti piacerebbe giocare a tennis?
– Ti piacerebbe andare da Marco?
– Ti piacerebbe fare del windsurf?
– Ti piacerebbe prendere un caffè?
– Ti piacerebbe visitare il museo?
– Ti piacerebbe andare a teatro?
– Ti piacerebbe giocare al computer?

C The students practise responding to suggestions by saying that they have already done it, e.g.

Teacher: Andiamo in piscina?
Student A: No, non vorrei. Siamo andati in piscina stamattina.
Teacher: Giochiamo a tennis?
Student B: No, abbiamo giocato a tennis ieri.

– Guardiamo un video?
– Suoniamo il pianoforte?
– Andiamo al cinema?
– Ascoltiamo la radio?
– Giochiamo al calcio?
– Andiamo in pizzeria?
– Compriamo un gelato?
– Guardiamo la televisione?
– Ascoltiamo la musica?
– Andiamo a pattinare?

8 Pronouns following prepositions (Book 3, Unit 9)

A Play 'Il gioco degli spazi'.

1 Buongiorno, signora. Questo è per _____ .
2 Ciao, ragazzi, ecco un regalo per _____ .
3 Dov'è Massimo? C'è una lettera per _____ .

4 Domani vado in piscina. Vieni con _____?
5 Jane e Patrick vanno al cinema. Vuoi andarci con _____?
6 La prossima volta che vieni in Italia, devi venire da _____ .
7 Barbara ha telefonato. Puoi andare da _____?
8 Ciao, Mauro. Senti, posso andare a scuola con _____?

B Ask a student to stand up and then ask the rest of the class to decide who is taller.

Teacher: Sarah è più alta di me?
Student: Sì, è più alta di te.
                 o
                 No, non è più alta di te.

Practise this with two or three students and then ask students to write answers to the following questions, e.g.

Domanda: C'è qualcuno nella classe che è più studioso(a) di te?
Risposta: Sì, Paul è più studioso di me.

Leave the example on the board as a guide.

1 C'è qualcuno nella classe che è più sportivo(a) di te?
2 C'è qualcuno nella classe che è più calmo(a) di te?
3 C'è qualcuno nella classe che è più serio(a) di te?
4 C'è qualcuno nella classe che è più timido(a) di te?
5 C'è qualcuno nella classe che è più socievole di te?
6 C'è qualcuno nella classe che è meno alto(a) di te?
7 C'è qualcuno nella classe che è meno allegro(a) di te?
8 C'è qualcuno nella classe che è meno sensibile di te?
9 C'è qualcuno nella classe che è meno sportivo(a) di te?
10 C'è qualcuno nella classe che è meno calmo(a) di te?

Main aim

~ To understand and talk about the weather

Materials

~ Tape
Previsioni meteorologiche (Teacher's Book page 128)
Che tempo farà? (Teacher's Book page 129)
Adesso, tocca a te! (Teacher's Book page 132)

~ Copymasters 53–58

Grammar in *Scoprite qualcosa di più*

~ Prepositions and the definite article: a, di, da, in, su

Revision

~ Arranging activities (Book 1, Unit 8)
~ Agreement of adjectives (Book 1, Unit 8)
~ Essere: present tense (Book 1, Unit 8)
~ Present tense of regular verbs (Book 3, Unit 1)
~ Staying at a campsite (Book 3, Unit 7)
~ Potere: present tense (Book 3, Unit 7)
~ Impersonal 'si' (Book 3, Unit 10)

Vocabulary

A: Productive

l'autunno	forte	la primavera
bello	freddo	sereno
brutto	l'inverno	il sole
caldo	la nebbia	la stagione
il cielo	la neve	il tempo
coperto	oggi	il temporale
domani	la pioggia	il vento
l'estate	piove	

B: Receptive

aumento	moderato	previsto
centrale	nevicare	la regione
il clima	il nord	il rovescio
diminuzione	la nuvola	settentrionale
gelare	nuvoloso	il sud
il ghiaccio	piovere	la temperatura
i gradi	prevedibile	variabile
mite	le previsioni	

Il tempo (page 95)

Main aim: To introduce the objectives of this unit

A The students read this short text in order to find out what the proposed objectives are. Discuss these with them, e.g.
- When is it useful to be able to talk, or read, about the weather in Italy?

You could make some suggestions, e.g.

- When you are wondering what clothes to wear on holiday there and where to go and at what time of the year.
- When you are planning what to do with Italian friends.
- When you want to 'break the ice' and start a conversation with a stranger, a comment on the weather can provide a good start.

Give the students every chance to make the above, and other, suggestions. This will help to involve them and train them in setting worthwhile learning objectives.

B Working in pairs, the students write two lists: one containing weather expressions they would like to learn for talking about the weather in their country, and the other for weather expressions they would need for talking about the weather in Italy. They should make sure that they have learnt the Italian for all these before the end of the unit and take responsibility for doing this.

Il tempo in Italia (pages 95-96)

Main aims: To introduce the key language of weather forecasts

To introduce the four seasons

A It is assumed that many weather expressions will already have been introduced incidentally by the teacher over several terms, as opportunities have arisen (e.g. a snowy or windy day, and days when the students arrive wet or hot). This unit will build on this earlier work.

B The students look at the symbols in the Students' Book. Check that these are all understood. Tell the students that the symbols are those used in Italian newspapers.
Read aloud the descriptions of the weather in spring and summer, as the students follow the text. You could repeat this, making a few deliberate mistakes to encourage students to correct you and to read the sentence correctly.
Base a few questions on these two maps, e.g.

- Che tempo fa di primavera vicino a Rimini (vicino a Roma, Arezzo, o in Sicilia)?
- Quando c'è sole in tutte le regioni d'Italia?

Then ask some similar questions about the other two maps before giving out Copymaster 53. Make sure that everyone knows what they are to do with these and give whatever help is needed to ensure success.

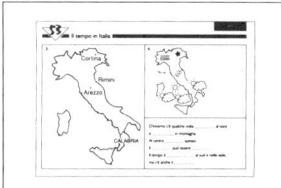

C Make sure that the students all understand the names of the seasons. Do some work to help them to learn these, e.g.

— Say any three: the students listen and add the fourth one. After a little while, this can be continued in pairs.
— Say a month: the students say which season(s) this month comes in. This can be continued in pairs.

In pairs, the students make up dialogues based on the model. Before they start, you could do this a few times with different students. While they work in pairs, move around, listening, helping and joining in.

D Divide the class into groups of three or four. Each group needs a copy of Copymaster 54, counters (pieces of paper with initials on) and a die (or a six-sided pencil with the numbers 1 to 6 on the sides). Explain how to play:

— they need a 6 to leave the 'pensione'
— scoring starts after this
— when a player lands on a square with a picture, he/she must follow the instructions
— anyone landing on square 45 must return to the 'pensione' and start again, including rolling a 6: you can't climb in fog
— the winner is the first to reach the mountain top
— players must speak Italian.

die = 'il dado'   counter = 'il gettone'

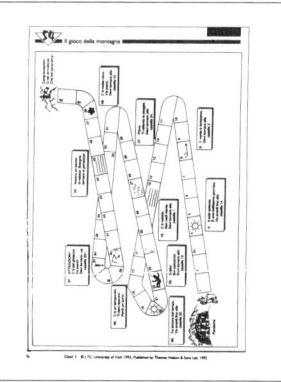

Le previsioni del tempo (page 96)

Main aim: Learning to understand the main points of a newspaper weather forecast

The students cover up the written weather forecast. They read the introduction, look at the map and then write some of the Italian words which they expect to see in the forecast. They then check with the forecast.

Encourage them to use a range of strategies to overcome any problems, e.g. visuals, the context (a weather forecast), words which they do know. If these fail, they could use a dictionary or ask you. Finally, ask what advice they would give.

Previsioni meteorologiche (page 96)

Main aim: To practise listening for specific purposes

A The students read the text to ensure that they know what to do and why. Before they listen, give them some practice in anticipation and prediction. For example, they could use what they know about the climate in Arezzo (referring back, if necessary, to page 95) and write down the Italian weather expressions which they expect to hear. With such anticipation exercises, the students must, of course, be aware of the need always to be ready for the unexpected and not to let what they expected to hear prevent them from hearing what is actually said.

B Play the first weather report twice. The students can take notes, if they wish. Ask some of the students to answer the question.

Clear up any problems and then play the recording once or twice more so that everyone understands it.

🔊 Previsioni meteorologiche

Numero 1

— Ecco le previsioni meteorologiche per l'Italia da mezzanotte alle ore 24.

Al nord, dalla Liguria fino al Friuli-Venezia Giulia persiste un periodo di tempo poco stabile con rovesci frequenti. Cielo nuvoloso con temperature in diminuzione.
Al centro e al sud, tempo più stabile, con cielo sereno. Possibilità di temporali sulla costa tirrenica a partire dal primo pomeriggio. Temperature in aumento: venti molto deboli. Per le isole si prevede la continuazione del bel tempo con temperature elevate attorno ai trenta gradi.

Numero 2

– Ecco le previsioni meteorologiche per l'Italia da mezzanotte alle ore 24.

Al nord tempo poco buono con piogge frequenti e temperatura in diminuzione.
Tempo molto simile al centro d'Italia dove la pioggia persisterà fino a sera. Temperature in notevole diminuzione. Bel tempo sulle isole.

Numero 3

– Ecco le previsioni meteorologiche per l'Italia da mezzanotte alle ore 24.

Continua il bel tempo sull'Italia settentrionale con temperature intorno ai trenta gradi.
Al centro, al sud e sulle isole, però, aumento di vento e di umidità, con forti possibilità di temporali fin dal primo pomeriggio. Temperature molto elevate.

Numero 4

– Ecco le previsioni meteorologiche per l'Italia da mezzanotte alle ore 24.

Nell'Italia settentrionale ci saranno rovesci frequenti per tutta la giornata, con possibilità di nevicate in montagna. Al sud ed anche al centro la giornata comincerà con cielo coperto. Ai primi del pomeriggio tornerà il sole e le temperature saranno in aumento.
Sulle isole persisteranno i venti forti di questi ultimi giorni.

C Play the other recorded weather reports. After each, the students suggest an appropriate activity. You could write some on the board or OHP for them to choose from.

D Give each student a copy of Copymaster 55. The students listen to *Che tempo farà?* Stop the tape after playing each report twice. The students enter the details, using words or symbols, on the map. Check their answers, clear up any problems, and move on to the next one.

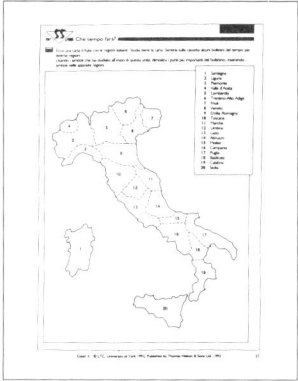

Che tempo farà?

– Ecco le previsioni meteorologiche per l'Italia per le prossime 24 ore.
– Sulle regioni centrali, dalle Marche fino al Lazio e l'Abruzzo, cielo nuvoloso o coperto con piogge frequenti.
– Sull'Emilia-Romagna e sulla Toscana persistono banchi di nebbia, particolarmente densi nella zona di Modena.
– Si prevede sole e bel tempo per il sud e per le isole. In Sardegna però, possibilità di temporali verso sera.
– Stamattina, fra la Sicilia e la Sardegna, venti forti, con mari molto mossi.
– L'inverno è già incominciato sulle montagne delle Alpi e delle Dolomiti, con neve dal Trentino-Alto Adige fino alla Valle d'Aosta ed al Piemonte. La Lombardia vedrà pure qualche nevicata in serata.
– Sulle regioni nord-orientali, ed anche in Liguria, piogge abbondanti che persisteranno per l'intera giornata.
– Come già detto, il sud avrà ancora una splendida giornata di sole. In Puglia però, possibilità di rovesci improvvisi a partire dalla sera.

E This would be a suitable time to start work on *Scoprite qualcosa di più* (pages 172-173).

Parliamo del tempo (page 97)

Main aim: **To present some of the key language needed for talking about the weather**

A Work on the list using techniques which have proved successful. This work should prepare the students to engage in simple exchanges about the weather, prompted by drawings, photos or the current weather conditions, e.g.

– Che tempo fa?
– Piove.
– Piove forte?
– No, non piove forte.
– Ti piace la pioggia?
– No, non mi piace molto.

B Display weather symbols on the board or OHP. Number them. The students can, after some class practice, work on these in pairs, e.g.

– Che tempo fa al numero due?
– C'è il sole: fa caldo.
– E al numero uno?
– Gela e nevica.

They could aim to discuss as many as possible in two minutes. The activity can be continued using the illustrations underneath the list.

C Ask for a volunteer to mime. Whisper a weather message to him/her or show him/her a weather picture. The volunteer mimes the weather and the others guess what the mime represents.

Andiamo (page 97)

Main aim: To practise suggesting activities which suit the weather conditions

A Give the students five minutes to revise the weather expressions.

B Ask students to say when they would suggest doing the activity in each picture on this page. Write the correct suggestions on the board or OHP.

C The students study and read aloud in pairs the short model dialogue. Each one then writes the four or five key words of the dialogue and uses these as a prompt to recreate the dialogue orally.
For each of the others, the students write the four or five key words and then, in pairs, expand these into short dialogues.

D At the end of a lesson, encourage the students to predict tomorrow's weather. Do this orally first and encourage disagreement and discussion. Each student then writes a weather prediction and gives it to you. You could give a small prize to the one which turns out to be the most accurate.

E This would be a suitable time to continue work on 'al' etc in *Scoprite qualcosa di più* (pages 172-173).

Com'è il clima da te? (page 98)

Main aim: To practise talking about the weather as a conversational strategy

A The students work on this item along the lines suggested in the Students' Book.

B Each student writes a list of three or four things that Italians visiting your country may say about the weather there. Then ask for contributions from them to produce a long list of these on the board or OHP.
You then read these out. After each one, encourage several students to respond. This could be continued in pairs.

C Using the list from **B** as a model, each student prepares an opening gambit using a weather expression, specifying where in Italy or Switzerland the conversation takes place. In turns, they say their gambits to the teacher, who has to respond appropriately. This could be continued in pairs.

Il tempo qui (page 98)

Main aims: To practise asking about the climate in another country and giving information about the climate in your country
To practise writing letters

A The students cover up the letter and read the introduction. On the basis of this, they predict orally what they expect to find in the letter, using specific Italian expressions. They then read the letter quickly to check on their predictions. Discuss how good the predictions were and how they could have used the available information to make better predictions.

B The students read the letter again and, in pairs, agree on the main points. Each one then lists the ten to twelve key words and, in pairs, then try to agree on twelve key words which sum up the text.

C Ask what conclusions they draw from the letter, e.g.
- Quali vestiti bisogna portare d'estate/d'inverno?
- Quali sono le migliori attività d'estate/d'inverno?
- In quale stagione vorresti andarci tu?

D Get the students to prepare their reply by:
- listing the key points to be made
- listing the key words to use.

This is a good technique in exams and real life: it helps you to use what you are confident about.
When the students have written their letters and had them back, corrected, ask them what conclusions their Italian friends would draw from their letters, e.g.
- i vestiti da portare
- quello che si può fare.

E This would be a suitable time to start work on 'del' etc in *Scoprite qualcosa di più* (pages 173-174).

Dove andiamo? (page 99)

Main aim: To practise finding relevant information in a holiday brochure

A Ensure that everyone understands the introduction and knows what to do.

B The students study what the first person wants. They then scan the text as quickly as possible to find where he should go. Do a number like this with the whole class. They then continue with this in pairs.

C Look again at what each person is looking for and invite the students to suggest suitable places, and seasons, for their own country. This should be done orally at first, and the advice could then be written.

Domani (Copymaster 56)

Main aim: To develop role-play skills on the topic of planning activities in the light of weather conditions

A Give each student a copy of Copymaster 56. Give the students ten minutes to read this item and to look back and revise anything which they need to revise.

B Each student works on the model dialogue and tries to learn it. When they are ready, they ask someone to test them. The tester can look at the whole page, but the other has to cover up the Italian on the left. They continue, helping each other as necessary, until everyone can do this.

C To prepare for making up similar dialogues, ask the students to say what sorts of things make for a good conversation on this topic. Encourage them to bear these points in mind as they make up more of their own.

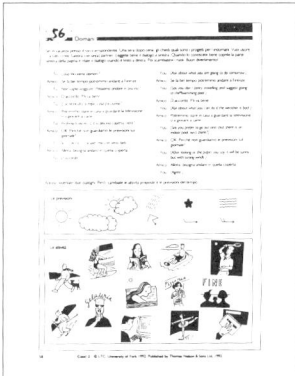

Quale cartolina? (page 100)

Main aim: To practise reading and writing postcards

A Before working on this item, play at word associations for a few minutes. You say a weather expression and the students reply with the name of a place. Then reverse this: you say the name of a place and the students say what weather this suggests.
Then repeat this, with the students writing their responses. After each one, ask them to read out their replies and see how many different ones there are. Students should be encouraged to justify, or explain, their responses.

B The students work on these postcards along the lines suggested in the Students' Book.

C The students read all the postcards again and look for key ideas which occur in several cards. They discuss these and try to agree on what they are. They then look for the key words and write these down, comparing their lists in pairs.

D Each student could now write the postcard which they think an Italian visiting their town today would write.

E This would be a suitable time to continue work on *Scoprite qualcosa di più* (pages 174-175).

Mandiamo una cartolina (page 101)

Main aim: To practise writing postcards

A Ensure that everyone knows what to do. Then instruct them to look back to page 100 to find phrases which they could use to write these cards, first phrases which could be used unchanged and then phrases which could be adapted.

B Discuss each place with the class and encourage them to say what they can do there. Able students could imagine that they have been to one of these places and say what they have done. Write key expressions on the board or OHP to help the others.

C Each student prepares to write the three postcards. To do this, they write for the first card the words and phrases they can use and feel confident about. Using this as a guide, they then write the cards. Encourage everyone to check what they have written. Go over these and help with any problems. Repeat this process with the next two cards. At the end, ask if the students felt that they made progress and if this is a good learning technique and a good technique for planning and writing a letter or postcard. They may be able to suggest other ways to help them to learn and to write.

D This would be a suitable time to continue work on *Scoprite qualcosa di più* (pages 175-178).

Adesso, tocca a te! (page 102)

Main aim: To demonstrate that the language of this unit has been mastered

Exercise 1
Language area: Weather and activities
Skill areas: Listening and writing

It may be advisable to work on the first two with the class to ensure that everyone knows what to do and how to do it.

Answers

lunedì:	ci sono andato(a)
martedì:	ci sono andato(a)
mercoledì:	non ci sono andato(a)
giovedì:	non ci sono andato(a)
venerdì:	ci sono andato(a)
sabato:	non ci sono andato(a)
domenica:	ci sono andato(a)

🔊 Adesso, tocca a te!

Numero 1

Ecco le previsioni del tempo per lunedì, 30 marzo. Oggi farà più caldo in tutto il paese ma farà ancora freddo in montagna dove sono buone le condizioni della neve.

Numero 2

Ecco le previsioni del tempo per martedì, 31 marzo. Oggi il primo bel sole di primavera: cielo sereno tutta la giornata, temperatura in aumento.

Numero 3

Ecco le previsioni del tempo per mercoledì, primo aprile. Oggi è prevista della nebbia in tutte le regioni. Sarà particolarmente intensa nei dintorni di Roma.

Numero 4

Ecco le previsioni del tempo per giovedì, due aprile. Oggi cielo nuvoloso con piogge abbastanza frequenti. Temperatura in diminuzione.

Numero 5

Ecco le previsioni del tempo per venerdì, tre aprile. Oggi, tempo incerto: pioggia e venti forti in mattinata, con temporali locali. Farà più freddo nel pomeriggio. Temperatura in diminuzione.

Numero 6

Ecco le previsioni del tempo per sabato, quattro aprile. Oggi la nebbia sarà densa in tutte le regioni. Visibilità ridotta a zero al di sopra dei mille metri.

Numero 7

Ecco le previsioni del tempo per domenica, cinque aprile. Oggi una bella giornata di sole con temperature primaverili. Temperatura in aumento.

Exercise 2

Language area:	Weather
Skill area:	Reading

The students should write down the advice they would give.

Exercise 3

Language area:	Weather and activities
Skill areas:	Listening and speaking

The students do this in pairs, each playing each part. Listen to as many as you can and keep notes about any problems which require revision or more work. If possible, get some students to record their dialogues. You can then listen carefully to these and report back, with suggestions, praise, etc.

Exercise 4

Language area:	Weather and activities
Skill area:	Writing

Each student prepares and writes a postcard, using the approach developed on page 131 in the Teacher's Book.

Ora sai (page 103)

Main aim: To act as a summary and reference point for the main language of this unit

A Present the following on the board or OHP to help the students to remember key words. They look on the right for the opposite of the word on the left:

caldo	scendere
sereno	debole
forte	scortese
partire	diminuzione
salire	brutto
apparecchiare	freddo
aumento	arrivare
anticipo	inverno
entrata	sud
arrivo	sparecchiare
cortese	coperto
nord	ritardo
estate	partenza
bello	uscita

B In this exercise, the students select the weather which best suits the activity:

il tennis – pioggia, nebbia, sole, neve
il calcio – vento, cielo coperto, caldo, gelo
una passeggiata – temporali, pioggia, freddo, cielo coperto
una gita al mare – sole, temporali, nebbia, neve
la spesa in centro – pioggia, nuvoloso, caldissimo, gelo
la piscina scoperta – vento, cielo coperto, caldo, nuvoloso
in cinema – sole, caldissimo, cielo sereno, neve
leggere un libro a casa – pioggia, sole, caldo, cielo sereno
il windsurf – temporali, neve, vento, sole
guardare la televisione – caldo, nebbia, bel tempo, cielo sereno

After working on **A** and **B** above, the students could produce similar exercises of their own for use in pairs.

Discuss these activities with the class. If they find them useful, they could make up others for other units when they revise them. They could also use now activities from earlier *Ora sai* which they liked and found helpful. Try to stress the importance for them of taking on the responsibility for their own learning and revision.

C Present this activity to the class, e.g.

– Il mese prossimo viene da te il tuo/la tua corrispondente italiano(a). Scrivigli/scrivile una cartolina in cui descrivi quello che fai di solito durante le vacanze. Spiega anche come l'attività dipende dal tempo. Domandagli/domandale di dirti quello che gli/le piace fare, e quello che detesta; così potrai fare dei progetti.

Esempio:

Quando fa bel tempo mi piace andare al mare. Ci sono andato(a) due settimane fa con i miei genitori.

Revision

1 Agreement of adjectives (Book 1, Unit 8)

A Present the following on the board or OHP. The students come out and cross out the adjectives which cannot be used to describe the noun. Ask them to explain why.

With the words which remain in each circle, the students make up sentences which describe the noun, ensuring that the adjective agrees. This should start off orally, but could become a written exercise.

B Give each student a copy of Copymaster 57. They read it and cross each square where the adjective can be used to describe the noun. As they do this, move round the class and prompt some oral use of the words, e.g.

– Si può dire che il tempo è grande?
– Come si dice di solito?
– Che tempo fa oggi?

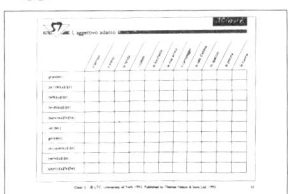

2 Essere: present tense (Book 1, Unit 8)

A Organise a brief period of verb circle practice, starting with, e.g.

– Sono di Parma.
– Sono italiano(a).
– Alassio è una stazione climatica della Riviera.
– Sono stato(a) in Inghilterra l'anno scorso.
– È stato(a) in ospedale.

B Name a topic, e.g. travelling by train, camping, eating a meal. The students then suggest useful sentences related to that topic which contain 'essere'. Encourage as many suggestions as possible.

After a while, all the students could have fifteen seconds in which to write an appropriate sentence for a given topic. They then read these aloud and see how many different sentences occur.

3 Present tense of regular verbs (Book 3, Unit 1)

A Organise a few minutes of verb circle practice, with, e.g.

– Guardo l'orario dei treni.
– Il treno parte alle undici.
– Non vedo posto libero.

B Give the students some intensive practice in asking and answering useful questions using the present tense. You could present some on the board or OHP for pair practice, e.g.

1 Alla stazione dove compri i biglietti?
2 Cosa fai se non c'è posto in uno scompartimento?
3 Cosa fanno i viaggiatori in una sala d'attesa?
4 Cosa fate se volete sapere a che ora parte il treno?
5 Cosa fate se vuoi essere sicuro di avere un posto a sedere in treno?
6 Allo spaccio di un campeggio che cosa fanno i campeggiatori?
7 Che cosa fai prima di partire da un campeggio?

8 Arrivi con la tua famiglia ad un campeggio ma è completo. Cosa fate?

9 Cosa fanno i bambini nel parco giochi di un campeggio?

10 Come scopri dove si trova il campeggio più vicino?

11 A che ora cenate di solito a casa tua?

12 Quando pranzate?

13 Che cosa prendi per la colazione?

14 Dimmi tre cose che fai per aiutare i tuoi genitori in casa?

15 Da te chi lava i piatti?

16 Cosa fa qualcuno quando vuole pulire il tappeto?

17 Cosa fai quando hai finito di mangiare con la famiglia?

18 Cosa fai quando un amico viene a casa tua per la prima volta?

19 Cosa dici se qualcuno ti domanda il tuo nome?

20 Quando incontri per la prima volta una persona simpatica che cosa fai per conoscerla meglio?

21 Se vuoi sapere dove abita qualcuno, quale domanda fai?

4 Staying at a campsite (Book 3, Unit 7)

A Begin by revising some of the key vocabulary. See how many words the class can correctly categorise in one minute, choosing one of these categories, which should be written on the board:

campeggio   stazione ferroviaria   il tempo

You could use the following, and any other suitable words:

piazzuola, tenda, sole, rapido, prenotare, piovere, docce, freddo, sala d'attesa, spaccio, temporali, giocare, nevicare, ritardo, terreno, scendere, vento, annunciare, rovesci, marciapiede, roulotte, nuotare, nuvoloso, biglietteria, coperto, comodo, sala TV, debole, orario, bello, direzione, deposito bagagli, lampi, presa luce, uscita, entrata, nebbia, previsioni, accelerato, alberi.

B Give each student a copy of Copymaster 58. Give whatever help may be needed to ensure successful completion of the task.

5 Potere: present tense (Book 3, Unit 7)

A Organise some verb circle practice based on, e.g.

– Non posso uscire stasera.

– Posso prendere un gelato?

– Mi può cambiare dei travellers cheque?

B Organise a 'University Challenge' (or similar) quiz between two teams, with ten points for each 'starter' and five points for other questions. All answers must use an appropriate part of 'potere'. The first team to score seventy wins.

La vostra domanda base per dieci punti

1 Che cosa non puoi fare bene quando c'è nebbia?

2 Quale sport si può fare quando c'è neve?

3 Puoi giocare a tennis quando c'è molto vento?

4 In Italia com'è il clima d'estate?

5 Dove si può trovare una piazzuola?

6 Ad un campeggio quando è vietato fare del rumore?

7 Che cosa puoi prendere ad una stazione?

8 In una stazione, dove si può mangiare qualcosa?

9 Che cosa puoi comprare alla biglietteria?

10 Se stai presso una famiglia italiana cosa puoi fare per aiutare in casa?

11 In Italia a che ora si cena di solito?

12 Dove si possono lavare i piatti?

13 Qualcuno ci presenta l'uno all'altro. Io ti dico: 'Piacere'. Tu, cosa mi dici?

Domande supplementari

1 Puoi dirmi un'altra cosa che non si fa bene nella nebbia?

2 Oltre alla neve, di che altra cosa hai bisogno per poter sciare?

3 Qual è il tempo ideale per giocare a tennis?

4 Come si può descrivere il clima della Sicilia d'inverno?

5 Perché tanti campeggiatori preferiscono i camping agli alberghi?

6 Cosa puoi comprare in uno spaccio?

7 Puoi pensare ad altre cose che sono vietate in un campeggio?

8 Qual è la stazione più vicina a noi?

9 Dove vai per poter bere qualcosa?

10 Perché guardi l'orario dei treni?

11 Chi fa i letti a casa tua?

12 A che ora cenate a casa tua?

13 A casa tua chi ha lavato i piatti stamattina?

6 Impersonal 'si' (Book 3, Unit 10)

A Play the following anagram game with the class. Write the questions on OHP/board, then copy at random the answers to each question, which are in anagram form. Explain that all the answers are there but the order of the letters is wrong. If you think it necessary, do the first one for them as an example.

– beaglitterii = biglietteria

You could give a small prize to the one who first succeeds in getting all the correct answers. The spellings must be spot on, of course.

1 Dove si comprano i biglietti alla stazione?
2 Ad un campeggio dove si va a comprare del gas?
3 Che tipo di treno si può prendere se si ha fretta?
4 Dove si portano i piatti sporchi?
5 Che cosa si mette in ordine prima di uscire la mattina?
6 A chi si presenta un nuovo amico che viene a casa per la prima volta?
7 Che tempo fa se si porta un ombrello?
8 A che cosa bisogna pensare se si fanno dei progetti per domani?

beaglitterii (biglietteria)
scopaci (spaccio)
pairod (rapido)
anucci (cucina)
macare (camera)
glimafia (famiglia)
vipeo (piove)
mopet (tempo)

B Reproduce the following table and sentences on OHP/board. Tell the students they have to translate the sentences into Italian by using the table. To find the Italian equivalent they must use one item from each of the columns. Do one or two with the class first, then get the students to write down their remaining translations.

Sentences

1 Where can one buy a newspaper?
2 Seats can be reserved a month in advance.
3 Where are the toilets?
4 The tickets were bought two days ago.
5 You can't have a shower after 11 p.m.
6 Pitches must be vacated by midday.
7 What is done for children?
8 The knives don't go there.
9 You put the dishes in the sink.
10 The butter must be put in the fridge.

Dove		fanno	dopo le 11.
Le piazzuole		possono prenotare	là.
I biglietti	si	può comprare	in frigo.
Il burro	non si	deve mettere	i gabinetti?
Che cosa		devono lasciare libere	un giornale?
I posti		mettono	due giorni fa.
I piatti		trovano	con un mese di anticipo.
I coltelli		fa	nel lavandino.
Le docce		sono comprati	per i bambini?
			entro mezzogiorno.

Main aims

~ To make arrangements for things to do during your free time
~ To see a film at the cinema

Materials

~ Tape
Cosa pensi di fare? (Teacher's Book page 137)
Vai spesso al cinema? (Teacher's Book page 139)
Che cosa ti piacerebbe fare? (Teacher's Book page 140)
Facciamo un giro in centro? (Teacher's Book page 141)
Alla cassa (Teacher's Book page 144)
Problemi, problemi! (Teacher's Book page 144)
Era proprio un bel film (Teacher's Book page 147)

~ Copymasters 59–63

~ TV and cinema guides, programmes for concerts, matches and plays
~ Advertisements and publicity material for different types of public entertainment

Grammar in *Scoprite qualcosa di più*

~ Using infinitives

Revision

~ Changing money (Book 1, Unit 9)
~ Collections, personality, appearance (Book 3, Unit 2)
~ Comparative adjectives (Book 3, Unit 2)
~ Lost property (Book 3, Unit 8)
~ Weather (Book 3, Unit 11)
~ Prepositions (Book 3, Unit 11)

Vocabulary

A: Productive

andare a trovare	una partita
una camminata	una passeggiata
un concerto	il pomeriggio
divertente	potremmo
domani	preferirei
dare (un film)	sarebbe possibile
era	la sera
una festa	sono rimasto un po' deluso
un giro	lo spettacolo
in bicicletta	ti è piaciuto
il luna park	vorresti
ottimo	

B: Receptive

di avventura	un programma
la cassa	riposo
chiusura estiva	sentimentale
di fantascienza	di spionaggio
in galleria	triste
un giallo	uscire
di guerra	uscita di sicurezza
musicale	vietato ai minori di 14 anni
dell'orrore	vietato fumare
in platea	volentieri
poliziesco	un western

Che cosa facciamo? (page 104)

Main aim: To discuss the objectives of this unit

A Suggest that the students read this item and that they write a list of the suggestions made for activities, copying the appropriate words from the text and writing next to them the English equivalents. Discuss the lists.

B Ask the students to add to their lists the English for activities they would like to be able to talk about in Italian. Before they finish work on this unit, they should ensure that they have added the Italian equivalents for these to their lists. Encourage them to ask the Italian assistant, students in higher classes, Italian visitors and you, to tell them how to say these phrases in Italian.

C Each student studies the text and writes what seem to him/her to be the twelve key words. In pairs, they read their key words to each other and tick those which they have in common. They then try to teach their partners the words which they have listed but which their partners have not: they will find out that the best way to learn something is to try to teach it to someone!

D Give the students three minutes to find and copy all the examples of the future tense. Ask them then to explain how they recognised them, and why a future tense is used in each case. Do not worry about taking this any further at this stage; concentrate on using the context to deduce meaning.

I preparativi per lo scambio (page 105)

Main aim: To introduce the main language associated with talking about leisure activities

A Read the item in the Students' Book with the class and ensure that everyone understands it. Base some question and answer work on the table, e.g.

– Ti piacerebbe andare ad una festa stasera?

Then write on the board:

– Ti piacerebbe ... ?
– Mi piacerebbe ... .

Each student chooses one activity in the list and uses it to complete in their exercise books:

– Mi piacerebbe ...

In pairs, they now try to guess what their partners have written, e.g.

– Ti piacerebbe andare al cinema?

B Give each student a copy of Copymaster 59. They put a tick or cross next to each activity. They then discuss their answers in pairs, using the model dialogue in the Students' Book.

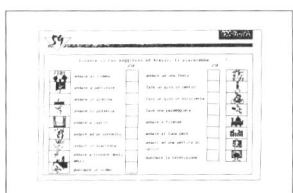

C Ask the class if it is possible to do all these activities where they live and discuss their answers, e.g.

– È possibile andare al cinema qui?
– Sì.
– Dove esattamente?
– Ci sono due cinema.

Working in groups of three, the students prepare a similar grid for Italian visitors to their town. These could be exchanged with similar work from a twinned class in Italy.

D Other activities which could be used to practise talking about activities, now or later, include:

• Ranking activities, e.g.
– Which eight do you most/least enjoy?
– Which eight do you think your partner/teacher would most/least enjoy?

This can lead to a comparison between predictions and what the people concerned say.

• Categorising activities, e.g.
– Which activities are suitable for
  the summer?   a village?
  the winter?   at the seaside?
  students in a city? in the mountains?

• Discussing and comparing, e.g.
– Che cosa si può fare dove abiti tu?
– Che cosa non si può fare dove abiti tu?
– Che cosa sarebbe bello poter fare dove abiti tu?

• Students draw or mime an activity: the others guess the activity. This can be done first in class and then in groups or pairs.

• Students could interview each other to try to find someone who likes four activities which they like and someone else who dislikes four activities which they dislike.

E Give each student a copy of Copymaster 60. The students listen to the following recordings and note the activities suggested by each speaker in the appropiate columns on Copymaster 60. They then say who they would most like to stay with, and why.

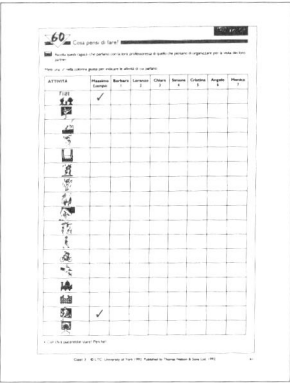

🔊 Cosa pensi di fare?

Esempio

Teacher:	Dimmi, Massimo, cosa pensi di fare la sera, la domenica, per esempio, quando avrai con te il tuo partner?
Massimo:	Beh ... il mio partner sembra abbastanza sportivo, gioca a pallavolo e s'interessa molto al calcio.
Teacher:	Sì ...
Massimo:	Allora, io ho pensato di andare ad una partita di calcio. So che c'è una partita domenica prossima.
Teacher:	Davvero?
Massimo:	Sì ... e poi se è d'accordo, potremmo giocare a calcio con degli amici ... e poi ho pensato di portarlo al cinema.
Teacher:	Che cosa danno?
Massimo:	In questo momento c'è un film comico, un film un po' buffo ... non è molto difficile capirlo.
Teacher:	Benissimo. Sembri molto ben organizzato.

Dialogo 1

Teacher: E tu, Barbara, ti sei organizzata? Sei pronta per lo scambio?

Barbara: Beh ... insomma. La mia amica suona il pianoforte e s'interessa molto alla musica.

Teacher: Musica classica o musica pop?

Barbara: Musica classica, musica rock ... tutto.

Teacher: Allora, cos'hai previsto?

Barbara: Beh ... mi piacerebbe portarla in discoteca una volta ... e poi sabato sera c'è un concerto di Pierangelo Bertoli a Firenze, allora pensavo di andare a Firenze, di passare la giornata lì, e poi la sera di andare al concerto.

Teacher: Buona idea. E per gli altri giorni?

Barbara: Beh ... a me piace tanto andare a pattinare, allora se lei è d'accordo, potremmo andare a pattinare insieme una sera.

Teacher: Brava!

Dialogo 2

Teacher: Buongiorno Lorenzo.

Lorenzo: Buongiorno signora.

Teacher: Allora, com'è il tuo partner, che tipo di persona è?

Lorenzo: Da quanto ho capito è un tipo abbastanza estroverso, allegro e dinamico.

Teacher: Ah, bene, e che cosa hai intenzione di fare con lui quando arriva?

Lorenzo: Beh, siccome a me piace nuotare, penso che andremo in piscina. Poi avrei anche intenzione di andare al Luna Park.

Teacher: Ah, ce n'è uno qui vicino?

Lorenzo: Sì, ce n'è uno ad una decina di chilometri.

Teacher: Ah, benissimo. E il fine settimana come lo passerete?

Lorenzo: Penso che ci guarderemo un video.

Teacher: Benissimo, mi sembra un'idea eccellente.

Dialogo 3

Teacher: E la tua partner com'è, Chiara?

Chiara: Oh lei è una ragazza a cui piace fare delle cose con altra gente, uscire, divertirsi. È una di quelle ragazze proprio socievoli.

Teacher: Uh, benissimo. E come avete intenzione di passare questo periodo?

Chiara: Io avevo programmato di portarla in una pizzeria con degli amici miei.

Teacher: Uhm, mi sembra un'idea eccellente. La pizza italiana le piacerà senz'altro.

Chiara: Oh sì, lo spero. Inoltre avevo programmato di organizzare una festa con tutto il gruppo.

Teacher: Ah che allegria. Dove, a casa tua?

Chiara: Sì, forse però affitteremo un locale. Inoltre la sera noi guardiamo la televisione e spero che piacerà anche a lei.

Teacher: Uhm, bene, brava.

Dialogo 4

Teacher: Simone com'è questo tuo partner?

Simone: Beh, non lo so. Spero che sia allegro e socievole. Mi sono messo d'accordo con i miei amici di uscire e portarlo con me.

Teacher: Dove avete intenzione di andare?

Simone: Beh abbiamo pensato di andare al Luna Park.

Teacher: Ah mi sembra un'idea buonissima.

Simone: O se il tempo è brutto di andare in piscina. Spero sappia nuotare.

Dialogo 5

Teacher: Cristina parlami della tua partner, che tipo di ragazza è?

Cristina: Oh ... dalle lettere è sembrata una ragazza abbastanza seria, studiosa, le piace andare a scuola.

Teacher: E che cosa avrete intenzione di fare quando arriverà?

Cristina: Beh, lei mi ha chiesto se potevamo andare a Firenze per la giornata. Io ne sono contenta, spero solo di non dover visitare troppi monumenti e ... ma di avere anche il tempo per un giro per negozi.

Teacher: Sì, sono sicura che anche a lei piacerà andare in giro per negozi. Eh per mangiare, dove hai intenzione di portarla?

Cristina: Beh, la sera potrebbe essere una buona idea portarla fuori a mangiare una pizza.

Teacher: Ah, tipicamente italiano, ma sono sicura che le piacerà senz'altro. E la sera?

Cristina: Beh, credo che quando resteremo a casa euhh ... potremmo vedere della televisione o affittare un video.

Teacher: Sì, sono sicura che con te non sì annoierà mai, Cristina.

Dialogo 6

Teacher: Angelo che tipo di persona ti sembra il tuo partner?

Angelo: Beh, carino però un po' timido, e non voglio stare troppo solo con lui.

Teacher: Gli farai incontrare i tuoi amici?

Angelo: Ah sì, certo.

Teacher: Ah bene, così socializzerà un po'.

Angelo: Beh, spero di sì.

Teacher: E la sera, come hai intenzione di passarla?

Angelo: Beh, la sera volevo andare a cinema, a vedere un film classico italiano.

Teacher:	Uh uh, bene.
Angelo:	E poi sabato prossimo avevo intenzione di portarlo a Firenze.
Teacher:	Benissimo. Firenze gli piacerà senz'altro. È bellissima.

Dialogo 7

Teacher:	Monica, parlami della tua partner.
Monica:	Penso di essere fortunata. Lei è una ragazza sportiva, anche io lo sono, penso che andremo d'accordo.
Teacher:	Che cosa avrete intenzione di fare?
Monica:	Ma guardi, ho qualche ... con qualche amico abbiamo pensato di andare a fare una scampagnata questo week-end. Andremo in bicicletta, forse affitteremo qualche bicicletta, andremo tutti insieme, così, a passare il week-end.
Teacher:	E in generale, che cosa pensi che farete?
Monica:	Mah forse o una sera o un pomeriggio dopo la scuola andremo a pattinare su ghiaccio. Non è che io sappia pattinare, però ci divertiremo, penso.
Teacher:	Ah sì, senz'altro. E la sera, hai qualche idea?
Monica:	Veramente, la sera di solito guardo la televisione con la mia famiglia e così sto a casa, spero che lei non sì annoi.
Teacher:	No, vedrai che con te sì divertirà.

Che cosa ti piacerebbe fare? (page 106)

Main aim: To practise discussing what to do

A Give each student a copy of Copymaster 61.
Each student tries to predict the results of the Italian class by writing in the first column S (spesso), O (ogni tanto), or R (raramente), according to whether they think most people in the Italian class do that activity often, occasionally or rarely.
The students then listen to the recording in which students from the Italian class say whether the majority of people in the class do that activity often, occasionally or rarely.
The students write the letter S, O or R in the second column beside each activity as it is mentioned.

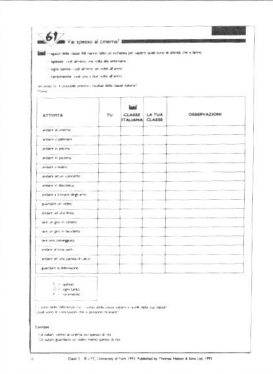

Vai spesso al cinema?

- Ecco i risultati dell'inchiesta fatta nella classe IIIB 'Vai spesso al cinema?':
- Andare al cinema: la maggioranza ha risposto che ci va ogni tanto.
- Andare a pattinare: la maggioranza va raramente a pattinare.
- Andare in piscina: la maggioranza ha risposto ogni tanto.
- Andare in pizzeria: la maggioranza ha risposto ogni tanto.
- Andare a teatro: la maggioranza ha risposto raramente.
- Andare ad un concerto: la maggioranza ha risposto raramente.
- Andare in discoteca: la maggioranza va raramente in discoteca.
- Andare a trovare degli amici: la maggioranza va spesso a trovare degli amici.
- Guardare un video: la maggioranza ha risposto ogni tanto.
- Andare ad una festa: la maggioranza ha risposto ogni tanto.
- Fare un giro in centro: la maggioranza ha risposto spesso.
- Fare un giro in bicicletta: hanno risposto ogni tanto.
- Invece, fare una passeggiata: hanno detto raramente.
- Andare al luna park: la maggioranza va raramente al luna park.
- Andare ad una partita di calcio: hanno detto raramente.
- Guardare la televisione: hanno risposto spesso.

B Each student now assumes responsibility for one activity. He/she interviews ten classmates, e.g.

- Vai spesso al cinema?
- Vai spesso in piscina?
- Guardi spesso la televisione?
- Fai spesso un giro in bicicletta?

You could write these questions on the board/OHP for reference.
You could also write up these answers as models, e.g.

- Sì, abbastanza spesso.
- Beh ... ogni tanto.
- No, raramente.

Each student records the number of answers in each category: 'spesso', 'ogni tanto', 'raramente'.
You could then collate the results. Students write the letters S, O or R in the third column, beside each activity.
Then compare the results of the Italian class with those of your students and ask them what observations and conclusions they can make.

C Students could then devise a similar questionnaire/survey to send to Italy. Instead of categories such as often, occasionally, rarely, they could find out which are the five most popular/least popular activities, for example,

a during the holidays
b during term time
c in summer
d in winter
e when the weather is good
f when the weather is bad.

They could collate the results for their class and record them on tape, ready to send to their exchange school.

D The students now look at page 106 of the Students' Book: they read the dialogues silently to themselves and ask about anything which puzzles or interests them. Praise warmly everyone who asks a question.
They now listen, and follow the texts in the Students' Book, as you play the recordings.

Che cosa ti piacerebbe fare?

Dialogo 1

– Che cosa vorresti fare stasera? Ti piacerebbe andare in pizzeria con Marco e Luisa?
– Eh, sì. Volentieri.
– Perfetto. Andiamo in pizzeria, allora.

Dialogo 2

– Che cosa ti piacerebbe fare domenica?
– Non lo so esattamente. Sarebbe possibile andare alla partita di calcio?
– Certo. Andiamo pure.

Dialogo 3

– Ti piacerebbe andare in discoteca domani sera?
– Mm ... non molto, mi dispiace.
– Non importa. Se preferisci, potremmo andare al cinema.
– Eh, sì. Che cosa danno?
– All'Odeon danno 'La casa 4'. È un film dell'orrore.
– Va bene.
– Andiamo al cinema, allora.
– Sì, dai.

Dialogo 4

– Che cosa facciamo stasera? Guardiamo la televisione o guardiamo un video?
– Che cosa c'è alla TV?
– Beh ... c'è Pentatlon; è un gioco a quiz.
– Io preferirei guardare un video, allora.
– Va bene, guardiamo un film.
– D'accordo.

E Encourage the students to play-read the dialogues in pairs. Then help them to adapt the key phrases to talk about their own interests, e.g.

– How would you say: Would you like to go to the theatre (the disco, a concert, etc.) with Marco and Luisa?

They then adapt the dialogues and make them suit their own interests and what is available locally.

F Practise again adapting the key phrases by asking the students to give you the Italian for, e.g.

– Let's go to the swimming pool (the disco, etc.), then.
– Would it be possible to go skating (to a concert, to Rome, etc.)?
– We could go round to some friends (to a party, to a football match, etc.).
– Let's watch a video (a film, the football match, etc.).
– I'd prefer to go for a bike ride (go swimming, go to a pizzeria, etc.).

After a while, do this against the clock: see how many the students can do in two minutes and then try a few more times to do more and better.

G Each student chooses one of these dialogues and tries to learn it. This could be a homework. You then display on the OHP heavily-gapped versions of the dialogues and, using these, each student tries to write in full the one he/she has learnt, e.g.

– Che . . . . stasera?
  Ti . . . . con Marco e Luisa?
– Eh ... .
– Perfetto. . . . . allora.

Ti piacerebbe andare al cinema? (page 107)

Main aims: **To practise discussing, negotiating and arranging what to do**

To develop fluency and independence

A The students should first read this quickly in order to find out what the item is about. Discuss this with them and encourage them to see the possibilities. You could base some questions on the visuals, e.g.

– Che cosa si potrebbe fare domani?

You could give the students two minutes to study the item again to learn what activities are available. They then close their books and answer your 'vero o falso' statements, e.g.

– Sarebbe possibile andare al luna park.
– Vero.

– Sarebbe possibile andare in piscina.
– Falso.

B Work on the list of useful phrases using techniques which have proved popular and effective. When the students are starting to become familiar with the expressions on the list, present some invitations, questions and suggestions on the OHP. Write each sentence in large handwriting: reveal each one slowly, starting with the top of the sentence and moving the mask down. The first student to recognise the sentence can put it to another student of his/her choice who must respond to it (with help from you, if necessary). If you do not have an OHP, use this activity by writing the sentences on the board before the class arrives and rubbing out the bottom half of the sentences.

C In pairs, the students read the model dialogue. They then adapt it to suit their own interests and what is available. You could suggest that they make up a dialogue in which they arrange activities for tomorrow. Make it clear that the visuals can be interpreted as they wish: so, the football match can be seen as a live match to go and watch or as something to be seen on TV.

D Working to the briefs given, the students make up dialogues for the three situations. They listen to and assess each other's dialogues, in a helpful and constructive way. They then use what they have learnt from this and make up more dialogues of their own on the same situations.

E Invite the students to think about and discuss the various techniques they use for getting their own way with different people. You say a number of expressions: after each one, the students say whether it sounds, for example: rude, agressive, arrogant, polite, diplomatic, e.g.

– Va bene, ci vado da solo(a).
– L'ho già visto; perché non andiamo a vedere 'Via col vento'?
– Decido io stasera.
– Non lo so, chiediamo a Stefano. Facciamo quello che vuole lui. È il suo compleanno.
– Facciamo così: oggi andiamo a pattinare e domani andiamo in piscina.

F In pairs, the students make up two dialogues:

● one in which one person is rude and selfish and uses this to get his/her own way
● one in which one person gets his/her own way without causing offence.

Facciamo un giro in centro? (page 108)

Main aim: To develop listening skills on the topic of free time

A The students read the introduction in the Students' Book. To help them to prepare to listen, ask them which of the following (which you could present on the board or OHP) they expect to hear on the tape you are about to play.

 1 Stasera cosa fai?
 2 Ti piacerebbe fare un giro in centro?
 3 Devo andare in banca a cambiare questi soldi.
 4 Ho perso il mio libro d'italiano; sai dov'è?
 5 Ci vediamo alle sette, davanti al cinema.
 6 No, oggi fa troppo freddo.
 7 Va bene, andiamo a trovare Letizia e Marco.
 8 Sarebbe possibile andare a Firenze oggi pomeriggio?
 9 Sei già stato al luna park?
10 Ma piove. Non mi piace uscire sotto la pioggia.
11 A più tardi, allora!
12 Sì, è una buona idea e poi fa proprio bello.
13 Ha trovato una macchina fotografica?
14 Potremmo guardare un video se preferisci.
15 Dove l'ha lasciato questo portafoglio?

B Play each dialogue twice. After each:

● ask which of the phrases they expected to hear they did hear
● then ask one or two factual questions and play it again for the students to find the answers.

When you have worked on all the dialogues along these lines, play them again without pausing to help the students decide which group they would prefer to go out with. Encourage them to justify their choices.

▬ Facciamo un giro in centro?

Numero 1

A: Enrica, voi due, cosa fate oggi pomeriggio?
B: Beh, non lo so ancora.
A: Facciamo un giro in centro, facciamo un po' di shopping, noi tre?
B: Va bene. E stasera, che cosa vorresti fare, allora? Ti piacerebbe andare al luna park o magari in discoteca?
A: Io no, grazie. Preferirei andare a trovare Antonio e il suo partner; Antonio deve stare a casa stasera.
B: Potrei venire anch'io?
A: Ma certo.

B: Va bene, allora, andiamo prima in centro e poi andiamo a casa di Antonio ...

A: Perfetto. A più tardi.

B: Ciao.

Numero 2

A: Senti, Silvana, cosa ti piacerebbe fare stasera? Hai voglia di uscire?

B: Sì, cosa hai intenzione di fare, tu? Non ho idea, io.

A: Beh ... potremmo andare in piscina se vuoi. La tua partner sa nuotare?

B: Sì, sì, nuota bene. E dopo, andiamo in gelateria? Che dici?

A: Mi dispiace, ma io non posso. Devo assolutamente tornare a casa dopo la piscina; ho troppi compiti da fare stasera.

B: Anch'io ho molti compiti.

A: O.K. Allora, andiamo in piscina. A che ora?

B: Alle cinque, va bene?

A: Benissimo. Ci vediamo alla piscina alle cinque.

B: Sì. Ciao.

A: Ciao.

Numero 3

A: Eh, oh! ... Daniele! Stasera, cosa fai?

B: Non lo so esattamente, faccio i compiti, guardo la televisione, perché?

A: Vorresti venire a casa mia a guardare un video?

B: Beh ... perché non andiamo al cinema? C'è un nuovo film che mi piacerebbe vedere ...

A: Che cosa danno?

B: È un film di avventura, di fantascienza. Penso che si chiami 'S.O.S. Fantasmi'.

A: Va bene. A che ora comincia il film?

B: Comincia alle nove.

A: Io vengo volentieri. Ci vediamo al cinema, allora?

B: Sì.

A: O.K. Davanti al cinema, alle otto e quaranta. Ti va?

B: Perfetto.

Numero 4

A: Ciao, Donatella. Ciao, Paola.

B, C: Ciao.

B: Senti, Massimo, ti piacerebbe andare a pattinare stasera? Noi due, ci andiamo con le nostre partner.

A: E dopo il pattinaggio che cosa fate?

C: Niente di speciale, perché?

A: Sarebbe possibile andare in pizzeria?

C: Sì, sì, sarebbe una buona idea. Io ho sempre fame dopo il pattinaggio.

B: Anch'io.

A: Va bene. A che ora ci andate, a pattinare?

C: Alle sei, sei e mezza.

A: O.K. Ci vediamo sulla pista.

C: Sì.

B: Sì.

A: A più tardi, allora. Ciao!

B: Ciao!

C: Ciao!

C Now would be an appropriate time to begin work on *Scoprite qualcosa di più* (pages 178-180).

La televisione italiana (page 108)

Main aims: To give information about Italian TV

To introduce the names of common types of film

To develop reading skills and communication strategies

A During work on this item, you could present a range of interesting information, e.g.

• De-regulation of Italian television has seen the rise of numerous private (often local) TV channels. In Arezzo it is possible to tune in to at least thirty different stations.

• It is not uncommon to see films at peak viewing times which would only be shown after 11 p.m. in the UK, and there is noticeably more pornography on Italian TV.

• RAIUNO programmes can be seen in the UK via satellite.

• Italian TV companies buy in many programmes from the USA and the UK. These are usually dubbed in Italian, e.g. Dallas, The Cosbys, M.A.S.H., Peyton Place, Lassie, Benny Hill, Perry Mason, Ironside, Superman.

You could bring in TV listings from Italian newspapers and magazines and ask the students to work out what proportion of programmes for one day are Italian/non-Italian in origin.

When talking about TV programmes with the class you may find the following programme types useful:

cartoni/disegni animati
le notizie, attualità, telegiornale
film (doppiato/sottotitolato)
telefilm
varietà
meteo/che tempo fa
sport
documentario
gioco quiz/gioco a quiz
... a puntate (prima puntata)
95° episodio
sceneggiato (in tre puntate)
spettacolo

B To develop scan reading techniques, ask the students to read this as quickly as possible to find certain specific information, e.g.

- examples of British programmes
- examples of American programmes
- the name of an Italian TV channel
- the title of an Italian TV magazine.

Then ask them to find and to tell you the Italian for, e.g.

- a musical
- a science fiction film
- a comedy
- a western
- an adventure film
- a spy film
- a cops and robbers film
- a horror film.

Ask the students to find and write down two words for types of film which they cannot understand or are not sure about. In Italian, they ask you what they mean. To explain, you could, e.g.

- give, in Italian, examples of, e.g. war films
- act out, with your own sound effects, a typical scene
- define the sort of film.

C To practise higher-level reading skills, you could encourage the students to look for links between different parts of the text, e.g.

Find two films which are in black and white (are American, have Italian actors, you could watch in the evening).
You could also ask them to recommend a film for, e.g.

- someone who hates violent films
- someone who likes films with some action in, but who wants to go to bed before midnight.

D Write on the board the words for types of film which your students should now understand. Make sure that everyone does understand them all. The students write these in a list, ranking them from the one they like most to the one they like least. They compare these in pairs. They then predict your order of preference.

E You could base a quiz on films and TV programmes, varying the questions to suit the class, e.g.

- Voglio il nome di un film western (poliziesco, etc.).
- Voglio il nome di un programma musicale (di fantascienza, etc.).
- 'Where eagles dare' ('Star wars', etc.), che tipo di film è?
- Sto pensando a un film musicale (poliziesco, etc.) : qual è?

Give the students five minutes only to list as many examples as they can of these types of film or TV programme, e.g.

Guerra, Giallo, Orrore, Poliziesco, Fantascienza.

F The students look again at page 108 and each chooses the film they would want to see. They also prepare to justify their choice, e.g.

- Perché sono appassionato di film dell'orrore.
- Perché vado matta per i film di fantascienza.

Each student then interviews several others to find out what they want to see and why. At the end, ask if anyone was surprised and, if so, by whom and why.

Che cosa danno all'Ariston? (page 109)

Main aims: To practise reading about films
            To practise arranging to go to the cinema

A Ask questions to encourage the students to scan the film advertisements several times, e.g.

- What is the most common price for going to the cinema?
- Which is the cheapest cinema?
- Find two cinemas which do not have air conditioning.
- Why do you think most cinemas do have air conditioning?
- At what time does the last performance start in all the cinemas?
- Find the title of an Italian (French, American) film.
- Find the title of a horror (science fiction, police) film.

B To develop communication strategies, including dictionary use, you could write the following on the board:

| criminale | il diavolo | soprannaturale |
| assassina | chiusura | estiva. |

Instruct the students to find these words in the text and to try to work out what each means. Only after they have written, in pencil, what they think each means do they check in a dictionary. Discuss with them how they worked out what each meant.

C Each student reads the dialogue silently, before they read it aloud in pairs. In pairs, they make up a new dialogue, changing the words underlined. They perform their dialogues for other pairs and compare the differences. You can move round, listening and helping.

D You could now return to, and continue with, *Scoprite qualcosa di più* (pages 178-180).

Al cinema (page 109)

Main aim: To introduce common signs and notices in cinemas

A The students read this silently to themselves and try to work out what each sign means, using a dictionary if necessary. Ask the questions under the signs and encourage several students to give different answers to each one.

B The students make attractive copies of the signs here which could be displayed in the school. Put these signs up in appropriate places.

C You, or students, make copies of these signs on pieces of card. Add these to signs from other topics. When you have a few minutes to spare at the end of a lesson, see how many of these signs the class can identify correctly in two minutes. They could tell you:
a what each sign means
b where they would expect to see each sign.

Alla cassa (page 110)

Main aim: To practise buying tickets for a film

A Each student reads these dialogues silently and asks about anything which is not clear. They then listen to the recording and follow the text as they do so. Give them five minutes to try to learn the dialogues either individually or in pairs. Then play the recording again: stop the tape from time to time and, without looking at the Students' Book, the students try to continue the dialogue.

🔲 Alla cassa

Dialogo 1

Employee:	Buonasera.
Man:	Buonasera. Due, per favore.
Employee:	Ecco. Uno ... due.
Man:	Quant'è?
Employee:	Ventimila lire.
Man:	Tenga. Grazie.
Employee:	Prego.

Dialogo 2

Employee:	Buonasera.
Woman:	Buonasera. Uno per 'La Casa 4', per favore.
Employee:	Ecco. Diecimila lire.
Woman:	A che ora comincia il prossimo spettacolo?
Employee:	Alle cinque e mezza: tra venti minuti.
Woman:	Ho capito, grazie.

B The students listen to *Problemi, problemi*. Play each one two or three times and then ask what the problem is.

🔲 Problemi, problemi!

Dialogo 1

Employee:	Buonasera.
Young person:	Due, per favore.
Employee:	Per quale film?
Young person:	Due, per 'Soprannaturale'.
Employee:	Quanti anni hai?
Young person:	Quattordici.
Employee:	E il tuo amico?
Young person:	Anche lui ne ha quattordici.
Employee:	Ne dimostrate di meno.
Young person:	Le giuro, abbiamo quattordici anni.
Employee:	Va bene. Ventimila lire.
Young person:	Ecco. Grazie.

Dialogo 2

Customer:	Scusi, scusi ...
Passer-by:	Sì?
Customer:	Senta, a che ora apre la biglietteria? Vorrei due biglietti per 'Un pesce di nome Wanda'.
Passer-by:	Ma il cinema è chiuso in questo momento. È chiuso per ferie.
Customer:	Mi dispiace, non lo sapevo. Quando riapre, allora?
Passer-by:	Riaprirà la prima settimana in settembre, penso.
Customer:	Grazie.
Passer-by:	Prego.

Dialogo 3

Customer:	Buonasera.
Employee:	Buonasera.
Customer:	Quattro, per favore.
Employee:	Mi dispiace, ma per questo spettacolo non ci sono più posti.
Customer:	Ah ... a che ora comincia il prossimo spettacolo, allora?
Employee:	Il prossimo spettacolo comincia alle sette e trentacinque e poi ce n'è un altro alle nove e dieci.
Customer:	Va bene. Mi può dare quattro biglietti per lo spettacolo delle nove e dieci, allora?
Employee:	Quattro, ha detto?
Customer:	Sì.
Employee:	Dunque ... trentaseimila lire.
Customer:	Grazie. Ecco.

Dialogo 4

Employee:	Buonasera.

Customer: Buonasera. Uno, per favore. Quant'è?
Employee: Diecimila lire.
Customer: Mi può cambiare un biglietto da centomila lire?
Employee: Centomila? Beh, sarà un po' difficile ... un momento ... Sì. Allora, dieci, venti, trenta, quaranta, cinquanta e centomila.
Customer: Grazie.
Employee: Prego.

Dialogo 5

Employee: Buonasera.
Customer: Buonasera. Vorrei cinque biglietti per 'Balla coi Lupi'.
Employee: 'Balla coi Lupi'? Ma è finito ieri quel film.
Customer: È finito? Oh, che delusione! Che cosa danno oggi?
Employee: 'Compagni di Scuola'.
Customer: Va bene. Mi fa cinque biglietti, allora?
Employee: Cinquantamila lire.
Customer: Tenga ... Grazie.
Employee: Prego.

Answers:

1 The cashier thinks they are under age.
2 The cinema is closed for a holiday.
3 There are no tickets for that particular performance.
4 The customer only has a 100.000 lire note.
5 The film they had hoped to see stopped running yesterday.

Play each dialogue again and ask the students to listen to how each person deals with the problems that arise. Can they suggest better ways of dealing with each problem?

C Now present the following on the board or OHP. Invite the students, in pairs, to continue each one and to find the best possible way to resolve the problem. Ask for volunteers to perform their dialogues for the class and ask the class to comment.

1
A: Buonasera.
B: Buonasera. Due per 'Arma Letale 2', per favore.
A: Seidicimila lire.
B: Ah no, ho dimenticato il mio portafoglio ...

2
A: Buonasera. Quattro, per favore.
B: Mi dispiace, ma siamo al completo ...

3
A: Scusi, mi sa dire a che ora apre?
B: Ma è chiuso per lavori ...

4
A: Buonasera.

B: Buonasera. Uno per 'Palombella Rossa'.
A: Mi dispiace ma stasera diamo "Poliziotto a 4 Zampe". L'altro film era diffettoso ...

D It is useful to know that membership of the Italian Institute (39 Belgrave Square, London SW1X 8NX) entitles you to borrow videos, films and slides from the Institute library. Catalogues are available.
Some Italian delicatessens keep a range of Italian videos: these can be hired.

E Give out copies of Copymasters 62A and B.
The students take turns to play the customer and the cinema employee.

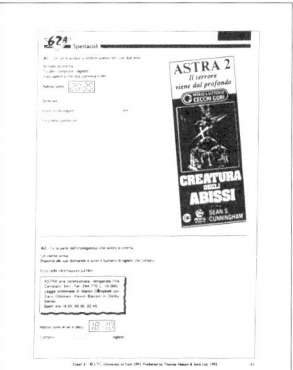 

F At a suitable time, you could explain that, in Italian cinemas, most feature films are shown in two sessions: 'primo tempo' and 'secondo tempo'. The 'intervallo' between the two provides an opportunity to sell drinks, pop corn, ice cream, etc.

Ti è piacuto il film? (page 110)

Main aim: To practise expressing opinions about a film, etc

A Work on the list using techniques which have proved successful.
When the students are starting to become familiar with the expressions, you could, e.g.

• ask the students to rank the replies given in the list from the most positive to the most negative. They could compare their lists.
• ask them to suggest the titles of films or TV programmes they have seen which could be described using these expressions, e.g.

– Era proprio divertente.
– Era molto bello.
– Era un po' noioso.

In pairs, they could compare their responses.

B The students look back at page 109. You ask several questions, e.g.

– Che film hai visto?
– Ti è piaciuto? Perché?

Write these questions on the board. The students now interview each other, using these questions as a guide, to find out what they have seen recently on TV or at the cinema. Ask a few students what they have discovered in these interviews.

C While the students interview each other, write on the board or OHP the titles of some films or TV programmes you have watched. The students all write down what they think you thought of each one. They then read these out. If possible, give a small prize for the best score.

D This would be a suitable time to do more work on *Scoprite qualcosa di più* (pages 178-180).

Come hanno risposto? (page 111)

Main aim: To practise expressing opinions

A Revise briefly the list on page 110, e.g.

● Invite the students to find as many ways as they can of completing, e.g.

– Era proprio ...
– Era molto ...
– Non era ...
– Era un po' ...
– Era ...

They could do this first as they look at the list and again without the list.

● Play a game of 'Il gioco degli spazi', e.g.
– Ieri sera ho visto 'Rainman': era ____ .
– Ho visto io 'Blue Peter': era ____ .

– Ti è piaciuta la partita di calcio alla televisione?
– Era ____ .

– Ti è piaciuto il concerto alla televisione?
– Era ____ .

– L'anno scorso siamo andati ad un campeggio vicino al mare. Il campeggio era ____ .
– Sono stata in un albergo di lusso. La mia camera era ____ .

– Come hai trovato la lezione di matematica?
– Era ____ .

– Ti è piaciuta la giornata a scuola?
– Sì, era ____ .

– La prima domenica di settembre siamo andati a vedere la Giostra del Saracino. Era ____ .

B The students study this item. When everyone understands what it is about, ask them to write a sentence to go with the first photo. They can then discuss their replies. Repeat this procedure with the other photos.
If you have an Italian assistant, you could ask him/her to say which expression goes best with each photo.

C Using blu-tack, stick to the board three or four photos of people, cut from newspapers. Ask the class to suggest a sentence for each one, describing what they imagine the people think about a film they have just seen. Write what they suggest under each photo, one sentence to each photo.
Use these to organise an experiment in telepathy. Ask who believes in telepathy, in the ability to know what someone is thinking before they say it. Choose one of these students to be the 'medium'. This person chooses one of the pictures on the board and concentrates on it, reading to him/herself the sentence under it. The others try to guess which picture has been chosen and read the corresponding sentence aloud: go round the class and tick a sentence each time a student reads it. Then ask the 'medium' to say aloud the sentence he/she has been saying to him/herself.

If this works well, try it again with another 'medium', perhaps asking the 'medium' to write the sentence beforehand on a piece of paper and give this to you: this removes the possibility of cheating.

If it does not work well with one 'medium', try it again with another.

Hai guardato la televisione ieri sera? (page 112)

Main aims: To develop listening skills

To practise asking for, and giving, opinions

A Spend a few minutes working again on the list on page 110 of the Students' Book to ensure that all the students are very familiar with the language needed for this activity.

B The students read the dialogue quietly to themselves and then ask about anything they do not understand. Clear up any problems and then ask them to play-read the dialogue in pairs, with appropriate gestures, expressions and intonation.
You could discuss the importance of non-verbal techniques in conveying opinions and give acting briefs for several students to interpret, e.g.

– Sei andato(a) a vedere un film con un amico. Non ti è piaciuto, ma al tuo amico è piaciuto molto e non vuoi offenderlo. Come rispondi quando lui ti chiede 'Ti è piaciuto il film?'
– La tua corrispondente ti invita al cinema a vedere un film che tu hai già visto. Ti è piaciuto il film però non hai voglia di vederlo per una seconda volta. Che cosa dici?

C The students listen to the following recordings. After each one, they describe the attitudes expressed. They then listen again to pick out the key expressions which communicated these attitudes and any other clues, e.g. tone of voice.

To practise higher-level listening skills, play all the dialogues without pauses: the students listen to find out:

* who sounded the most enthusiastic
* who sounded the least enthusiastic
* if anyone seemed to be exaggerating.

🎞 Era proprio un bel film

Dialogo 1

Interviewer:	Buonasera.
Woman:	Buonasera.
Interviewer:	Senta, vedo che Lei è appena uscita dal cinema. Le è piaciuto il film?
Woman:	Eh sì, moltissimo. È proprio un bel film. Era un po' triste ma ...
Interviewer:	Un po' triste?
Woman:	Sì. È la storia di una madre che viene separata da suo figlio, che soffre, che ha tanti problemi, ma ...
Interviewer:	Le è piaciuto?
Woman:	Sì, sì. Era molto bello.

Dialogo 2

Woman:	Allora, Marco, non è ancora finito quel video?
Boy:	Beh ... finisce adesso; è la fine ora.
Woman:	Meno male. Ti è piaciuto almeno?
Boy:	Eh sì, era divertentissimo. Mi è piaciuto moltissimo, soprattutto quando ha mangiato i pesciolini, vivi!
Woman:	Sono contenta.
Boy:	Sì, mi sono veramente divertito.

Dialogo 3

Woman 1:	Hai guardato la televisione ieri sera, Maria Luisa?
Woman 2:	Io, sì. Ho visto il film su Italia Uno.
Woman 1:	Anch'io l'ho visto. Ti è piaciuto?
Woman 2:	Beh, non molto. Ne sono rimasta un po' delusa.
Woman 1:	Sì, pensavo che sarebbe stato più bello, più interessante.
Woman 2:	Sì. Peccato, eh?

Dialogo 4

Man:	Uffa ... finalmente è finito.
Woman:	Dai ... andiamo ...
Man:	Allora, ti è piaciuto?
Woman:	Assolutamente, no. Prima di tutto il rumore - era troppo forte.
Man:	Io l'ho trovato proprio noioso. Era troppo lungo.
Woman:	Io sono rimasta proprio delusa.
Man:	Anch'io. È l'ultima volta che vado a vederlo.

Dialogo 5

Man:	Usciamo di qua, c'è meno gente.
Woman:	OK. Vai prima tu.
Man:	Che bel concerto, mi sono proprio divertito.
Woman:	Ti è piaciuto, allora?
Man:	Euh, sì, tanto. Sono rimasto un po' sorpreso. Di solito la musica classica non mi piace ...
Woman:	Ma stasera la musica era proprio bella, no?
Man:	Sì. Il programma era ottimo. Hai scelto bene.
Woman:	Grazie.

D In pairs, the students practise adapting the dialogue on page 112, finding as many variations as they can in six minutes.

E Present this grid on the board:

	Nome	Ha guardato	L'ha trovato
1			
2			
3			
4			
5			
6			
7			
8			

Each student copies it. Ask a few students some appropriate questions and make appropriate notes on your grid on the board to ensure that everyone knows what to do.

The students fill in the first line of the grid for themselves. They then interview seven others in order to find three other people who have watched the same programme as them and who share their opinion of it. Give them ten minutes in which to do this.

12ª Unità

Adesso, tocca a te! (pages 112-113)

Main aim: To demonstrate that the main points of this unit have been mastered

Exercise 1
Language area: Leisure activities
Skill area: Writing

Make sure that everyone understands clearly what to do before they write their lists.

Exercise 2
Language area: Planning leisure activities
Skill areas: Speaking and listening

Both students play both roles. They should help each other to do as well as possible: this is not a competition.

Exercise 3
Language area: Going to the cinema
Skill area; Speaking

Again, in pairs, the students play each role in turn and again they help each other to do this as well as possible.

Exercise 4
Language area: Information regarding films
Skill areas: Reading and speaking

The students read these advertisements and then, in pairs, negotiate about which one they will go to see together.

Exercise 5
Language area; Going to the cinema
Skill area: Speaking

In pairs, the students prepare this together, helping each other. They then perform each role in turn. If possible, get them to record this and mark the recordings.

Exercise 6
Language area: Television programmes
Skill areas: Speaking and listening

As the students conduct their interviews keep an eye open for students who finish early and pair those who are free.

Listen and keep a note of any linguistic problems: use your notes as a basis for any necessary remedial work.

Ora sai (page 114)

Main aim: To act as a summary of the main learning objectives of this unit

A Encourage the students to use any techniques which they have previously found enjoyable and effective for working on

these lists. Move around and listen to find out which activities they use.

B Each student copies any three of the sentences in this item, writing each sentence on a different piece of paper: encourage them to write sentences which they are finding difficult to learn.

They form groups of five or six and put their sentences on a desk. A student picks one at random and mimes the sentence which is on it. The others guess what the sentence is. The first student to do so has the next go.

Collect in the sentence cards. Form new groups of three or four. Give each group three sentence cards. They make up a mime which uses all three sentences. Each group in turn performs its mime for the class who try to say what the three sentences are.

C At the top of the board write the words 'molto divertente'. At the bottom write 'molto noioso'. The students copy these and, between them, write as many other 'opinion' words as they can, placing them at appropriate places on the page to grade them from very enjoyable to very boring. They can compare in pairs what they have written.

Revision

1 Changing money (Book 1, Unit 9)

A Give each student a copy of Copymaster 63. Working individually, they write out the sentences. They then compare what they have done, in pairs, and help each other to get them all right.

B In pairs, the students make up a dialogue using as many of these sentences as possible. Invite the pairs which manage to include the most sentences to perform their dialogues for the class.

Answers:

1 Vorrei cambiare questi soldi.
2 Vorrei cambiare questo travellers cheque.
3 Mi può cambiare cinquanta sterline.
4 Firmi qui per favore.
5 Si accommodi alla cassa.
6 Mi dà cinque biglietti da diecimila lire.

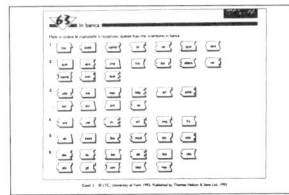

2 Collections, personality, appearance (Book 3, Unit 2)

A The students revise Unit 2 on their own, using their own preferred techniques. This could be done at home. Ask several students how they went about this, if they found it effective and enjoyable, and why.

B The students imagine that they are going to a party with a group of Italians. They want to get to know the Italians and try to make friends. To prepare for this, they write a list of ten to twelve questions they will ask people at the party.
Correct these questions. Then ask the students to move around and to put their questions to each other.

C Ask the students to help you to write on the board as long a list as possible of adjectives which can be used to describe characters in TV soaps. Then use the words on the list to describe a soap character, e.g.

– È australiana. Non è molto alta. È magra. Non porta gli occhiali. Ha i capelli biondi e ricci. È abbastanza bella. È sportiva e estroversa.

The students guess who it is. As soon as possible, let the students take over. They can continue this in pairs.

3 Comparative adjectives (Book 3, Unit 2)

A Present these sentences on the OHP. The students choose and copy only those which compare two things or people:

1 Mia madre lavora come stilista.
2 Ciao! Vorrei corrispondere con ragazzi(e) dai 16 anni in su.
3 Faccio collezione di portachiavi.
4 Nella classe, Massimo ha la più grande collezione di compact disc.
5 Non mi piace la scuola perché ho sempre molti compiti da fare.
6 La seconda lettera che ha scritto Federica è più lunga della prima.
7 Ho quindici anni.
8 Il sabato pomeriggio mi piace praticare diversi sport.
9 Mio padre è molto meno calmo di mia madre.
10 La mia collezione di adesivi è più grande di quella di cartoline.
11 I miei genitori dicono che non sono molto studioso.
12 Il tuo cane è più vecchio del tuo gatto?
13 Sono nata a Magenta il tre settembre 1979.
14 Il ragazzo più alto della classe è Jacopo.
15 Ho gli occhi azzurri e i capelli scuri.
16 Abito in un appartamento nella periferia di Arezzo.
17 La persona meno sportiva è Claudio.
18 Mio padre porta gli occhiali.
19 Di tutte le ragazze, io sono la più bassa.
20 Ho due sorelle; una più grande di me e l'altra più piccola.

Use the comparative sentences to remind the students of the principles of how to compare. Get the students to adapt the sentences orally to compare other things and people.

B Now present on the board or OHP the titles of well-known TV programmes and characters, in pairs, e.g.

Eastenders – Neighbours
Blue Peter – Blockbusters
Blankety-blank – Bull'seye
Dallas – Dynasty

Each student prepares a sentence comparing the two programmes in each pair. You ask about them in turn, e.g.

– Secondo te, qual è la differenza tra 'Eastenders' e 'Neighbours'?

Students read out their comparisons. Give a small prize to anyone who says a correct comparison which no other student has thought of.

4 Lost property (Book 3, Unit 8)

A As suggested in **2A** above, get the students to revise Unit 8 on their own. This is important for them to develop useful study skills.

B All the students write a list of things they might lose, or leave behind, in a cinema (e.g. gloves, wallet, sunglasses). They then cross off their lists anything which would not be worth crossing town and giving up four hours of a holiday to go back to the cinema for.
Looking back to Unit 8 if they need to, the students now write a list of eight to ten sentences which they would find useful when enquiring about something valuable they left behind in a cinema in Italy. They use these as a basis for role-play in pairs: each takes a turn to be the customer and the cinema employee.

5 Weather (Book 3, Unit 11)

A The students all look again at page 95. You say a weather condition, e.g.

– Nevica. (Piove. Il tempo è variabile.)

The students say which of these activities they would choose to do. Keep changing the weather and try to maintain a fast pace.

B Play a game of 'Il gioco degli spazi' (see Teacher's Book 1 page 110), e.g.

1 Fa ___ oggi.
   Domani farà ___ .
2 Vado a pattinare quando ___ .
   Giochiamo a calcio quando fa ___ .

3 Il tempo è bello qui d' __ .
   Ma piove molto in __ .

4 Mi piacerebbe fare un giro in bicicletta se domani fa __ tempo.
   Preferirei andare al concerto se stasera __ .

5 È possibile andare a pattinare anche quando __ .
   Andiamo in piscina soprattutto quando __ .

6 **Prepositions (Book 3, Unit 11)**

A Present the following prepositions on the board:
   a, di, da, su, in.
Get the students to look again at Unit 11 and *Scoprite qualcosa di più* (pages 172-178) and to find examples to revise the rules for changing these words when they are followed by a definite article.

Then ask everyone to try to draw a picture and to write a caption which will help the others to remember each of these five words. Correct these and encourage the students to produce large and attractive versions: they use these to teach each other these words and to create an attractive wall display.

B Play a game of 'Dino dice'.
The students obey your commands only if these are preceded by the words 'Dino dice'.
You score a point every time you catch someone out. See how long it takes you to score ten. Then play again and see if you can score ten faster.
You could say, e.g.

— Da' una matita alla persona alla tua destra.
— Prendi un quaderno nello zaino.
— Metti una penna sul tuo libro d'italiano, ecc.

C Give a volunteer a piece of paper with a sentence written on it, e.g.

— Il mio portafoglio è sulla tavola.
— Vado all'ufficio oggetti smarriti.
— I francobolli nella mia collezione sono in un album.
— Il nostro appartamento è al secondo piano.
— Il mio cane è più grande del mio gatto.
— Il tempo è variabile al sud e nelle isole.

The volunteer has lost his/her voice so has to mime or draw an illustration. The class tries to work out what is written on the piece of paper from the mimes or drawings. The volunteer can use some of the devices used when playing charades, e.g. indicate how many words there are; indicate which word(s) he/she is miming/drawing.

13ª Unità
A ROMA

Main aims

~ To be able to understand announcements, information and notices on guided coach tours
~ To be able to understand the working of the 'metropolitana'
~ To book tickets on guided coach tours and to use the 'metropolitana'

Materials

~ Tape
Avete delle informazioni? (Teacher's Book page 152)
Come scegliere e prenotare (Teacher's Book page 153)
È il pullman giusto? (Teacher's Book page 155)
Conosci Roma adesso? (Teacher's Book page 156)
Adesso, tocca a te! (Teacher's Book page 158)

~ Copymasters 64–69

Grammar in *Scoprite qualcosa di più*

~ Perfect tense: 'avere' and 'essere' verbs, regular and irregular past participles

Revision

~ Getting a penfriend (Book 2, Unit 1)
~ Avere (Book 2, Unit 1)
~ Talking about your town (Book 3, Unit 3)
~ Comparative and superlative adjectives (Book 3, Unit 3)
~ Staying with an Italian family (Book 3, Unit 9)
~ 'Noi' and 'voi': present and perfect tenses (Book 3, Units 1, 5, 9)
~ Going to the cinema (Book 3, Unit 12)
~ Potere (Book 3, Unit 7)
~ Perfect tense

Vocabulary

A: Productive

bisogna	libero	quanto ci mette
giro	la linea	una sosta
una gita	la metropolitana	turistico(a)
la guida	occupato	una visita
le informazioni	il pullman	

B: Receptive

l'aereo	la durata	la partenza
il centro storico	l'ingresso	il secolo
costruito	la nave	il Tevere

A Roma (page 115)

Main aim: To develop reading skills and to arouse interest in a visit to Rome

A Start by asking if anyone has been to Rome. If anyone has, encourage them to talk about Rome and to bring any souvenirs, photos, slides into the class and talk about them. If possible, have a wall display based on Rome to begin work on this unit: you can add to the display as work progresses and use it several times as a basis for discussions.

B To practise the technique of finding specific information in a text as quickly as possible, ask the students to look first at these questions on the board:

– Quali sono i luoghi più importanti da vedere a Roma?
– Ci sono delle visite di Roma in pullman?
– C'è una metropolitana a Roma?

When everyone is familiar with the questions, give them thirty seconds only to look at page 115 and to decide where in the text they will find the answer to each question. Ask how they knew and discuss the various clues which are mentioned.

The students look again at the questions: then give them two minutes to find the answers. Put the questions orally to several students. Encourage discussions, e.g.

– about famous monuments (e.g. Why do they think the traffic is shown on the photo of the Colosseum? Does it spoil the effect?)
– what the two tours offer and which extras are available; put into order of attraction the points in the Green Line advert and compare different replies
– on the advantages of a guided tour of a big city
– on the various answers to: Come si può andare a Roma?

C Discuss the main aims of this unit. The students then choose from this page what they think will be key words in the unit. They write these down. At the end of the unit, return briefly to these and check how accurate their predictions were.

I preparativi (page 116)

Main aim: Using reading and writing skills to find out about Rome

A Give the students one minute to look at this section and to work out what its function is (to give information about how to prepare for a visit to Rome). Discuss the clues they used.

B The students read the letter and list the information it asks for. They compare their lists in pairs.

They then read the rest of the section to find out what else is available in Rome. They use this information and any other (e.g. from the wall display, from what you and others in the class have said about Rome) to write a letter asking for the information they would like, adapting the letter on this page. Encourage them to send their letters and to bring into the class whatever they receive in reply.

C Discuss the advantages of carefully planning a visit to Rome. Useful books, publications and addresses include:

Pianta di Roma (detailed city plan)
Carnet di Roma (monthly events and general features)
Qui Roma (basic information)
Roma giovane (useful tips and hints for young visitors)
Musei e monumenti

All the above are available free of charge, in English or Italian, from the Ente Provinciale per il Turismo, Via Parigi 11, 00185 Roma.

Tuttocittà – Roma (detailed city plan plus hints on what to see, how to travel, and services available), from Edizioni Stet, Via Bertoli 28, 10122 Torino.

Trovaroma (weekly supplement to the newspaper *La Repubblica*, with details of coming films, concerts, festivals etc.) from Stabilimento A.G.R., Via Costarica 11, Pomezia, 00182 Roma.

Blue Guide to Rome and environs (Benn)
Baedecker's Rome (A.A. publications in U.K.)
Frommer's Rome (Simon and Schuster)
Rough guide to Italy (Harrap)
L' Istituto Italiano di Cultura (Films, slides, videos, etc., membership fee), 39 Belgrave Square, London SW1.

Avete delle informazioni? (page 116)

Main aim: To introduce the main language needed for enquiring about guided tours

A Work on the list using techniques which have previously proved effective and enjoyable.
You could start 'una scalinata' on the board. The students look at the list and try to find a word beginning with the same letter as the last letter of the previous word and thus take the stairs down, e.g.

QUANTO
     R
     AVETE

When they cannot find a suitable word in the list, they can use another word. Play this game for a few minutes in a number of lessons, trying each time to produce a longer staircase. Students can play the game in pairs.

B The students read the information about coach tour A and write down the questions they would ask about it. They put these questions to you, and you give suitable replies. They then use and adapt the questions in the list to ask about tour B.

C The students listen to the recordings: after each one, they say which advert it refers to. Warn them that one advert does not have a conversation based on it. Discuss their answers and clear up any problems before going on to the next one.

Avete delle informazioni?

Dialogo 1 (Advert D)

Employee:	Buongiorno. Desidera?
Woman:	Buongiorno. Avete delle informazioni sulle gite in pullman?
Employee:	Sì, signorina. Ecco qualcosa sul panorama di Roma.
Woman:	Quanto costa, per favore?
Employee:	Costa 25.000 lire.
Woman:	A che ora parte, per favore?
Employee:	Ci sono delle partenze alle 10, alle 12, alle 14 ...
Woman:	E ci mette molto tempo?
Employee:	Ci mette circa due ore.
Woman:	Da dove parte, per favore?
Employee:	Parte da Piazza Barberini.
Woman:	C'è una guida?
Employee:	No. Non c'è una guida. Ma avete una cuffia acustica.

Dialogo 2 (Advert B)

Employee:	Buongiorno.
Man:	Buongiorno. C'è un pullman che fa il giro di Roma di notte?
Employee:	Sì, certo, parte dall'agenzia alle 20.00.
Man:	Quanto ci mette?
Employee:	Circa tre ore.
Man:	E c'è una guida?
Employee:	Sì, signore. C'è una guida italiana.
Man:	Grazie.

Dialogo 3 (Advert A)

Employee:	Buongiorno. Posso aiutarLa?
Girl:	Buongiorno, quanto costa questa gita, per favore?
Employee:	Costa 30.000 lire per persona.
Girl:	Gli ingressi sono inclusi nel prezzo?
Employee:	Sì, signorina, ingressi e guida sono inclusi.
Girl:	Da dove parte, per favore?
Employee:	Parte dall'Albergo Nuovo, alle nove.
Girl:	Ci mette molto?
Employee:	Circa quattro ore.
Girl:	Grazie.
Employee:	Prego, signorina.

D The students make up, write down and act out the dialogue about notice C. Move around as they do this, listening, helping and joining in. As students finish this, ask them to make up a similar dialogue on another of the notices.

E If the work on **D** above shows that more practice is needed you could, e.g.

- Ask ten students to ask you the time a coach leaves for somewhere: the class note your replies.
- As above, for the time a coach returns.
- As above, for where a coach leaves from.
- As above, for prices, with replies between 20.000 L and 80.000 L.

F The students close the Students' Book and listen again to the recorded conversations. They say if the following (on the board or OHP) are true or false.

Dialogo 1

a Costa 25.000 lire. (V)
b Parte da Piazza Navona. (F)
c C'è una guida. (F)

Dialogo 2

a Il pullman torna all'agenzia alle 20. (F)
b Non c'è una guida. (F)

Dialogo 3

a Costa 20.000 lire. (F)
b Parte dall' Albergo Nuovo. (V)
c Ci mette circa quattro ore. (V)

Come scegliere e prenotare (page 117)

Main aim: To introduce the key language needed when booking and reserving seats and tickets for a coach tour

A Before working on the list, present the task in order to explain the usefulness of the list. Then work on the list using techniques which have previously proved effective.

Ask students to read out the phrases that they would probably need to say. Then ask them to pick out and read aloud the phrases that the employee would be more likely to say. Ask one student to play the part of the employee and another to be the tourist: they make up a dialogue using phrases from the list. The students can then do this in pairs, and add to and adapt the phrases in the list.

B The students look again at the adverts on page 116. They then listen to the four people booking places, noting down the information they are asked to look for.

Come scegliere e prenotare

Dialogo 1 (Advert D)

Man: Buongiorno, che cosa avete per domani mattina?
Employee: C'è il Panorama Tour che parte alle dieci, e Roma Cristiana alle 9.
Man: E quale ritorna prima?
Employee: Allora il Panorama – ritorna alle 12: ma il giro di Roma Cristiana è molto più interessante.
Man: Sì, grazie, ma non ho molto tempo. Bisogna prenotare?
Employee: No, signore, non bisogna prenotare.

Dialogo 2 (Advert B)

Employee: Buongiorno, signora. Desidera?
Woman: Le gite per domani – bisogna prenotare?
Employee: Beh ... dipende, signora ... per il Panorama non bisogna prenotare ma poi ...
Woman: Sì, sì, ho capito. Il Tour Roma di Notte viene con cena inclusa?
Employee: Ah, no, signora. Se vuole la cena deve prendere la gita Tivoli ...
Woman: Sì, ma costa troppo – non ho soldi da buttare via ... No, prendo Roma di Notte ... Posso pagare domani?
Employee: Ah no. Mi dispiace, signora, se vuole prenotare deve pagare adesso.
Woman: Va bene, va bene. Speriamo che valga la pena!

Dialogo 3 (Advert A)

Man: Buonasera, signorina. Vorrei fare una gita domani. Non avrebbe qualcosa per me, per piacere?
Employee: Sì, signore, posso raccomandare la gita Tivoli con cena – è molto buona – i giardini e le fontane sono bellissimi.
Man: Quanto costa, per favore?
Employee: Costa 65.000 lire per persona.
Man: Sessantacinque – Caspita! Mi piacciono i giardini, ma, mi scusi, costa troppo. Non ci sarebbe qualcosa di meno caro per domani?
Employee: Certo, signore. Abbiamo Roma di Notte che parte alle 20.
Man: Ma, forse è troppo tardi per me, mi scusi.
Employee: Non c'è di che – forse Le interesserà la gita Roma Cristiana?
Man: Quanto costa, per favore?
Employee: Trentamila lire.
Man: Bisogna prenotare?
Employee: Sì, sarebbe meglio.
Man: Va bene, due biglietti, per favore, e grazie tante.

Dialogo 4 (Advert C)

Man:	Buongiorno ... per sabato prossimo vorrei una gita per me e mia moglie – qualcosa di ... come dire ... romantico.
Employee:	Allora – la gita Roma di Notte sarebbe perfetta.
Man:	Grazie – ma la cena è inclusa?
Employee:	Ah no, signore ... ma potrebbe cenare al ritorno.
Man:	Mi scusi, ma non possiamo mica celebrare il nostro anniversario di matrimonio senza mangiare. Potrebbe trovarci qualcosa con cena inclusa, per favore?
Employee:	Sì certo, signore ... c'è sempre il giro di Tivoli e Villa d'Este ... con cena inclusa ... ed è molto, molto romantico.
Man:	Che bello. Mille grazie. Bisogna prenotare?
Employee:	Sì signore, bisogna prenotare.

C   The students listen again and decide which tourists were polite, which were rude, and who was in a hurry. When presenting this activity, use the words 'cortese' and 'scortese': write these on the board, ensure that everyone understands them, and leave the words on the board. Once the students have identified who was rude, they should make up more polite conversations to achieve the same ends.

D   Talk with the class about coach tours in their area. If they don't know about them, set the task of finding out as a homework. Then play the part of an Italian visitor and ask about them, including prices and whether it is necessary to book.

E   The students make up dialogues in pairs, based on the adverts on page 116. One asks about the information he/she wants and if it is necessary to book, then buys a ticket. Before they do this in pairs, it may be necessary to produce a model orally with the class and to write this on the board or OHP.

Quale gita scelgono? (page 117)

Main aim: **To develop reading skills, with information about tours**

A   The students read what the people say and think, and summarise the sorts of things that they all need. They read the tourist information and find the best tour for each person. They should be prepared to justify their choice. It would help some students if you dealt with one person at a time.

B   The students read the information again and ask about anything they do not understand and would like more information on. They each choose the tour they prefer and list what they like about it. They then look for someone who has

chosen a different tour. In pairs, they both try to persuade the other to change tour.

Che pensi tu di questi tour? (page 118)

Main aim: **Expressing and justifying opinions**

A   The students read again the details about the three tours on page 117 with a view to expressing their opinions about them. They then use the table to help them to do this: do some orally first with the class.

B   Each student writes 15 opinions, using the table. They should write something about each tour. Move around the class and ask questions, e.g.

– Ti piace questo tour?
– Quale tour preferisci?
– Non ti piace il numero 3? Perché?

C   The students work in pairs along the lines suggested in the Students' Book.

Bisogna comprare questi biglietti (page 118)

Main aim: **To practise buying tickets for a coach tour**

A   Give the students one minute to find out what this activity is about and what they have to do. Ask some to explain and to demonstrate by doing the example, and a few more examples from the board, e.g.

2 x Napoli ore 10.15.
1 x Roma Moderna ore 8.30.

B   Each student writes down how to ask for each set of tickets. In pairs, they ask for the tickets in random order: the partner points to what is asked for and replies appropriately.

È il pullman giusto? (page 119)

Main aim: **Finding the right coach and a seat on it**

A   Make sure that the students understand the point of the list and the value of the phrases in it. Then use previously successful techniques to work on the list.
After some work on the list, you could play a game of 'il gioco degli spazi', e.g.

1 È questo il pullman per la gita di ___ ?
2 C'è un posto ___ ?
3 C'è una ___ a Firenze?
4 Ci sono posti ___ ?
5 Questo posto è ___ .

6 C'è una sosta di ___ minuti.

7 C'è un posto ___ al finestrino?

8 Sì, è ___ questo posto.

B Explain that students will hear five conversations and, for each one, they should write down:

– whether the correct coach is found

– whether a seat is available.

Play each conversation twice and discuss the students' replies before going on to the next one. You could ask additional questions, e.g.

– Dove hanno trovato il posto?

– Qual era il problema? (numbers 4 and 5)

È il pullman giusto?

Dialogo 1

Man:	Scusi, mi sa dire se questo è il pullman che va a Firenze?
Driver:	Certo. Si accomodi.
Man:	C'è un posto libero?
Driver:	Sì, c'è ne uno in fondo.

Dialogo 2

Woman:	Scusi, mi sa dire se è questo l'autobus per la gita Roma Cristiana?
Driver:	Eh no, signorina. Noi andiamo a Tivoli.

Dialogo 3

Boy:	Cerco il pullman per la visita dei Castelli Romani.
Driver:	È questo.
Boy:	Grazie. C'è un posto vicino al finestrino?
Driver:	Sì, guarda, ce n'è uno lì, a sinistra.

Dialogo 4

Man:	Scusi, è questo il pullman per la gita Roma Imperiale?
Driver:	Sì, signore – ma non c'è posto – siamo al completo.
Man:	Ma, non capisco ... ho prenotato ... ecco il mio biglietto.
Driver:	Faccia vedere – ah sì ... è per la gita di mezzogiorno ... deve aspettare una mezz'ora e dovrà salire sul prossimo pullman.

Dialogo 5

Woman:	Buongiorno. Vorrei un posto accanto al finestrino, per favore. E siccome soffro il mal di macchina, vorrei un posto davanti.
Driver:	Si sieda qui, vicino a me, signora, ... va bene?
Woman:	Grazie. Che fortuna. Sono arrivata proprio a tempo. Quanto ci mette per arrivare ad Assisi?

Driver:	Ma io non vado ad Assisi. Vado a Napoli e a Sorrento.
Woman:	Ho sbagliato! Si fermi, per favore! Si fermi subito!

C Each student works on the activity below the list and works out what each person needs to say. They help their partners to improve and practise in pairs. Move around, listening, joining in and helping.

D You say that you are in a coach going to an Italian city. The students try to find out which city by asking:

– È questo il pullman per ... ?

The student who guesses correctly takes over.

Vedute di Roma (pages 120-121)

Main aims: To develop reading skills and to present interesting information about Rome

A Give the class just sixty seconds to work out what this item is about. They then close their books and tell you. Write their ideas on the board or OHP. Then give them three minutes to check their original ideas. Discuss their findings and, if appropriate, ways of finding out quickly and accurately what a text is about using, e.g.

– titles

– visuals

– captions

– first and last sentences of paragraphs

– words which appear several times.

B Practise finding specific details quickly by asking the students to scan the text to find, e.g.

– The name of the biggest ancient monument.

– When the Colosseum was built.

– The name of the biggest church in the world.

– The name of the artist who painted the Sistine Chapel.

– The tradition about throwing coins into the Trevi Fountain.

– The name of the oldest square in Rome.

– The name of the boys who were raised by wolves and who founded Rome.

– When and why the Arch of Constantine was built.

C Form groups of six or seven students. Each student studies one or two of the seven texts, so that each text is studied by someone in each group. They then tell each other all about the monument they have studied.

D The students study this text for homework. Then base a quiz on it. This could be a 'Blockbuster' type quiz with two competing teams.

E Present some of the key words from the text on the board, e.g.

a.C.	imperatore
d.C.	antichità
colle	secolo
antico	costruito

The students find these words in the text and explain what they mean. Use this to develop their communication strategies by sharing ideas about how to work out the meanings of such words.

F You could develop project work about Rome. Students could use information they have received in response to their letters, some of the books suggested, others available in school and local libraries and materials provided by you.

Conosci Roma adesso? (page 122)

Main aim: To develop reading and listening skills

A Work on the first part of this activity with the class.

B Give each student a copy of Copymaster 64. Use the map as a basis for discussion about Rome, what they know about the monuments on the map and to practise giving directions. Each student then plans the best order of visiting the monuments. They must begin at Piazza Barberini and stop for lunch in Trastevere.

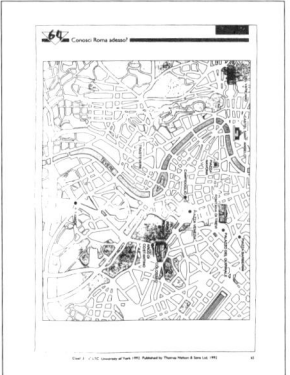

C They listen to the commentary and see if the tour took the same route as they had planned. They could discuss the differences and decide which is the best order.

🔊 Conosci Roma adesso?

– Signori e signore, mi chiamo Franco Rannari, e sono la vostra guida. Siete pronti ... andiamo.

Partendo da Piazza Barberini, a destra, la prima cosa importante che vedrete è il Palazzo del Quirinale, che ospita il Presidente della Repubblica.

Da qui entriamo nel pieno centro storico. Soffre molto per l'inquinamento: ecco perché ci sono certe vie e piazze pedonali.

Qui siamo a Piazza Venezia dove vedete il Mausoleo del Rè Vittorio Emmanuele II e la Tomba del Militare Ignoto.

Siamo arrivati adesso al Campidoglio che bisogna visitare a piedi. Il Campidoglio è sempre stato il cuore politico della Città. La splendida piazza è stata progettata da Michelangelo nel Cinquecento.

Da qui abbiamo una bella veduta del Campo Marzio. Davanti avete il Foro Romano, il centro di ciò che era il cuore politico, economico e religioso della civiltà romana. È la più antica piazza di Roma. Qui, secondo la leggenda, Romolo e Remo furono trovati e allattati da una lupa.

Il Colosseo è il maggior monumento dell'antichità, simbolo della grandezza e dell'eternità di Roma. Fu eretto fra il 72 e l'81 d.C. e fu destinato a pubblici spettacoli e giochi. La croce che vedete ricorda le persecuzioni dei primi cristiani che venivano mangiati dagli animali feroci durante i giochi.

Accanto al Colosseo vedete l'Arco di Costantino. Fu costruito per celebrare la battaglia e la vittoria sul tiranno Massenzio.

Qui siamo alla Piazza di Porta S. Paolo dove avete una bellissima veduta della Piramide.

Da qui proseguiamo verso il Tevere, che attraverseremo per poter fare una sosta di 2 ore nel quartiere che si chiama Trastevere. È il quartiere più popolare e genuino di Roma e gli abitanti si considerano i 'veri' Romani. Se volete mangiare qui troverete delle trattorie tipiche. Qui potete anche visitare il mercato di Porta Portese, dove vendono di tutto. Ma, attenzione – qui è il paradiso del borsaiolo – fate attenzione al portafoglio, alla macchina fotografica, e a tutto quello che avete di valore! Eccoci, adesso. Siete pregati di essere di ritorno per le due. Buon shopping – e buon appetito.

Bene. Siamo tutti qui? Avete tutti mangiato bene?

E adesso, la Città del Vaticano. Dentro potete ammirare le stanze di Raffaello con i meravigliosi affreschi del maestro, la Cappella Sistina, con i famosi affreschi di Michelangelo, e tante belle opere d'arte – quadri, sculture – tutto. Se permettete vi dirò ciò che io amo di più – è la Pietà di Michelangelo ... Vi consiglio di andare a vederla.

Per tornare, passiamo davanti al Castel Sant' Angelo, attraversiamo di nuovo il Tevere e possiamo avvicinarci a Piazza Navona con le sue tre fontane, e a Piazza di Trevi con la sua famosissima fontana conosciuta in tutto il mondo.

Siamo adesso nella zona elegante e commerciale di Roma, ma purtroppo siamo alla fine della nostra visita. Ecco di nuovo Piazza Barberini. Vi ringrazio di avermi ascoltato con tanto interesse, e non mi rimane che dirvi buonasera e arrivederci.

D Play the commentary again. Base some questions on which places are visited and what is said about them.

E Use the language of this item to adapt the first part of the activity. Make up statements about places of interest in your town and region: the students guess where you have been. They could then try to do this, making up the statements and guessing.

F This would be a good time to start work on *Scoprite qualcosa di più* (pages 180-183).

Prendiamo la Metropolitana (pages 122-123)

Main aim: To present the language and information needed to travel on the Rome underground

A Although the 'metro' is not a major means of transport in Italy, there are systems in Rome, Milan and Naples, all of them fairly small.

B Before the students read the information, give them thirty seconds to scan it and to work out what it is about. Discuss their impressions and clear up any misapprehensions. Present the following questions and give the students three minutes to find the answers.

1 How much is a single ticket?
2 Where can you buy a book of tickets?
3 How much does each ticket in a book cost?
4 What is the English for 'obliterare'?
5 How many lines are there in the Rome underground system?
6 What are Termini, Ottaviano and Laurentina?
7 Which station is on two lines?
8 At what times does the metro start and finish?

C When the students have answered the questions, ask them to read the information again. Then ask them to tell you what they have found out about the Rome 'metro'. At first, ration each student to one fact, but towards the end allow students to sum up with several things they have learnt.

D Each student lists the ten words which they would find most useful when using the 'metro'. They compare and discuss their lists in pairs.

E They read the text again. Then, referring only to their ten key words, they take turns to talk for thirty seconds about the 'metro'.

Students who are familiar with another underground system could use the Italian they have learnt to describe that system.

F The students read the statements about the Rome 'metro'. They say which are true and which false. They then correct the false statements.

G You could continue work on *Scoprite qualcosa di più* (pages 180-183).

Quale linea? Quale stazione? (page 124)

Main aim: To practise how to use the Rome underground

A The students read this item to themselves and then ask any questions they have. They read it again and summarise it as briefly as possible.

B In pairs, the students play–read the dialogue. They then adapt it to ask how to get to other monuments. The students should play each role two or three times, changing the dialogue each time.

C You could complete work on *Scoprite qualcosa di più* (pages 180-183).

Adesso, tocca a te! (pages 124-125)

Main aim: To demonstrate that the language of this unit has been mastered

Exercise 1
Language area: Tourist information
Skill area: Reading

The students answer the three questions as fully as possible.

Exercise 2
Language area: Coach travel
Skill area: Speaking

In pairs, the students help each other to perform both roles, practising together until they are quite satisfied with their performance.

Exercise 3
Language area: Coach travel
Skill area: Speaking

The students work on this as with exercise 2.

Exercise 4
Language area: Tourist information
Skill area: Listening

Play each announcement twice. The students write down what they would say.

🔊 Adesso, tocca a te!

Durante la gita

Esempio

– Qui facciamo una sosta di trenta minuti. Potete visitare la chiesa, se volete, ma attenzione. C'è una messa, e, si prega di non fare rumore. Mi raccommando, signori, silenzio per favore.

Numero 1

– Per visitare questo museo ci si mette almeno un'ora. Vedrete molti bei quadri e sculture. Ma devo dirvi che è vietato fare fotografie. Potete sempre comprare cartoline all'ingresso.

Numero 2

– Mi dispiace dire che per alcuni di voi non sarà possibile visitare la Basilica, perché portate calzoncini, minigonne, tee shirt eccetera. Vedete bene l'insegna: 'L'accesso è vietato alle persone in abbigliamento indecoroso'.

Numero 3

– Se volete andare in cima a questa collina per visitare il castello vi consiglio di fare attenzione, perché la strada è un po' difficile. Se non avete buone scarpe dovreste forse rimanere di sotto.

Numero 4

– Allora, da qui potete andare a mangiare, e forse dopo fare un po' di shopping. Ma attenzione, in queste piccole vie ci sono borsaioli – allora attenzione alla macchina fotografica ed al portafoglio. La settimana scorsa un signore è stato derubato di 100.000 lire in questo quartiere.

Exercise 5

Language area: Travel by 'metro'
Skill area: Speaking

The students work on this as for exercise 2.

Ora sai (page 126)

Main aim: To act as a summary and reference point for the main language of this unit

A The students study this page and then test each other in pairs, using their own preferred techniques.

B The students tell their partners what they have found difficult to learn and ask their partners for help.

C Play a game of 'Categorie'. Say as many words and phrases as you can which relate to travel by coach or 'metro'. After each one, the students say 'Pullman' or 'Metro'.

See how many the class can correctly categorise in one minute. After a while, the students can play this in pairs.

D The students study and practise the questions on this page. They then cover them up and look at the advert. They ask their partners as many questions as they can about the advert and their partners have to try to answer.

Revision

1 Getting a penfriend (Book 2, Unit 1)

Give each student a copy of Copymaster 65. They could work on this in class or at home. If there are any general problems which you note when marking their work, you could explain these and practise them with the class.

2 Avere (Book 2, Unit 1)

A Organise some verb circle practice, starting with, e.g.

– Ho un biglietto per la gita.
– Ha un posto accanto al finestrino.
– Non hai visto il pullman.
– Abbiamo fatto la visita.

B Play 'Categorie'. You say as many infinitives as possible: after each one, the students say 'avere' or 'essere' to show which of these the verb goes with in the perfect tense. See how many the students can correctly categorise in one minute. They can continue this in pairs.

C Play another game of 'Categorie'. This time, you say any part of the verbs 'avere' and 'essere' which the students should know, saying these in short sentences, e.g.

– Quanti hanni hai? Questi ragazzi hanno tutti 13 anni. Siamo cinque in famiglia. Sono figlio unico. Abbiamo tre canarini a casa. Il mio compleanno è il 15 dicembre. Quali sono i tuoi hobby? Secondo me questa donna ha una grande famiglia. Firenze non è vicino al mare. Rimini ha una lunga spiaggia.

Alassio è un gran centro balneare. Avete una cattedrale nella vostra città? Hai fame? Abbiamo sete. Sei stanco? Questi libri sono per voi. Questa gonna è per te. Ci sono dei film divertenti? Questo è un film per i soli adulti.

After each sentence, the students say 'avere' or 'essere'.

3 Talking about your town (Book 3, Unit 3)

A Present the following words on the board.
Ask the students to list them in order of difficulty. Then, in pairs, they compare their lists and help each other to learn the words they find difficult.

si trova	la questura	una piscina
bello(a)	visitare	uno stadio
i monumenti	vedere	un centro
i negozi	importante(i)	vivo(a)
gli abitanti	andare	

B The students now prepare to talk for thirty seconds about their town and region. They can use only the list of words in **A** above to help them and they must use all the words. If possible, they could record this, at school or at home.

4 Comparative and superlative adjectives (Book 3, Unit 3)

Give out copies of Copymasters 66A and B, one part to each student in each pair. Demonstrate with an assistant or able student how they can complete this quiz by helping each other, by working on one or two of the questions. You could also write a model on the board for everyone to refer to, e.g.

Student A:	Qual è la più grande di queste città? Cosa ne pensi?
Student B:	Secondo me, è Bologna.
Student A:	Secondo me, è Bari. Bari ha quanti abitanti?
Student B:	358,000.
Student A:	Bologna ha 492,000 abitanti. Allora, hai ragione. Bologna è la più grande di queste due città.

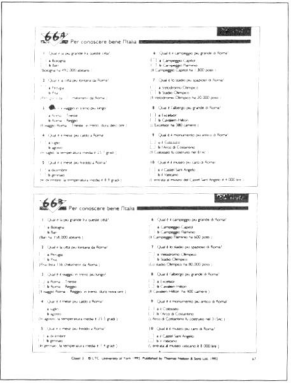

5 Staying with an Italian family (Book 3, Unit 9)

Give each student a copy of Copymaster 67. In pairs, students help each other to master these roles: they practise until perfect and then, if possible, record their performance.

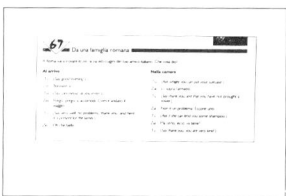

6 'Noi' and 'voi': present and perfect tenses (Book 3, Units 1, 5, 9)

A Write down the following questions on the board. The students answer, saying what they and their friends (or family) did on holiday. Students giving a correct answer choose another question to ask one of the other students.

- Siete andati in vacanza, l'anno scorso?
- Dove siete andati?
- Avete comprato dei regali?
- Che cosa avete mangiato?
- Che cosa avete bevuto?

B Present on the board the following sentences spoken by young Romans about life in Rome. The students adapt each sentence to talk about their own town or region.

- Prendiamo la metropolitana molto spesso.
- Compriamo i biglietti dal tabaccaio.
- Partiamo alle sette per andare a scuola.
- Torniamo alle due.
- Visitiamo molti monumenti.
- Andiamo al cinema ogni settimana.
- Mangiamo in ristoranti tipici.
- Facciamo dello shopping ogni giorno.
- Abbiamo delle bellissime piazze.
- Siamo contenti di abitare a Roma.

The students make up short monologues based on these sentences, such as they might say to a visitor from Rome, e.g.

- Qui partiamo alle otto per andare a scuola, mentre voi partite alle sette, non è vero?

7 Going to the cinema (Book 3, Unit 12)

Give each student in each pair Copymaster 68A or B. Make sure that everyone knows what to do and, as they work in pairs, move around listening, helping and joining in.

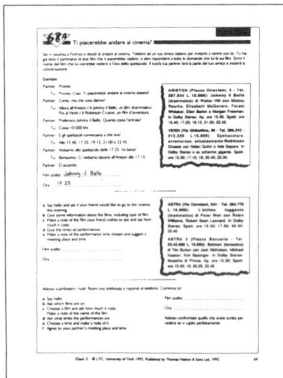 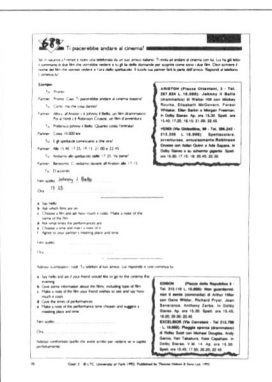

8 Potere (present tense) (Book 3, Unit 7)

A Organise a few minutes of verb circle practice, starting with, e.g.

- Posso andare al luna park?
- Possiamo fare una passeggiata adesso.
- Nella mia città si può pattinare.
- Potete guardare un video stasera.

B Present the grid below on the blackboard or OHP. Divide the class into two teams. Each team asks the other a question from the grid. The team answering has to say it is able to do the activity, but make up an excuse for not doing so, e.g.

Team A: Sa sciare?
Team B: Sì, sa sciare, ma oggi non può perché va al cinema.

Domande		
Sai Sa Sapete Sanno	sciare giocare a tennis pattinare fare del windsurf nuotare fare la vela	?
Risposte		
Sì,	so sa sappiamo sanno	sciare, giocare a tennis, pattinare, fare del windsurf, nuotare, fare la vela,	ma oggi ...

9 Perfect tense

Copymaster 69 is provided so that students can have their own revision reference sheet on the perfect tense. It summarizes all the information covered so far. You could make copies of it and issue it now, or at a later stage, for revision and practice purposes.

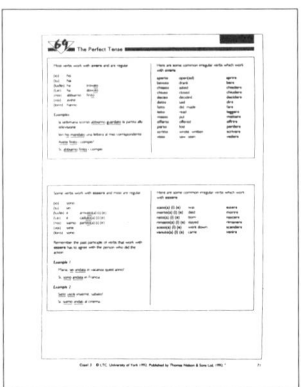

14ª Unità
AI GRANDI MAGAZZINI

Main aims

~ To be able to buy clothes and shoes
~ To ask for the correct size
~ To ask to try a different size or colour

Materials

~ Tape
Senta, sto cercando il reparto calzature (Teacher's Book page 162)
Un'inchiesta (Teacher's Book page 162)
Sconto del 15% sulle scarpe (Teacher's Book page 164)
Che cosa desidera? (Teacher's Book page 165)
Buoni affari! (Teacher's Book page 166)
Adesso, tocca a te! (Teacher's Book page 167)

~ Copymasters 70–74

Grammar in *Scoprite qualcosa di più*

~ Demonstrative adjectives: questo, quello

Revision

~ Phoning home (Book 2, Unit 2)
~ Possessive adjectives (Book 2, Unit 1)
~ Avere: present tense (Book 2, Unit 1)
~ Mealtimes and offering to help (Book 3, Unit 10)
~ Impersonal 'si' (Book 3, Unit 10)
~ Guided tours (Book 3, Unit 13)
~ Bisogna + infinitive (Book 3, Unit 13)

Vocabulary

A: Productive

le calze	lo/la/li/le posso provare?
una camicetta	una maglietta
una camicia	i pantaloni
cercare	pratico
che numero ha?	quello
che taglia porta?	questo
elegante	il reparto
una felpa	le scarpe
una giacca	sportivo
una gonna	gli stivali

B: Receptive

abbigliamento	(di) cotone
un abito	(di) lana
acrilico	un magazzino
calzature	(di) pelle
i calzoncini	saldi
il camerino	sconto
il cappotto	i vestiti

Ai grandi magazzini (page 127)

Main aim: To introduce the objectives of this unit

A Give the students one minute to read this and one more minute to write notes of the key points in it. Discuss their notes.

B Discuss the students' knowledge about Italian fashion and fashion stores. You could report that many young Italians consider it very important to be dressed in designer clothes, 'capi firmati'. Benetton is popular, and your students may also know of Armani, Fiorucci, Ferragamo and Gucci. Do your students wear designer clothes and do they consider them to be important?

C Each student could write a list, in English, of clothes they would like to buy, or may need to buy, in Italy. They could also write the English for expressions they think they would need to buy clothes and shoes. They compare and discuss their lists. They should make sure that they learn the Italian for everything in their lists before leaving this unit.

D Try to bring in some fashion magazines and encourage students to do so. Make a wall display of appropriate illustrations, articles and advertisements. Refer to these during discussions and question and answer work.

Senta, sto cercando il reparto calzature (page 128)

Main aims: To present the key language needed in a department store

To practise finding a specific department

To revise buying souvenirs and presents

A The students read and study the store guide, asking for help if they need it. They then tell you, in Italian, what they can buy on each floor. Give them two minutes to try to learn the words on the guide. They then cover up the words and, looking only at the visuals on the guide, say what they can buy on each floor. After some class practice, the students could continue this in pairs.

B Write the names of departments on cards and display them around the room. You could include other appropriate signs, e.g. 'Entrata', 'Uscita'. You ask the way to different departments and the students point to the appropriate sign, e.g.

Teacher: Sto cercando il reparto elettrodomestici.
Student: Si trova lì, accanto al reparto giochi.

One student chooses an item to buy and the others guess:
a the department
b the floor
c the item.

C Work on the dialogues along the lines suggested in the Students' Book:

– the students listen and sum up each dialogue
– they follow the text and listen again
– they play-read them in pairs
– they make up, in pairs, dialogues based on the four lists.

📼 Senta, sto cercando il reparto calzature

Dialogo 1
Client: Vorrei vedere un pullover come quello in vetrina.
Assistant: Dunque, deve andare al reparto Moda Donna al terzo piano. C'è un ascensore accanto all'ufficio informazioni.

Dialogo 2
Client: Sto cercando il reparto calzature.
Assistant: Sì, signore. Il reparto calzature si trova al secondo piano.
Client: C'è un ascensore?
Assistant: Sì, si trova accanto all'ufficio informazioni.

Dialogo 3
Client: Mi sa dire dove posso comprare dei dischi, per favore?
Assistant: Certo. Deve salire al primo piano. I dischi si trovano accanto al reparto Articoli Sportivi.

D If necessary, practise the language needed for buying presents and souvenirs, e.g.

● Play at 'Pictorial noughts and crosses' (see Teacher's Book 1, page 41).

● Display a selection of pictures. Each student chooses five that they would buy and lists them in order of priority. In pairs, they take turns to guess what their partner has chosen and in the correct order. They count the questions asked and the

student with the fewer questions at the end is the winner.

● See how long a sentence the class can make up, helping each other as needed, e.g.

– Vorrei comprare un pullover.
– Vorrei comprare un pullover e un disco.
– Vorrei comprare un pullover, un disco e un poster.

Abbigliamento (page 129)

Main aim: **To present and practise some of the language needed to buy clothes**

A Give the students some time to study this page: they could do this at home. Then encourage them to express their opinions, e.g.

to pick out something they like, e.g.
– Mi piace questa camicia.

to pick out things they do not like, e.g.
– Non mi piacciono quei pantaloni.

to say what they think you would like, e.g.

Student A: Secondo me, Le piacciono quegli stivali.
Student B: Secondo me, Le piace questo cappotto.

B The students ask you how to say in Italian the words for clothes they would like to buy, e.g.

Student: Come si dice 'swimming costume' in italiano?
Teacher: Si dice 'costume da bagno'.

They all select four or five items on this page that they would like to buy and write a list of them in Italian. Next to each item, they write the price given on this page. They compare their lists in pairs.
For homework, each pair of students makes a set of 'Happy Family' cards. They each divide a piece of A4 paper into eight equal parts and cut out the eight cards. One writes the name of four outside garments and four items of sportswear on the cards. The other writes the name of four woollen garments and four top–half garments. They use these to play 'Happy Families' in class, in groups of four.

C The students listen to this recorded interview and say:

– what each teenager suggests wearing
– which of them they like the sound of and why.

📼 Un'inchiesta

Interviewer: Buongiorno, signori e signore. Oggi, parliamo di moda. I vestiti sono importanti per i giovani? Vi presento Claretta, Fabio e Silvia che stanno discutendo di moda.

Claretta: Ciao. Mi chiamo Claretta. Non è importante per me essere alla moda. E in più non ho molti soldi. Secondo me, è più importante inventarsi un proprio stile.

Fabio: Ciao. Io sono Fabio. È vero – c'è sempre il problema dei soldi. Ma secondo me, Claretta, a te piace la moda. Hai una giacca Levi's adosso.

Claretta: Be' lo so, ma non mi piace vestire come Silvia. Indossa sempre le stesse cose che indossano le sue amiche.

Silvia: Ma semplicemente mi piace essere come i miei amici. Ci piacciono le stesse cose. E poi, se tu vedi qualcuno che non conosci, dal modo in cui è vestito ti fai già un'idea del tipo.

Interviewer: Allora ragazzi, che cosa indossate per andare ad una festa? Una festa da amici?

Claretta: Per me, è semplice. Indosso un abbigliamento sportivo: una camicetta, i jeans Levi's, le scarpe belle.

Interviewer: E tu Fabio, che cosa indossi?

Fabio: Be' non lo so. Una festa da amici, hai detto? Potrei indossare un paio di jeans, una maglietta bianca e delle scarpe comode.

Interviewer: E tu Silvia, che cosa indossi?

Silvia: Telefonerei alle mie amiche per chiedere loro che cosa indosseranno. Perché non voglio fare brutta figura. Ma per una festa, non so; sono incerta ... be' magari indosserei una gonna elegante, una camicetta, un vestito bello nuovo, insomma, non lo so!

Interviewer: Bene ragazzi, vi ringrazio.

D As a follow-up, you could, e.g.

• Start a discussion on school uniform.

• Ask the students to write a list of the clothes they would need to buy if their case were lost when they flew to Italy for a two-week holiday. Then ask what they have chosen in various categories, e.g. 'pratico', 'sportivo', 'elegante'.

• Give each student a copy of Copymaster 70. They could work on this at home or at school.

Solution:

camicetta
giacca
camicia
cappotto
stivali
maglietta
calze
golf
scarpe
sciarpa
pullover
pantaloni
slip
gonna
sandali
jeans
abito
cintura

C	A	M	I	C	E	T	T	A	N
H	A	C	C	A	I	G	K	I	T
L	O	T	T	O	P	P	A	C	N
S	T	I	V	A	L	I	G	I	A
A	T	T	E	I	L	G	A	M	U
T	R	I	E	V	U	B	N	A	G
U	R	N	T	Z	L	Y	D	C	O
R	I	G	O	A	L	E	N	A	R
F	L	O	G	S	C	A	R	P	E
S	A	N	D	I	I	N	C	R	V
N	D	N	A	P	N	O	R	A	O
A	N	A	B	I	T	O	I	I	L
E	A	T	O	L	U	G	U	C	L
J	S	O	X	S	R	E	R	S	U
A	I	N	O	L	A	T	N	A	P

E Now would be a good time to begin work on *Scoprite qualcosa di più* (pages 183-184).

Che numero ha? (page 130)

Main aim: To develop the ability to buy shoes and clothes

A Before the students work on the list, ask them to brainstorm for a few minutes:

– to list the Italian they already know for buying shoes and clothes
– to list, in English, what else they would like to know.

Then work on the list, and add to it what the students have asked for. With the list you could, e.g.

– match up orally questions and answers.
– write questions or answers on the OHP or board with a word missing: the students complete these.
– see how many different answers the class can give you in sixty seconds to each question: they could continue this in pairs.

B Revise numbers, e.g.

• Games, e.g. 'Tombola', 'Noughts and crosses'.
• Fill the boxes and add up the numbers, e.g.

Answer:

	16		= 54
		12	= 42
22			= 40

= 52 = 46 = 38

20	16	18
10	20	12
22	10	8

Explain that there are differences between British and continental sizes and work on this, asking some questions, e.g.

- Che taglia porti? Che numero hai?
- Che numero di scarpe hai?
- Che taglia di vestiti porti?

Sizes										
GB It	Shoes	3 36	4 37	5 38	6 39	7 40	8 41	9 42	10 43	
GB It	Women	8 36	10 38	12 40	14 42	16 44	18 46	20 48	22 50	
GB It	Men (trousers)	26 40	28 42	30 44	32 46	34 48	36 50	38 52	40 54	waist in inches
GB It	Men (jackets)	34 40	36 42	38 44	40 46	42 48	44 50	46 52	48 54	chest in inches

• Encourage the students to write a grid with their own sizes, for reference: point out how useful this will be if they buy clothes in Italy.

• A mail order catalogue, which can be ordered from Postalmarket, Casetta Postale 11000, 20194 Milano, has a grid of sizes at the back: this could be used to practise numbers and sizes. Postalmarket can also be bought at Italian news stands.

The class may also need to revise colours, e.g.

• Play a game of 'Fammi vedere qualcosa di bianco'. Anyone who does not, in five seconds, has to pay a forfeit (e.g. count from 1 to 10, 100 to 90, 500 to 1000 in hundreds).

• Ask each other about 'colour sums', e.g.

- Rosso più bianco fa ...? (rosa)
- Azzurro più giallo fa ...? (verde)
- Rosso più giallo fa ...? (arancia)

C The students make up dialogues based on the drawings, along the lines suggested in the Students' Book.

D Give each student a copy of Copymaster 71. Before listening to the cassette, ask the students to suggest the type of announcement they are likely to hear in a department store, e.g. announcements of discounts, staff announcements. Play the examples and make sure that all the students know what they have to do. If it is a staff announcement, they put a cross next to the appropriate department. If it is an announcement that concerns the customer, they should complete the grid as in the example. Draw their attention to the difference in tone. Announcements of discounts tend to be more lively. Play the cassette twice. Finally ask students which

department they would visit as a result of hearing the announcements.

- A quale reparto vuoi andare?
- Perché?

🔊 Sconto del 15% sulle scarpe

Numero 1
- Signore e signori. Benvenuti al magazzino più grande della città. Non mancate di visitare il reparto calzature. C'è uno sconto del 15% su tutte le scarpe. Non dimenticate, c'è uno sconto sulle scarpe fino alla fine di agosto.

Numero 2
- Attenzione, prego. Il Signor Bianchi è desiderato al reparto Elettrodomestici.

Numero 3
- Attenzione, prego. La Signora Baresi è attesa al telefono al reparto Profumeria.

Numero 4
- Signori e signore. Oggi c'è uno sconto del 20% su tutte le sciarpe e tutti i guanti al reparto Accessori. Sbrigatevi – quest'offerta finisce stasera!

Numero 5
- Attenzione prego. La Signorina Mancini è richiesta al reparto Sport.

Numero 6
- Avviso alla clientela. Vi ricordiamo che al reparto Abbigliamento Giovane vi sono offerte speciali sulle maglie, sulle magliette e anche sui pantaloni. Abbigliamento Giovane si trova al secondo piano. Ci sono sconti fino al 20%, fino a venerdì.

Numero 7
- Signore, signorine, vi ricordiamo che c'è un'offerta speciale sulle gonne eleganti, fino a sabato! C'è uno sconto del 10% su tutte le gonne.

Numero 8
- Attenzione, prego. Il Signor Conti è atteso al telefono al reparto Abbigliamento Uomo.

Che cosa desidera? (page 131)

Main aims: To develop speaking and reading skills on the topic of buying clothes

To practise the use of direct object pronouns

A Work on the dialogues in the Students' Book along the lines suggested. Play the recording *Che cosa desidera?*. Students listen to the dialogues and then read them with a partner.

🔲 Che cosa desidera?

Dialogo 1

Assistant: Buongiorno. Mi dica.
Client: Vorrei vedere una gonna come quella in vetrina.
Assistant: Che taglia porta?
Client: Quaranta.
Assistant: E di che colore la vuole?
Client: Azzurra, per favore. La posso provare?
Assistant: Sì, certo. Il camerino è lì in fondo.

Dialogo 2

Client: Cerco un paio di scarpe da ginnastica.
Assistant: Di che colore le vuole?
Client: Nere.
Assistant: Vediamo ... sì, abbiamo queste nere, ed anche quelle lì.
Client: Mi piacciono queste qui.
Assistant: Va bene. Che numero porta?
Client: Quarantuno. Le posso provare?
Assistant: Sì, certo. Va bene?
Client: Sì. Le prendo.

Dialogo 3

Client: Buongiorno. Sto cercando dei pantaloni come quelli marrone in vetrina.
Assistant: Sì. Che taglia porta?
Client: Mi dispiace, non lo so. Che taglia mi consiglia?
Assistant: Ecco, questi pantaloni, taglia quarantaquattro.
Client: Li posso provare?
Assistant: Sì, certo. Il camerino è lì, in fondo ...
Client: Mi dispiace, posso provare la misura più grande?
Assistant: Sì. Di quei pantaloni abbiamo anche la quarantasei.
Clienti: Grazie. Vanno meglio questi.

Dialogo 4

Client: Buongiorno. Vorrei comprare degli stivali.
Assistant: Di che colore li vuole?
Client: Nero.
Assistant: Che numero ha?
Client: Trentanove.
Assistant: Le piacciono questi stivali?

Client: Li posso provare?
Assistant: Faccia pure. Vanno bene?
Client: No, mi dispiace, non li piacciono. Non li prendo.

B Now would be a good time to continue work on *Scoprite qualcosa di più* (pages 185-186).

Ti piace seguire la moda? (page 132)

Main aim: To practise reading and writing a letter about clothes

A Give the students sixty seconds to skim–read the letter to find out the gist. When you have discussed their first responses, practise scan reading by getting them to race to answer your questions, e.g.

- How many questions does Silvia ask?
- What is her last question?
- How many times does she use:

    giacca?   mi?   vestiti?

- What is her favourite item of clothing?
- How did she get it?

B The students each write a letter. Give whatever help they need to ensure success. They could do this at home or in class.

C Give out Copymaster 72. The students complete the quiz and then find someone else who has done it: they discuss their answers and the conclusions in pairs.

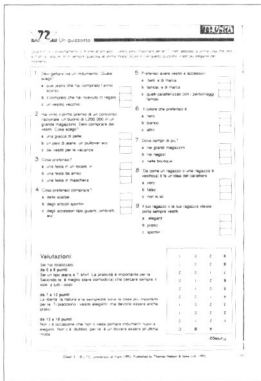

Problemi! (page 132)

Main aim: To practise coping with difficulties when buying clothes

A Each student works on this alone. They then compare their answers in pairs and make any necessary corrections. Still in pairs, they adapt all the sentences to bring in other problems and other clothes.

B Each student makes up a complete dialogue based on any one picture: this should include everything involved in asking for the clothing, trying it on, overcoming the problem and paying.

Le prendo (page 133)

Main aim: To practise role-play on the topic of buying shoes and clothes

A Each student prepares this role-play, looking back through the unit to check anything about which he or she is not sure. They then perform it in pairs, playing each role in turn.

B The students now make up their own dialogues to buy clothes or shoes. Encourage them to use their imaginations and their sense of humour. Get volunteers to act out their roles for the class.

C You could tell the students about Italian shoes, saying how good and how reasonably priced they are. They could brainstorm for a few minutes to produce a list of key words and expressions they might need for buying shoes in Italy.

Buoni affari! (page 133)

Main aim: To develop listening and reading skills on the topic of shopping for shoes and clothes

A Give the students two minutes to skim–read these notices and to say what they are. Then practise scan reading for key points by asking questions and encouraging the students to race to find the answers, e.g.

– What are the dates of the sales at Cesarina?
– At which shop can you get the most discount?
– Which words tell you that there is a special offer?
– Sometimes, advertisers exaggerate in order to attract your attention. Which of the words in these advertisements exaggerate the discount in order to attract your attention?

As a follow-up, you could, e.g.

– base a memory game on these notices
– encourage students to make similar signs to attract Italians to sales in local shops: you could offer the results to the shops!

B Play the unscripted recording. After hearing it twice, the students could, e.g.
– report on what the girls say
– report on links between what they say and the advertisements
– draw conclusions (e.g. about where they think the girls will go and why; where *they* would go).

Buoni affari!

Woman 1:	Senti, devo assolutamente comprare un completo per un matrimonio. Voi venire con me?
Woman 2:	Sì, vengo volentieri. Guardiamo sul giornale, per vedere quali sono i negozi che hanno degli sconti in questo periodo.
Woman 1:	Sì va bene.
Woman 2:	Allora, vediamo un po'. C'è la boutique 'Lydia'. Cosa ne dici della boutique 'Lydia'?
Woman 1:	Ma guarda, ci sono stata, non avevano dei buoni vestiti. Erano fuori moda, erano fatti male e anche se c'è lo sconto del 10% erano abbastanza cari.
Woman 2:	Umm. Invece hai mai sentito parlare di 'Sabo-Sabo'?
Woman 1:	Non ci sono mai stata. Ma mi hanno detto che è un negozio molto buono. Cosa ne pensi di 'Welt Mode'?
Woman 2:	Ah sì, sì, 'Welt Mode' ne ho sentito parlare. Hanno sconti tutto il tempo. Ma i commessi sono incredibili. Non ti lasciano mai in pace.
Woman 1:	E 'Cesarina', che tipo di negozio è? Buono?
Woman 2:	Sì 'Cesarina' normalmente ha dei buoni vestiti. Perché non ci andiamo? Andiamo a vedere che cosa hanno?
Woman 1:	Sì, dai, mi sembra una buona idea. Andiamo. Poi, se c'è tempo facciamo anche un salto da 'Sabo-Sabo'.
Woman 2:	Sì, d'accordo.
Woman 1:	OK. Andiamo.

Adesso, tocca a te! (pages 134-135)

Main aim: To demonstrate that the language of this unit has been mastered

Exercise 1
Language area: Buying clothes and shoes
Skill areas: Reading and writing

Work on the example with the class to ensure that everyone knows what to do. The students then do the others unaided.

Exercise 2
Language area: Buying clothes and shoes
Skill area: Reading

Work on the example with the class to ensure that everyone knows what to do. The students then do the others unaided.

Exercise 3
Language area: Buying clothes
Skill area: Listening

The students listen to each announcement twice and write a summary, in English, of the main points.

📼 Adesso, tocca a te!

Numero 1

– Signore e signori, buongiorno. Oggi, non dimenticate di visitare il reparto calzature. C'è un'offerta speciale su tutte le scarpe. Vi ricordiamo che fino a stasera vi sono prezzi eccezionali non solo sulle scarpe, ma anche sugli stivali e sui sandali. Non mancate quest'offerta incredibile.

Numero 2

– Da Gran Bazaar ci sono sempre dei vestiti bellissimi e di marca. Ora, c'è ancora più scelta. Fino a sabato c'è un'offerta speciale su tutte le maglie e le camicie. Cos'è quest'offerta? Facciamo uno sconto del 15%. Ma quest'offerta finisce sabato.

Numero 3

– Siete in cerca d'occasioni? Volete trovare qualcosa di bello, senza pagare troppo? Non dovete cercare oltre. Per un mese facciamo uno sconto del 10% su tutti gli articoli sportivi. Venite al reparto Articoli Sportivi, c'è una scelta incredibile.

Exercise 4

Language area: Buying shoes and clothes
Skill area: Speaking

In pairs, the students help each other to play each role as well as they can. They practise until perfect and then ask you to listen to them.

Excercise 5

Language area: Buying clothes
Skill areas: Reading and writing

Each student writes a card along the lines of the brief. They can base what they write on the model or be completely original.

Ora sai (page 135)

Main aim: To act as a summary and reference point for the main language of this unit

A   By now, the students should have a good repertoire of techniques for using these lists to practise and revise. Ask them to use the techniques they know, to plan how they will work on this page. Go over their plans and comment and advise as appropriate. The students then put their plans into action. When they have finished, discuss how their plans worked and if the students are satisfied with the results. Offer advice for improving learning strategies, if these are wanted.

B   You could give students a copy of Copymaster 73. It offers a chance to extend their language to include fabrics.
Each student reads the grid: they try to work out the meaning of all the words and then to tick all the appropriate boxes. They compare and discuss their completed grids and use them as a basis for class discussion, e.g.

– Di solito, di quale tessuto sono le magliette?
– Quale tessuto preferisci?
– Quali vestiti si possono fare in lana?
– Quando fai dello sport, che cosa ti metti?
– Secondo te, quali vestiti sono eleganti (sportivi, pratici)?

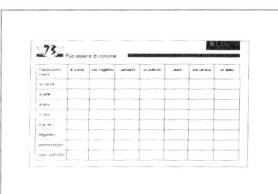

Revision

1   Phoning home (Book 2, Unit 2)

The students could revise numbers with a team game. The teacher reads out a telephone number, and the first team to write it down correctly wins a point e.g.

99.22.51
32.89.21
60.83.00 and so on.

Remind the students how to make an international call from Italy.
They need to know:

1   il prefisso internazionale 00

2   l'indicativo dello stato:
GB = 44
Australia = 61
USA/Canada = 1

3   l'indicativo interurbano (the code of the town, omitting the first digit)

4   il numero dell'abbonato (the number they require)
Therefore to phone Dover (0304) 207447 they need to phone:
00 44 304 207447.

Give the students ten seconds to work out their own telephone numbers.

2 Possessive adjectives (Book 2, Unit 1)

A Collect eight to ten objects from students, e.g.

– Ian, mi puoi dare la tua cravatta, la tua penna, il tuo pullover? ecc.

Then see if any student can identify what belongs to whom, e.g.

Teacher: Questo guanto è di Anna?
Student A: Sì, è il suo guanto.
Student B: No, non è il suo guanto, quel guanto è di Mary.

B A student gives you one of his/her possessions and leaves the room. You hide the possession somewhere in the room. The student returns and asks where it is. Whoever is asked passes the question on to someone else who can only point and say where the object is. This will ensure that first, second and third person forms are practised e.g.

A: Dov'è la mia penna?
B: Non so dov'è la tua penna, Mandy.
   John, sai dov'è la sua penna?
C: Sì. La sua penna è lì.

The owner can ask as often as he/she wishes: in each case, the question is passed on and answered in the same way until the object is found.

3 Avere: present tense (Book 2, Unit 2)

A Organise some brief verb circle practice, e.g.

– Quanti fratelli hai?
– Ho due sorelle e un fratello.
– Hai un cane?
– No, non ho un cane.
– Hai finito i compiti?
– Sì, ho finito i compiti.

B Each student writes five questions which contain 'avere' and which they would find useful to ask in Italy. Encourage them to use their imaginations. They then practise asking and answering these questions.

4 Mealtimes and offering to help (Book 3, Unit 10)

A Start a 'word tree' on the board, e.g.

IL PRANZO

una forchetta   la sala da pranzo

un coltello   l'acqua

un bicchiere

Ask the students for suggestions and write these in. Stop before the tree is complete. The students copy your tree and then see how much they can add to it.

B Try a drama exercise with the class. The students say a given sentence in different ways to show different moods and emotions, e.g. shyness, anger, sarcasm, politeness, rudeness, indifference.
Sentences used could include, e.g.

– A che ora si mangia la sera?
– Non mi piace il pesce.
– Mi piacciono i fagioli.
– Mi dispiace, ma non mangio la carne.
– Vuoi un po' di minestra?
– No, preferisco il pollo arrosto.
– Mi puoi passare il sale, per favore?
– Posso aiutare?
– Il latte si mette nel frigo.
– Dove si mette il pane?

5 Impersonal 'si' (Book 3, Unit 10)

A See how quickly the class can give you the answers to the following questions without looking at the Students' Book. e.g.

Teacher: Come si dice 'dress' in italiano?
Student: Si dice abito.

– Come si dice 'gloves' in italiano?
– Come si dice 'jacket' in italiano?
– Come si dice 'soldi' in inglese?
– Come si dice 'camerino' in inglese?
– Come si dice 'reparto' in inglese?
– Come si dice 'shoes' in italiano?
– Come si dice 'socks' in italiano?

B Write the following categories on the blackboard:

di lana   di cotone   di pelle   di acrilico

See how quickly the class can correctly categorise the following items:

il pullover	l'impermeabile	la giacca
la camicia	la maglietta	la maglia
le scarpe	i jeans	il golf
i sandali	il cappotto	la gonna
gli stivali	le calze	l'abito

Then students race to complete the sentence:

– Il pullover si fa di ...

The first student to answer then starts the next sentence. Students can use the same item more than once, if that item can be made from several fabrics.

6 Guided tours (Book 3, Unit 13)

A Give each student a copy of Copymaster 74. The students read the text carefully and write their answers to all the questions.

Each student chooses a tour. They then role–play in pairs: one books a tour and the other plays the part of the clerk. If necessary, you could put some of the sentences likely to be needed by the clerk on the board or OHP.

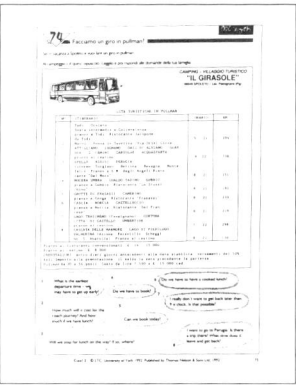

B Play a game of 'Categorie' with 'il pullman', 'la Metropolitana', 'il treno'. See how quickly the class can correctly categorise the following words:

una gita guidata	la linea A
aria condizionata	il binario
prenotare	l'orario
sedili reclinabili	la sala d'attesa
il biglietto	un'andata e ritorno
una sosta di dieci minuti	seconda classe
un carnet	

Repeat the game at least once with a view to improving on the time taken.

7 Bisogna + infinitive (Book 3, Unit 13)

A See how quickly the class can give you good advice, using 'bisogna' + infinitive, to cope with the following problems:

- Ho perso i miei guanti.
- Ho freddo.
- Vorrei comprare delle scarpe.
- Ho perso il mio passaporto.
- Mi hanno rubato la valigia.
- Non ho il dentifricio.
- Vorrei andare a Firenze in pullman.
- Non ho più soldi.
- Ho mal di testa.
- Ho fame.

Repeat this at least once with a view to improving on the time taken.

B Discuss things that are done differently in Italy and in your country. You say a list of statements, some of which are true for Italy. The students say which are true and then work out the equivalent for their country, e.g.

In Italia:
- bisogna guidare a destra.
- bisogna andare a scuola il sabato.
- bisogna cominciare la scuola alle otto la mattina.
- bisogna avere una carta d'identità.
- bisogna fare i compiti ogni giorno.
- bisogna continuare a studiare fino ai 14 anni.
- bisogna andare in chiesa ogni domenica.
- bisogna offrire regali a Natale.
- bisogna parlare inglese a scuola.
- bisogna andare a scuola il pomeriggio.

After this oral work, each student could write a table, saying what must be done in Italy on the left and comparing this with their country on the right. The results could be displayed and discussed.

15ª Unità
LA TUA SCUOLA, COM'È?

Main aim

~ To talk about your school, how you get there and its facilities

Materials

~ Tape
Ci vado in macchina (Teacher's Book page 171)
Una giornata tipica (Teacher's Book page 172)
E la tua scuola, com'è? (Teacher's Book page 173)

~ Copymasters 75–76

Grammar in *Scoprite qualcosa di più*

~ Uscire: present tense
~ Di, da: further uses

Revision

~ Introductions, saying hello (Book 1, Unit 1)
~ At a petrol station (Book 3, Unit 6)
~ Indirect object pronouns (Book 3, Unit 6)
~ Main verb + infinitive (Book 3, Unit 12)

Vocabulary

A: Productive

un alunno	un laboratorio di scienze
un'aula	il liceo
una biblioteca	una palestra
circa	a piedi
la corriera	il preside
il cortile	la sala dei professori
entrare	la segretaria
l'istituto	uscire
un laboratorio di lingue	venire

B: Receptive

l'aula magna	il greco
bocciare	un intervallo
una divisa	un motorino
l'entrata	una sala

La tua scuola, com'è? (page 136)

Main aim: To introduce the topic of school life in Italy

A Give the students two minutes to read the text, with the task of finding out the main aims of this unit. Encourage them to discuss these aims, e.g.

– to say what they know already about schools in Italy and

what else they would like to know
– to suggest five questions which they would like to ask about schools in Italy
– to suggest five questions which they would expect an Italian visitor to ask about their school.

Each student could write five questions which he/she would like to ask about Italian schools: they should make sure, by the end of the unit, that they can ask them all.

B To arouse more curiosity about schools in Italy, you could organise a mini-quiz on the topic. You could give the same quiz at the end of the unit to show the students how much progress they have made.

Quiz

1 Italian children start attending the 'scuola elementare' at the age of:
a 4   **b** 5   **c** 6
(Answer = **c**)

2 True or false:
In Italy, children go to school on Saturday   (True)

3 The average school day in Italy is:
a 8–12   **b** 8.30–13.30   **c** 9–5
(Answer = **b**)

4 13-year-old Italians go to the:
a liceo   **b** scuola media   **c** scuola media superiore
(Answer = **b**)

5 True or false:
At the age of 14 all Italian students have to choose what type of school they will go to next   (True)

6 How old are Italians when they start at the 'liceo'?
a 14   **b** 16   **c** 18
(Answer = **a**)

7 If you wanted to study business studies you would go to:
a un liceo classico   **b** un istituto commerciale
c un istituto tecnico
(Answer = **b**)

8 True or false:
All Italian schools have half-term holidays   (False)

9 The summer holidays in Italy last:
a 1 month   **b** 2 months   **c** 3 months
(Answer = **c**)

10 The teachers in a 'liceo' are addressed as:
a maestro / maestra   **b** professore / professoressa
(Answer = **b**)

C This would be a good time to revise school subjects. Divide the board into two columns headed 'Mi piace' and 'Non mi piace'. Ask students to suggest school subjects for each column: encourage discussion and, in the event of disagreement, take a vote. When the list is complete, the students question each other in pairs, e.g.

– Ti piace la ginnastica?

Each student then writes a list of his/her four favourite subjects. Their partners have five questions to discover what these are.

Come vieni a scuola? (page 137)

Main aim: To introduce and practise the language needed to talk about travelling to school

A Make sure that the students realise the aim of this item. They could then write a list of all the new words they can find in it. They then try to work out what all these mean and to write the English equivalent next to each Italian word: they could use dictionaries to check their guesses before writing.

B The students try to learn by heart the speech bubbles to all the photos: this could be a homework. To help them to learn, you could suggest some activities, e.g.

- In pairs, student A covers up the bubbles, student B reads the speech bubbles aloud in random order and student A points to the appropriate photo.

- Working alone, the students cover the speech bubbles with a piece of paper and then try to write them from memory. They should then check and keep on doing this until they can write all the sentences correctly.

- In pairs again, both cover the bubbles and, in turn, point to a photo and challenge their partners to say the appropriate sentence. In the event of a disagreement, they check with the original.

C The students should now be ready to work on the dialogue, e.g.

- read it silently
- ask about any problems and help each other to understand
- play-read it in pairs
- adapt it to match the other pictures.

Those who finish first could write one of their dialogues.

D This would be a good time to work on 'uscire' in *Scoprite qualcosa di più*, Parts 1 and 2 (pages 186-187).

E Encourage the students to look again at the photos on page 137 and to see how much they can discover from them about life in Italy, e.g.

1 Italian students do not wear school uniform.

2 They should notice the mopeds. Many Italian students have their own 'motorino'.
The most popular is 'La Vespa'.
In Italy you can drive a moped from the age of 14.

3 Crash helmets: at present it is not compulsory to wear a crash helmet in Italy. Do they think this is a good idea?

4 Encourage them to notice any differences between school buses in Italy and buses in their country.

F Play *Ci vado in macchina*, giving different tasks to different students, e.g.
- some listen just for the form of transport used
- others listen to find out why that form of transport is chosen.

🚌 Ci vado in macchina

Dialogo 1

Interviewer:	Mi scusi, signore. Stiamo facendo un'indagine sui mezzi di trasporto. Mi potrebbe concedere un attimo?
Man:	Certo, mi dica.
Interviewer:	Come va a lavoro ogni giorno?
Man:	Beh, abito abbastanza vicino al mio lavoro, quindi è pratico andarci a piedi.
Interviewer:	Grazie, signore.
Man:	Prego.

Dialogo 2

Interviewer:	Scusi, signora. Potrebbe rispondere a una domanda per cortesia?
Woman:	Sì, certo.
Interviewer:	Mi può dire come va a lavoro?
Woman:	Abito in un piccolo paese che si chiama Subbiano. È a tredici chilometri da Arezzo. Devo prendere l'autobus per andare al mio lavoro.
Interviewer:	Grazie, signora.
Woman:	Prego.

Dialogo 3

Interviewer:	Signore, mi scusi. Vorebbe rispondere a una domanda su come va a lavoro?
Man:	Certo. Vado dappertutto in motorino, anche a lavoro.
Interviewer:	Grazie, signore.
Man:	Prego.

Dialogo 4

Interviewer:	Mi scusi, signorina. Volevo farLe una domanda.
Woman:	Va bene, ma ho fretta.
Interviewer:	Ci può dire come va a lavoro ogni giorno?
Woman:	Vado sempre a lavoro in macchina. Così sono indipendente.
Interviewer:	Grazie, signorina.
Woman:	Prego.

Dialogo 5

Interviewer:	Signora, mi può rispondere ad una domanda?
Woman:	Mi dica.
Interviewer:	Come va a lavoro?
Woman:	Devo andarci in macchina. Abito lontano dalla città, e quindi è più pratico viaggiare in macchina.
Interviewer:	La ringrazio, signora.
Woman:	Di niente.

Una giornata tipica (page 138)

Main aim: To practise talking about a school day

A The students could work on this on their own, e.g.

- read it silently
- ask each other and, if necessary, use a dictionary or ask the teacher about anything they do not understand
- listen to the tape
- discuss the tape
- play read the questions and answers.

Revise numbers and times to prepare the students for the activities to come, e.g. 'Tombola', 'Noughts and crosses', 'Blockbuster', 'Wordchain', or with clocks drawn on the board.

B Put each question to the class and encourage several students to answer so as to get a range of answers to each question. You could write key expressions used in these answers on the board or OHP. To help the students to learn all these expressions, you could play 'Kim's game' with them (see Teacher's Book page 6).

C Each student prepares an interesting answer to each question in the table. They could write these in their exercise books and learn them. Then, in pairs, they take turns to ask and answer all the questions. Students who finish first could ask about different days and see if their answers change.

D The students look at the text again as they listen again to the recording. They listen to spot differences between Giancarlo's typical day and theirs. They discuss these differences with you and each other.

🖭 Una giornata tipica

Interviewer:	Buongiorno, Giancarlo. A che ora esci di casa la mattina?
Giancarlo:	La mattina esco alle otto meno dieci.
Interviewer:	Come vai a scuola?
Giancarlo:	Ci vado in motorino.
Interviewer:	A che ora arrivi a scuola?
Giancarlo:	Arrivo a scuola verso le otto.
Interviewer:	A che ora entri a scuola?
Giancarlo:	Entro alle otto e un quarto quando comincia la prima ora.
Interviewer:	A che ora finisce la scuola?
Giancarlo:	Finisce all'una e mezza.
Interviewer:	A che ora esci?
Giancarlo:	Esco alle due meno venti.
Interviewer:	E infine, a che ora torni a casa?
Giancarlo:	Torno a casa verso le due.

E Give out copies of Copymaster 75. The students work on this in pairs. The second line is for the interviewers to put their partners' answers. These can be checked by reversing roles: the interviewers give the answers they have written.

All the facts needed to complete the grid are on Copymaster 75, but some deduction will be needed. Encourage the students to work in pairs and to write their answers, in pencil, on one grid only.

When the grids are completed, the students compare the days, say which they prefer and why.

For more speaking practice, the students could repeat the interviews in pairs, this time as Luc, Luisa or Monika.

F This would be a good time to work on Parts 3 and 4 of *Scoprite qualcosa di più* (pages 187-188).

The completed grid for Copymaster 75

Nome:		Dove abita?	A che ora parte?	Come va a scuola?	A che ora arriva?	A che ora entra?	La scuola finisce a che ora?	Esce a che ora?	Torna a casa a che ora?
Giancarlo	(Italia)	Arezzo	7.50	motorino	8.00	8.15	13.30	13.40	14.00
Il tuo/La tua partner									
Luc	(Francia)	Tours	7.15	autobus	7.45	8.00	17.00	17.15	17.45
Monika	(Germania)	Dortmund	7.45	macchina	8.00	8.10	13.30	13.45	14.00
Luisa	(Spagna)	Santander	8.40	piedi	8.50	9.00	18.00	18.10	18.20

A che ora esci la mattina? (page 139)

Main aim: To develop reading and writing skills on the topic of schools

A Give the students three minutes to read the letter and to find the gist of it: they can compare ideas about what the gist and the main points are.
To practise reading quickly to find specific details ask, e.g.

– How old is Chiara?
– How does she go to school?
– What happens when it rains?
– At what time does she get to school?
– When does she leave school on Thursdays?
– What subject doesn't she like?
– What does she do on Saturdays?
– What does she ask about your school?

B Help the class to work out a strategy for answering letters like this, e.g.

– make a note of the questions you should answer
– search the letter for information and language you can use to answer these questions
– write a list of expressions which you think are useful and would want to use again, and try to learn them.

When the students have noted the questions, work through them and find different answers to each one. You could put suggestions on the board or OHP.

C The students write a letter in reply to Chiara's. Encourage those who can do it to ask different questions at the end of their letters, e.g. about family, pets or holidays.

D Some students could imagine that they have to interview Chiara to find out the information given in her letter. They prepare their questions. They put their questions to their partners who can refer to the letter when they answer and adapt it appropriately. The interviewers take notes in Italian. At the end of the interview, the pairs compare the notes with the letter to see if any information has been omitted or changed.

E Now would be a good time to work on 'di', in *Scoprite qualcosa di più* (pages 188-189).

E la tua scuola, com'è? (page 140)

Main aim: To practise talking about schools

A Give the students the task of preparing to talk about their own school. They should study this interview and use it to help them to answer these, and similar, questions about their own school. After a few minutes, play the recording of the interview which they listen to as they follow the text.
When they have produced some draft answers, play the recording of the cassette sent from an Italian school. They listen to find more ideas for their own answers, and change their answers accordingly.
In pairs, they put the questions to each other and answer them. If possible, they should record this. They can then listen to their recording, discuss what they could do better, and then do it again.

▸ E la tua scuola, com'è?

Dialogo 1

Interviewer: Che scuola frequenti?
Boy: Frequento l'istituto tecnico ad Arezzo.
Interviewer: Ti piace la tua scuola?
Boy: Sì, mi piace abbastanza. Mi piace soprattutto l'informatica.
Interviewer: E la scuola com'è?
Boy: È una scuola abbastanza moderna e grande, e si trova in centro.

Dialogo 2

Interviewer: E tu, che scuola frequenti?
Boy: Frequento la scuola media ad Arezzo.
Interviewer: Quanti alunni ci sono nella tua scuola?
Boy: Beh ... circa settecento alunni, credo.
Interviewer: E quanti professori ci sono?
Boy: Non sono sicuro. Forse ce ne sono quaranta.

Dialogo 3

Interviewer: Frequenti il liceo classico, vero?
Girl: Sì, frequento il liceo qui ad Arezzo.
Interviewer: Quanto tempo dura una lezione?
Girl: Una lezione dura un'ora e faccio cinque lezioni al giorno.
Interviewer: Quale materia preferisci?
Girl: Mi piacciono le lingue (classiche e moderne), l'inglese, il greco e anche il latino.
Interviewer: C'è una materia che non ti piace?
Girl: Sì. Non mi piace la filosofia.

B Some students could adapt the questions to suit reporters from different newspapers preparing an article about their school, e.g. **The Sun, The Times, The Guardian, The Mirror.**

Sono il bidello (page 141)

Main aims: To present more information about Italian schools and to develop speaking skills on this topic

A Give the students just one minute to read this and to work out the meaning of 'un bidello'. Then ask them to say how they did this. Repeat this process for some other words, e.g.

segretaria	cortile
preside	laboratorio di lingue
biblioteca	laboratorio di scienze
palestra	aula d'informatica

By analogy with 'aula d'informatica', students should be able to work out how to say, in Italian, a French room, an Italian room, etc.

To help the students to learn the key words in this text, and to help them to develop further their ability to learn useful words when they meet them, you could present the following activities. These could be used by the students to learn words which they need to talk about their own school.

• The students copy this crossword from the board or OHP. It should be empty, except for the word 'bidello'. They then try to fit into it the nine words that follow. They could then add to it other words about school which they wish to learn.

```
                              L
                P A L E S T R A
        B       R       C     B   B
      L I N G U E       I     O   I
        D       S       E     R   B
S E G R E T A R I A     N     A U L A
        L       D       Z     T   I
        L       E       E     O   O
  S C U O L A             R   T
                              I   E
                              O   C
                                  A
```

palestra	segretaria	scienze
laboratorio	scula	aula
lingue	biblioteca	preside

• The students write the words they want to learn in two different lists, e.g. words which they find easy and words which they find difficult; words which they like and words which they dislike. They compare their lists with their partners' and discuss any differences.

B You could present orally some more information about schools in Italy, e.g.

• Generally, Italian schools are not very modern, and are often quite basic. They are also very traditional.

• P. E. and Religion are compulsory although some schools do not have a gym and P.E. takes place in the courtyard.

• The students usually have all their lessons in one room.

• Italian schools do not have a canteen as school finishes at lunchtime. However during the 'intervallo' many schools have people who sell slices of pizza and 'panini' in the corridor.

• The library is usually only for use by the staff!

C Using this text to help them, the students could all write a monologue to present what they see as the ten most interesting features of their school, including suitable illustrations. They could make an interesting wall display with these and then send them to their Italian penfriends, or twinned school, and ask for something similar in return.

Insomma, non è male andare a scuola (page 142)

Main aim: To practise reading and writing about life in school

A Give the students one minute only to study this item and to find out the gist of it and as much detail as possible, using the title, the introduction, the visuals and key words. They then shut the Students' Book and report on everything they have found out. This should be an encouraging experience as they will probably have picked up a lot of information in one minute.

B Now ask the students to read the text more carefully and to write two lists: one containing favourable comments made by Paolo and the other unfavourable comments. When you have discussed these lists, ask the students to write two similar lists presenting their favourable and unfavourable comments about their own school. They could present, and discuss, these with their partners and others.

These lists could form an interesting wall display. They could be used to stimulate discussion in several lessons.

C Now would be a good time to work on 'da', in *Scoprite qualcosa di più* (pages 189-190).

D Give out copies of Copymaster 76. This survey could act as preparation for writing a short article.

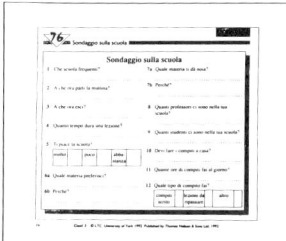

Adesso, tocca a te! (page 143)

Main aim: To demonstrate that the language of this unit has been mastered

Exercise 1
Language area: School
Skill area: Speaking

Working in pairs, the students help each other to play both roles as well as possible, practising together until they are quite satisfied with their performance.

Exercise 2
Language area: School
Skill areas: Reading and writing

Each student writes a description of their school. In pairs, they then help each other to improve what they have written.

Exercise 3
Language area: School
Skill areas: Speaking and listening

The students work on their dialogue in pairs until they are happy with it. If possible, they should then either record it or perform it for you and/or the class.

Ora sai (page 144)

Main aim: To act as a summary and reference point for the main language of this unit

The students work on this alone, and in pairs, to make sure that they have really mastered the language of the unit. They could do this before moving on to Book 4 and also later, as revision.

B You could introduce more techniques for language learning for the students to try out and add to their repertoire, e.g.

- Students write a bilingual list of words which they find difficult to learn. They try to learn three, then cover up the Italian words with a piece of paper and write the Italian on the piece of paper. They repeat until they can write all three correctly, then move on.

- Students make four columns, headed:

Le materie   La gente   Il trasporto   La scuola

They write four lists, as long as possible, and then compare their lists with a partner's. They try to correct and to add to their partner's lists.

C The students adapt the sentences in this grid to talk about themselves and their school.

D Each student adds some questions and answers about their school: they try these out on their partners and aim to be able to hold a really interesting conversation about their school.

Revision

1 Introductions and saying hello (Book 1, Unit 1)

Each student imagines how a famous person or TV character would introduce him/herself on a visit to their school. In groups, they then perform their introductions: the others have to guess who they are pretending to be.

As a follow-up, each student could imagine how they would introduce themselves if they met the person they most wanted to meet in the world.

2 At a petrol station (Book 3, Unit 6)

A To revise some of the key language of this topic, play a game of word association. You say a word and students write another word which your word makes them think of. They then read out their words and, if need be, explain the association. You could use the following words:

la benzina	senza piombo
una cartina della regione	una stazione di servizio
un distributore	super
il gasolio	il parabrezza
normale	la gomma
l'olio	controllare

B Present this role play on the board/OHP.
You and your family stop at a service station in Italy. Your partner will play the part of the employee.

A: Buongiorno.

B: (Ask for 10,000 lire of unleaded petrol.)

A: Certo. Le serve altro?

B: (Ask if you can buy a map in the shop.)

A: Deve chiedere nel negozio.

B: (Say thank you. [Entra nel negozio] Ask if there is a telephone.)

A: Sì, subito dietro l'officina.

B: (Say thank you. Ask how far it is to Siena.)

A: Circa diciotto chilometri.

B: (Say thank you and goodbye.)

A: Di niente. Arrivederci.

3 Indirect object pronouns (Book 3, Unit 6)

A You could organise a game of 'Il gioco degli spazi', with, e.g.

1 Scusi, mi sa dire quanto è _____ Arezzo?

2 Vi presento il _____ di inglese, Signor Paoli.

3 Gli dia una _____ Margherita, per favore?

4 Ti piacerebbe _____ al cinema, stasera?

5 _____ può controllare l'olio, per favore?

6 Ecco signora _____ posso dare uno sciroppo per la tosse.

7 Senta, _____ sa dire se c'è una farmacia qui vicino?

8 E per mio fratello ... _____ può portare un gelato alla fragola, per favore?

B Present the following questions on the board or OHP. Point out that they are the sorts of questions which the students will often be asked in Italy and in exams. They should prepare interesting answers to them so that they can answer the questions confidently and well. Help individuals with their answers and, as they practise them in pairs, move around helping and advising.

– Ti piace la tua scuola?

– Ti piace uscire la sera con gli amici?

– Le piacerebbe venire in Italia a studiare?

– Le piacciono gli esami orali o preferisce gli esami scritti?

– Le piace mangiare all'italiana?

– Ti piace andare al cinema?

4 Main verb + infinitive (Book 3, Unit 12)

A Organise a short period of verb circle practice starting with, e.g.

– Ti piace uscire la sera?

– Volete andare in pizzeria?

– Possiamo partire presto la mattina.

– Deve prendere l'autobus.

B Present on the board or OHP the following incomplete sentences:

1 Se vuoi _____ con Maria, devi chiamare più tardi.

2 Mi piace _____ alla scuola con gli amici.

3 Ci piace _____ con gli amici la sera.

4 Vi piacerebbe _____ al cinema?

5 Dobbiamo _____ fino alle sette.

6 Mi può _____ l'olio, per favore?

7 Vorrei _____ quanto è lontana Torino.

8 Deve _____ il modulo.

sap-	aspett-	
parl-	controll-	-ire
ven-	usc-	-are
compil-	and-	-ere

The students complete the sentences with the infinitives in the box, choosing the right ending for each one. Those who finish first could be asked to work in pairs and to make up dialogues which use as many as possible of the completed sentences.